African Economic Outlook

2009

OECD

AFRICAN DEVELOPMENT BANK

DEVELOPMENT CENTRE OF THE ORGANISATION
FOR ECONOMIC CO-OPERATION AND DEVELOPMENT

ORGANISATION FOR ECONOMIC CO-OPERATION AND DEVELOPMENT

The OECD is a unique forum where the governments of 30 democracies work together to address the economic, social and environmental challenges of globalisation. The OECD is also at the forefront of efforts to understand and to help governments respond to new developments and concerns, such as corporate governance, the information economy and the challenges of an ageing population. The Organisation provides a setting where governments can compare policy experiences, seek answers to common problems, identify good practice and work to co-ordinate domestic and international policies.

The OECD member countries are: Australia, Austria, Belgium, Canada, the Czech Republic, Denmark, Finland, France, Germany, Greece, Hungary, Iceland, Ireland, Italy, Japan, Korea, Luxembourg, Mexico, the Netherlands, New Zealand, Norway, Poland, Portugal, the Slovak Republic, Spain, Sweden, Switzerland, Turkey, the United Kingdom and the United States. The European Commission takes part in the work of the OECD.

OECD Publishing disseminates widely the results of the Organisation's statistics gathering and research on economic, social and environmental issues, as well as the conventions, guidelines and standards agreed by its members.

*
* *

The Development Centre of the Organisation for Economic Co-operation and Development was established by decision of the OECD Council on 23 October 1962 and comprises 23 member countries of the OECD: Austria, Belgium, the Czech Republic, Finland, France, Germany, Greece, Iceland, Ireland, Italy, Korea, Luxembourg, Mexico, the Netherlands, Norway, Poland, Portugal, Slovak Republic, Spain, Sweden, Switzerland, Turkey and the United Kingdom. In addition, the following non-OECD countries are members of the Development Centre: Brazil (since March 1994); Chile (November 1998); India (February 2001); Romania (October 2004); Thailand (March 2005); South Africa (May 2006); Egypt, Israel, and Viet Nam (March 2008); Indonesia (February 2009); Costa Rica, Mauritius, Morocco and Peru (March 2009). The Commission of the European Communities also takes part in the Centre's Governing Board.

The Development Centre, whose membership is open to both OECD and non-OECD countries, occupies a unique place within the OECD and in the international community. Members finance the Centre and serve on its Governing Board, which sets the biennial work programme and oversees its implementation.

The Centre links OECD members with developing and emerging economies and fosters debate and discussion to seek creative policy solutions to emerging global issues and development challenges. Participants in Centre events are invited in their personal capacity.

A small core of staff works with experts and institutions from the OECD and partner countries to fulfil the Centre's work programme. The results are discussed in informal expert and policy dialogue meetings, and are published in a range of high-quality products for the research and policy communities. The Centre's Study Series presents in-depth analyses of major development issues. Policy Briefs and Policy Insights summarise major conclusions for policy makers; Working Papers deal with the more technical aspects of the Centre's work.

For an overview of the Centre's activities, please see www.oecd.org/dev

 The opinions expressed and arguments employed in this publication are the sole responsibility of the authors and do not necessarily reflect those of the OECD, its Development Centre or the governments of their member countries; the African Development Bank; the European Commission; the Economic Commission for Africa or the Secretariat of the African, Caribbean and Pacific Group of States or its member states.

This publication has been produced with the financial assistance of the European Commission. A generous grant from the European Development Fund, jointly managed by the Commission of the European Communities and the African, Caribbean and Pacific Secretariat, was essential to initiating and sustaining the project.

Également disponible en français sous le titre :
PERSPECTIVES ÉCONOMIQUES EN AFRIQUE

THE AFRICAN DEVELOPMENT BANK GROUP

The African Development Bank Group is a regional multilateral development finance institution the members of which are all of the 53 countries in Africa and 24 countries from Asia, Europe, North and South America. The purpose of the Bank is to further the economic development and social progress of African countries, individually and collectively. To this end, the Bank promotes the investment of public and private capital for development, primarily by providing loans and grants for projects and programmes that contribute to poverty reduction and broad-based sustainable development in Africa.

The non-concessional operations of the Bank are financed from its ordinary capital resources. In addition, the Bank's soft window affiliates – the African Development Fund and the Nigeria Trust Fund – provide concessional financing to low-income countries that are not able to sustain loans on market terms.

By the end of 2008, the African Development Bank Group cumulatively approved 3 276 loans and grants for commitments of close to UA 44.7 billion (approximately USD 61.80 billion). The commitments were made to 52 regional member countries and institutions to support development projects and programmes in agriculture, transport, public utilities, industry, education and health services. Since the mid-1980s, a significant share of commitments has also gone to promoting economic reform and adjustment programmes that help to accelerate socio-economic development. About 43.5 per cent of the total Bank Group commitments were financed on non-concessional terms, while the balance benefited from concessional financing.

ECONOMIC COMMISSION FOR AFRICA

The Economic Commission for Africa (ECA) was established by the Economic and Social Council (ECOSOC) of the United Nations (UN) in 1958 as one of the UN's five regional commissions. ECA's mandate is to promote the economic and social development of its member States, foster intra-regional integration, and promote international cooperation for Africa's development.

ECA's dual role as a regional arm of the UN, and a part of the regional institutional landscape in Africa, positions it well to make unique contributions to member States' efforts to address their development challenges. Its strength derives from its role as the only UN agency mandated to operate at the regional and subregional levels to harness resources and bring them to bear on Africa's priorities.

ECA's work programme now focuses on achieving results in two related and mutually supportive areas:

Promoting Regional Integration in support of the African Union vision and priorities. ECA's support to the implementation of AUC's regional integration agenda focuses on undertaking research and policy analysis on regional integration issues, strengthening capacity and providing technical assistance to institutions driving the regional integration agenda, including strengthening and supporting the Regional Economic Communities (RECs), and working on a range of trans-boundary initiatives and activities in sectors vital to the regional integration agenda.

Meeting Africa's special needs and emerging global challenges. ECA recognizes the importance of focusing attention on Africa's special needs, particularly within the context of achieving the Millennium Development Goals (MDGs). In this regard, ECA places emphasis on supporting efforts to eradicate poverty, placing African countries on the path of growth and sustainable development, reversing the marginalization of Africa in the globalization process, and accelerating the empowerment of women. It aims to provide significant technical support to the African Peer Review Mechanism (APRM) and also to promote peer learning and knowledge sharing in a range of development areas.

Foreword

Nine years ago, when the *African Economic Outlook* project began, the world was in the midst of what seemed to be a robust growth path. There were bumps, of course, but the general trend was upwards and the interruptions were relatively localised and short-lived. In 2009, however, the picture is very different: the financial crisis has spread throughout the world economy, which is now caught in the deepest and most widespread recession for more than 50 years.

Africa has not been spared. The continent is severely affected by plummeting levels of FDI and remittances, falling commodity prices and depressed export demand from OECD countries. The risk of reversals in recent development progress is looming, which in turn poses serious threats to the hard-won gains in political and social stability. A growth cycle of several years has just been interrupted.

The promising news is that shifting trade patterns, prudent macroeconomic reforms, debt relief, the use of new information and communication technologies – the special focus of this edition of the *Outlook* – and improvements in the business environment suggest that African economies are better positioned to deal with the crisis than in the past. 2010, however, will be crucial for understanding the medium-term macroeconomic prospects for the continent, and for Sub-Saharan Africa in particular.

To strengthen the foundations of growth and development, Africa should continue to pursue structural reforms, investment in infrastructure, poverty reduction; and to foster regional integration. The drop in external financial flows due to the crisis calls for an expeditious response with targeted initiatives, such as accelerating fiscal reforms to increase government revenue, and scaling up resources to finance public programmes, including trade finance. A key challenge will be to find the right balance between these efforts and the preservation of macroeconomic fundamentals. In support of this endeavour, OECD countries and Africa's other development partners must stand by their pledges – more and better aid, and an open trading system.

The *African Economic Outlook* has become a vital source of detailed analysis of African economies; it helps to provide evidence-based policy advice on key development challenges on the continent. We recommend it to policy makers and decision makers in all fields, both within and outside the African continent.

We salute the partnership of the European Commission and its unwavering faith in this project from its inception. Its financial support has been a critical factor for the success of the AEO.

Above all, we reaffirm our own commitment to sound and objective research and analysis, promoting peer learning and good governance, all goals to which the *African Economic Outlook* makes an essential and invaluable contribution.

Donald Kaberuka,	**Angel Gurría**,	**Abdoulie Janneh**,
President,	Secretary-General,	Executive Secretary,
African Development Bank Group,	Organisation for Co-operation	United Nations Economic
Tunis	and Development,	Commission for Africa,
	Paris	Addis Ababa

African Economic Outlook

Country Studies

Full-length country notes available at www.africaneconomicoutlook.org

- Algeria
- Angola
- Benin
- Botswana
- Burkina Faso
- Burundi
- Cameroon
- Cape Verde
- Central African Republic
- Chad
- Congo, Democratic Republic
- Congo, Republic
- Côte d'Ivoire
- Djibouti
- Egypt
- Equatorial Guinea
- Ethiopia
- Gabon
- Gambia (The)
- Ghana
- Guinea
- Kenya
- Lesotho
- Liberia

- Libya
- Madagascar
- Malawi
- Mali
- Mauritania
- Mauritius
- Morocco
- Mozambique
- Namibia
- Niger
- Nigeria
- Rwanda
- Senegal
- Seychelles
- Sierra Leone
- South Africa
- Sudan
- Swaziland
- Tanzania
- Togo
- Tunisia
- Uganda
- Zambia

5

Acknowledgements

The *African Economic Outlook* project is a joint initiative of the African Development Bank, the OECD Development Centre and the United Nations Economic Commission for Africa. The Report was drafted by a core team from the three partner institutions, supported by resource people in selected countries. The AfDB team was led by Barfour Osei and Beejaye Kokil in the Complex of the Chief Economist. The team at UNECA was led by Adam Elhiraika, and the team at the OECD Development Centre was led by Jose Gijon, Head, Africa and Middle East Desk, and Federica Marzo. Kenneth Ruffing served as Co-ordinator. The Outlook was prepared under the overall guidance of Louis Kasekende, Chief Economist, AfDB; Léonce Ndikumana, Director, AfDB Development Research Department; Désiré Vencatachellum, Acting Manager, Networking and Research Partnership Division, AfDB; Kiichiro Fukasaku, Head, Regional Outlooks Division, OECD Development Centre; Javier Santiso, Director, OECD Development Centre; and Mahamat Abdoulahi, Officer-in-Charge of the Trade, Finance and Economic Development Division, UNECA.

The Overview was drafted by Kenneth Ruffing and edited by Colm Foy, with significant inputs and comments from the following: Valérie Bérenger on behalf of the AfDB; Thomas Dickinson, Jose Gijon, Federica Marzo, Andrew Mold, Annalisa Prizon and Papa Amadou Sarr of the OECD Development Centre; and Joseph Atta-Mensah, Adam Elhiraika, Stephen Karingi and Ben Idrissa Ouédraogo of UNECA. Laura Recuero Virto drafted the chapter on Innovation and ICT in Africa, which was edited by Timothy Witcher, with the assistance of Gregory de Paepe and Papa Amadou Sarr, and with significant inputs from Ibrahima Ndiaye, Roble Egal Noor, Marcellin Henri Ndong Ntah, Enock Yonazi (AfDB); and Aida Opoku-Mensah (UNECA).

6

The country notes were drafted by John Anyanwu, Abou Amadou Ba, Farid Benyoucef, Mohammed Chemingui, Shirley Chinien, Victor Davies, Derrese Degefa, Mamadou Diagne, Thomas Dickinson, Adam Elhiraika, Alain Fabrice Ekpo, Jose Gijon, Theophile Guezodje, Tonia Kandiero, Kavazeua Katjomuise, Christian Kingombe, Marianne Kurzweil, Albert Mafusire, Olivier Manlan, Federica Marzo, Ahmed Moummi, Tijani Najeh, Peter Ondiege, Barfour Osei, Ben Idrissa Ouédraogo, Nooman Rebei, Laura Recuero Virto, Leila Saidi-Hammami, Adeleke Salami, Marco Stampini, Ignacio Tourino Soto, Philippe Trape, Désiré Vencatachellum, Audrey Verdier-Chouchane, Susanna Wolf, Jamal Zayid. Nine country notes were prepared by authors from national research institutions. These were the following: Ibrahim Thione Diop and Aly Mbaye, Centre de Recherches Economiques Appliquées (CREA, Sénégal); Gaston Eloundou, Centre d'Etudes et de Recherche en Economie et Gestion (CEREG, Cameroun); Twimukye Evarist, Economic Policy Research Centre (EPRC, Uganda); Ibrahim Bun Kamara, Botswana Institute for Development Policy Analysis (BIDPA); H. Bohela Lunogelo and Rose Aiko, Economic and Social Research Foundation (ESRF, Tanzania); Jean-Sylvain Ndo, Laboratoire d'Économie Appliquée (LEA, Gabon); Alain Niyubahwe, Institut de Developpement Economique (IDEC, Burundi); Malak Ali Reda, Egyptian Centre for Economic Studies (ECES); and Klaus Schade, Namibian Economic Policy Research Unit (NEPRU).

The work on the country notes greatly benefited from the valuable contributions of local consultants: Laura Marie-Therese Ahtime (Seychelles), Fatima-Zohra Alaoui M. (Morocco), Souberou Bachir Olatoundji (Benin), Alimamy Bangura (Sierra Leone), Obi Benneth Prince (Nigeria), Saidy Buah (Gambia), Ghazi Boulila (Tunisia), Modibo Dolo (Mali), Peter Draper and Gilberto Biacuana (South Africa), Kodjo Evlo (Togo), Malik Garad (Djibouti), Artur Gobe (Mozambique), Péma Guilavogui (Guinea), Ousseini Hamidou Siddo (Niger), Aloysius Heagbetu (Liberia), Abdellah Ali Khalifa (Libya), Alain Serge Kpassokro Gnabroyou (Côte d'Ivoire), Sarah O. Latigo (Zambia), Rebih Labeche (Algeria), John McGrath (Malawi), Michel Matamona (Congo), Patrick Musila Mwaniki (Kenya), Alexandre Nshue Mokime (Democratic Republic of Congo), Adesida Olugbenga (Cape Verde), Teodoro Ondo Mba (Equatorial Guinea), Ndang Tabo Symphorien (Chad), Laza Razafiarison (Madagascar),

Alves da Rocha (Angola), Sawkut Ally Rojid (Mauritius), Sita Malick Sawadogo (Burkina Faso), Kabbashi M. Suliman (Sudan), Ahmed Taki Ouled Mohamed (Mauritania), Festus Turkson (Ghana), Félicien Usengumukiza (Rwanda) and Jean Baptiste Wago (Central African Republic).

The committee of peer reviewers of the country notes included: Elizabeth Asiedu, Maria João Azevedo, Janet Ceglowski, Sylvain Dessy, Kwabena Gyimah-Brempong, Anne-Marie Geourjon, Stephen Golub, Mwangi Samson Kimenyi, Paul Koffi Koffi, Bertrand Laporte and Kenneth Ruffing.

Valuable statistical inputs were provided by Feidi Amel, Anouar Chaouch, Hilaire Kadisha, Beejaye Kokil, Koua Louis Kouakou, Fetor Komlan, Fessou Emessan Lawson, Nirina Letsara, Mboya De Loubassou and Maurice Mubila at the AfDB Statistics Department and Imen Chorfi and Laureline Pla provided research assistance. Hee-Sik Kim and Victor Davies reviewed the political risk indicator. At the UNECA, the ICT and Science and Technology Division (ISTD), led by Sizo Mhlanga, provided valuable information on ICT in the countries covered by ECA, Mamo Girma and Berhanu Haile-Mikael provided research assistance while Thérèse Ouédraogo and Rahel Desta provided administrative support. At the OECD Development Centre, Gregory De Paepe provided research assistance.

The macroeconomic framework and database used to produce the forecasting was updated and managed by Federica Marzo at the OECD Development Centre and Beejaye Kokil, Riadh Ben Messaoud and Nooman Rebei at the African Development Bank. The statistical annex is the product of a joint work carried out by a team from the AfDB Statistics Department led by Beejaye Kokil and Federica Marzo at the OECD Development Centre.

The project also benefited from the assistance provided by Papa Amadou Sarr and Yvette Chanvoédou, at the OECD Development Centre, and Rhoda Bangurah and Nelson Abiana at the AfDB Development Research Department. Michèle Girard, Librarian at the OECD Development Centre, was also of assistance.

The country maps were produced in Paris by Magali Geney and Roland Pourtier. The maps and diagrams used in this publication in no way imply recognition of any states or political boundaries by the African Development Bank Group, the European Union, the Organisation for Economic Co-operation and Development, the Development Centre or the authors.

A large number of African government representatives, private-sector colleagues and civil society members provided extremely valuable inputs and comments, including all the participants in the joint AfDB/OECD Development Centre expert meeting on Information and Communication Technologies. Several institutions also contributed to the project at various stages: the AfDB country operations departments and Field Offices, the *Agence Française de Développement*, the African Partnership Forum Support Unit, the European Commission delegations in Africa, OECD Centre for Tax Policy and Administration, the OECD Economics Department, the OECD Development Co-operation Directorate, the OECD Directorate for Financial and Enterprise Affairs, and the World Bank Economic and Prospects Group.

Adrià Alsina, Kathryn Bailey, Colm Foy, Vanda Legrandgérard, Sheila Lionet, Olivier Puech and Henri-Bernard Solignac Lecomte at the OECD Development Centre ensured the production of the publication, in both paper and electronic form. Sheila Lionet managed the editorial process and was responsible overall for transforming the manuscript into the publication.

Typesetting by Vif Argent, Paris.

Preface

This eighth edition of the African Economic Outlook reflects an important advance over previous editions, bringing us within striking distance of covering the entire continent. This has been made possible by an expanded partnership. In addition to continuing a particularly fruitful collaboration among the African Development Bank, the OECD Development Centre and the United Nations Economic Commission for Africa (UNECA), we have expanded the number of independent African research institutions involved in preparing country studies and participating in the dissemination of the AEO. And within the Bank, the country economists of the Operations Departments have played a greater role than ever before. Thus, this year's edition sees a further increase in the coverage of the continent to 47 countries, up from 35 in 2008, covering 97 per cent of Africa's population and 99 per cent of its economic output.

Unfortunately, the international environment facing Africa has turned decisively negative. GDP in the OECD countries is expected to contract by 4.3 per cent in 2009 and to be virtually flat in 2010. Growth in emerging economies is also expected to slow dramatically. In turn, world trade is expected to contract by 13.1 per cent in 2009 – the first decline in world trade in 60 years. The global economic recession in which the world now finds itself has led us to slash forecasts of growth in Africa for 2009 to 2.8 per cent, less than half of last year's level. And even this may turn out to be optimistic as projections for OECD and major emerging market countries have continued to be marked down even while this volume was going to press. This somewhat overshadows the good news that growth in Africa was estimated to have been 5.7 per cent in 2008, the fifth consecutive year with growth above 5 per cent.

The slower growth which is now forecast for Africa is accompanied by deteriorating fiscal balances and current account balances, and countries with large projected deficits may find them difficult to finance. At the same time, the contraction of bank lending may make it difficult even for credit-worthy governments to finance them. Thus, enhanced support by the international financial institutions will be essential. The USD 1.5 billion Emergency Liquidity Facility, the Framework of Accelerated Resource Transfer to ADF Countries, and the USD 1 billion Trade Finance Facility announced by the AfDB in March, and the enlargement of resources for the IMF agreed in April will be especially important if these projected deficits are to be fully financed.

Moreover, most of the countries in Africa are grappling with inflation that surged to double-digit levels in 2008, considerably limiting the room for manoeuvre of central banks that would find it problematic to monetise a significant portion of fiscal deficits, especially in the 28 countries with inflation above 10 per cent in 2008.

As has been true in the past, there are marked differences between the oil-exporters and the others. The collapse in oil prices means that the public finances of the former group will come under pressure in 2009 and 2010, including those that had accumulated large reserves during the period of high oil prices. Those must take care to safeguard planned investment in infrastructure and human resource development and to diversify the sources of economic growth.

Net oil-importing countries face a different set of challenges. GDP growth in many of them is expected to fall sharply in 2009 and 2010. Meanwhile, inflation has been rising, mainly due to a more complete pass-through to consumers of international oil price increases combined with the persistence of high international prices of grains and vegetable oils. Most of them must either contain or finance expanding current account deficits which have been heavily impacted by the same factors.

Some countries continue to face the challenge of conflict and instability. In the first quarter of the year, three governments (Madagascar, Guinea and Guinea Bissau) were removed using undemocratic means, in addition to a military takeover in Mauritania in August 2008. However, there have been positive moves by international organisations, including the African Union and the African Development Bank, to help bring an end to conflict. One encouraging development was in the Democratic Republic of Congo (DRC) where a peace agreement was recently signed between the government and the main rebel group in eastern Congo. In Zimbabwe, the opposition party holds the portfolio of prime minister and is now in charge of several ministries. However, conflict resolution will also require the goodwill of African leaders in government and in opposition. The continent's political leaders must continue to show determination to end armed conflict and political instability. This is arguably Africa's greatest challenge.

However, this edition of the AEO sheds light on the ability of Africa to confront the crisis. Over the past years, improved macroeconomic management, debt relief, better governance and greater integration into the world economy have made Africa more resilient to international economic shocks. Moreover, intensified trade with emerging powers such as China, India and Brazil makes Africa less dependent on OECD markets. Growing Sino-African economic relations, in particular, have forged strong linkages and have recast Africa as a global trading partner.

Despite better prospects for tackling the crisis, Africa faces the daunting task of mitigating the negative effects of the downturn on its populations, particularly the most vulnerable. A key challenge is to secure adequate resources for private and public investment as well as trade financing. African countries are doing their level best to minimise the impact of the crisis, but they lack adequate resources and policy space to sustain the various initiatives undertaken at national and sub-regional level. In this context, the fight against protectionism – particularly on the part of OECD countries – and donor country commitments to maintain or increase Official Development Assistance (ODA) are essential for the continent. It will not be enough to scale up ODA, however. Donor countries must also improve the effectiveness of their aid. Now, more than ever, ODA should act as a countercyclical tool in Africa, especially for highly aid dependent countries.

This edition of the AEO provides an analysis of network infrastructure by surveying the Information and Communication Technology (ICT) infrastructure sector and its contribution to innovation in Africa. Sub-Saharan African countries on average have the lowest internet penetration rate in the world. North African countries are relatively better-off than their Sub-Saharan counterparts. However, even in North Africa the penetration rate for broadband internet is low. International backbone infrastructure to connect Africa to the rest of the world is being built and will soon be operational. However, governments will need to play a more active role in attracting inland network investment and in regulating prices in order to increase usage in Africa,

Despite the low penetration rates, innovative applications of ICT, especially in telecommunications, have been proliferating: e-banking, e-payments, e-agriculture, e-trade, e-government, e-education, and capacity building programmes for developing ICT skills and, more generically, for driving innovation. Innovative business models have also been gradually expanding the customer base to include significant numbers of low-income households. Innovation, however, requires better public policies

Government's role as a regulator will be particularly important in realizing the promise of ICT and the innovative applications it makes possible. The regulatory framework must be streamlined to encourage private investment in the sector and promote competition for increased efficiency and access. The report identifies many examples of good practice in this respect and it is our hope that they will become more widespread in future.

Louis Kasekende,
Chief Economist,
African Development Bank,
Tunis

Javier Santiso,
Director,
OECD Development Centre,
Paris

Mahamat Abdoulahi,
Officer-in-Charge,
Trade, Finance and Economic
Development Division,
United Nations Economic
Commission for Africa,
Addis Ababa

April 2009

Executive Summary

The *African Economic Outlook 2008/09* comprises an Overview Chapter (synthesising the results of the country analyses), a chapter on the *AEO* special topic, *Innovation and Information and Communication Technologies in Africa,* a separate chapter on each of the 47 countries covered in the report[1], and a Statistical Annex. The Overview situates its analysis of the short term prospects of Africa's economies in a global context, which this year is dominated by the global financial crisis and widespread recession.

African Economic Outlook 2009: an Overview

The international environment facing Africa has turned decisively negative. GDP in the OECD countries is expected to contract by 4.3 per cent in 2009 and to be virtually flat in 2010. Growth in emerging economies is also expected to slow dramatically. In turn world trade is expected to contract by 13.1 per cent in 2009 – the first decline in world trade in 60 years. In 2010, growth in world trade is expected to exhibit positive growth of 1.5 per cent as recovery in economic activity gets underway in the countries of the OECD. A factor depressing trade beyond the impact of slowing demand has been the sharp contraction in trade credit in OECD countries, along with the freezing of bank lending in general. This situation is not expected to be alleviated much by the modest progress made in regional trade liberalisation, whether between African countries and the EU or among themselves. Most commodity prices have fallen back to their 2005 or 2006 levels, many of them registering declines of 40 per cent or more. As a result, prices of exports have fallen by more than prices of imports, inflicting a significant negative terms of trade shock on most countries. For many countries, the persistence of high prices for internationally trade of food continues to contribute to a food crisis situation, especially for the urban poor.

Official development assistance (ODA) to Africa, which was driven largely by debt relief and emergency assistance, fell by 18 per cent in real terms in 2007, mostly due to the end of exceptional debt relief operations, and, while growth was positive in 2008, ODA may well grow more slowly in 2009 and 2010. According to donor nations' pledges, aid levels are expected to increase further during the next two years and Africa is likely to benefit more than other regions. However, ballooning fiscal deficits and dwindling political support for greater aid levels in major donor countries could trigger a downward revision of aid levels. Moreover, less of it is likely to be in the form of debt relief or humanitarian assistance. Thus, the rate of increase is likely to slow, making it highly unlikely that the Gleneagles commitments to double aid to Africa by 2010 will be met. New estimates consider that the shortfall of Gleneagles aid commitments already amounts to USD 20 to 25 billion, a figure that will probably increase with reduced political support for aid policies.

Flows of foreign direct investment appear to have decreased by about 10 per cent in 2008. For 2009, they are likely to contract further as investment in extractive export industries is being postponed in many countries. Portfolio investment has also been affected by the global financial crisis, becoming negative in net terms and causing many countries to draw upon their international reserves.

---

1. Available on a CD-ROM for certain editions of this report. The 47 countries examined in this eighth edition of the *African Economic Outlook* account for some 97 per cent of Africa's population and 99 per cent of its economic output. The countries are classified by sub-region: in North Africa: Algeria, Egypt, Libya, Mauritania, Morocco, Sudan and Tunisia; in West Africa: Benin, Burkina Faso, Cape Verde, Côte d'Ivoire, the Gambia, Ghana, Guinea, Liberia, Mali, Niger, Nigeria, Senegal, Sierra Leone, and Togo; in Central Africa: Cameroon, Chad, Central African Republic, the Republic of Congo, the Democratic Republic of Congo, Equatorial Guinea, and Gabon; in East Africa: Burundi, Djibouti, Ethiopia, Kenya, Rwanda, Seychelles, Tanzania and Uganda; In Southern Africa: Angola, Botswana, Lesotho, Madagascar, Malawi, Mauritius, Mozambique, Namibia, South Africa, Swaziland and Zambia.

Not surprisingly, the outlook for Africa has been adversely affected by the global recession. Economic growth in Africa is expected to be only 2.8 per cent in 2009, less than half of the 5.7 per cent estimated for 2008. It is then expected to rebound partially to 4.5 per cent 2010. Growth in oil-exporting countries, which continued to outpace that of oil importers by a substantial margin in 2008 (2 percentage points), is slowing as well and is expected to be 2.4 per cent in 2009 compared to 3.3 per cent for the net oil importers. Moreover, some countries continue to face particularly serious problems – including the humanitarian catastrophe in the Darfur region of Sudan, the economic collapse in Zimbabwe, conflicts and political unrest in Guinea, Guinea Bissau, Equatorial Guinea, Madagascar and Somalia, which are likely to further impede economic progress. The hard-won macroeconomic stability achieved recently in African countries was also affected by food price inflation in the first three quarters of 2008 and could be challenged further by the worsening of economic conditions. A slowdown of investment in oil and mineral production is also expected to be a drag on growth in 2009 and 2010.

Inflation has become a problem in many countries. It increased in net oil-importing countries (excluding Zimbabwe), to double-digit levels of 13.5 per cent in 2008, up from 7.9 per cent in 2007, mainly due to increasing oil, fertiliser and food prices. But it also increased in oil exporters, reaching 10 per cent in 2008 compared to 7.2 per cent in 2007, reflecting not only higher import prices but also supply constraints in the face of strong growth of domestic demand.

The windfall gains from commodity prices strengthened public finances for both oil exporting and net oil importers through 2007. However, for net oil importers as a group, the overall budget deficit deteriorated in 2008, to 1.8 per cent, and is projected to increase to 2.7 per cent in 2009. On the other hand, the public finances of oil exporters were supported by revenues from the high oil prices that prevailed through most of 2008. However, as a result of their subsequent collapse, they are expected to exhibit an overall deficit of 7.5 per cent in 2009.

Current account balances deteriorated in many countries in 2008, especially among net oil importers, whose aggregate deficit increased to 7.1 per cent of GDP, up sharply from 5.4 per cent in 2007. Many of them were adversely affected by higher import bills despite some improvement in the prices of agricultural export products, cocoa, coffee, and cotton in particular. As a result, many of them are facing severe pressure on the level of international reserves. Their deficits are expected to remain high in 2009 and 2010. Oil exporters continued to register a large current account surplus in 2008 but, as a group, the surplus is expected to give way to a deficit of 3.5 per cent in 2009. The emergency USD 1.5 billion "bailout facility" announced by the African Development Bank (AfDB) in March and the enlargement of resources for the International Monetary Fund (IMF) agreed on 2 April at the G20 in London will be especially important if these projected deficits are to be fully financed.

With public finances coming under pressure in 2009 and 2010, net oil exporters must take care to safeguard planned investment in infrastructure and human resource development to continue to diversify the sources of economic growth. Diversification is all the more important with the collapse of the boom in commodity prices. Most of them are in the fortunate position of having accumulated large reserves during the period of high oil prices.

Net oil-importing countries face a different set of challenges. GDP growth in many of them is expected to fall sharply in 2009 and 2010. Meanwhile, inflation has been rising, mainly due to a more complete pass-through to consumers of international oil price increases combined with increases in the international prices of grains and vegetable oils. Containing inflation to single-digit levels may preclude monetising their global budget deficits,

11

and this may well further dampen growth. Moreover, the GDP growth forecasts in this edition of the *AEO* are associated with increasing current-account deficits that result from a weakening in demand for their exports, reflected in part by weakening non-oil commodity prices – only partially offset by declines in the prices of imported food and oil (assumed to be USD 50 per barrel in 2009 and USD 55 in 2010). Thus, another assumption underpinning the forecasts is that the additional funds required to finance the deficits will be forthcoming, despite the difficulties of raising finance on international capital markets at present.

Another major uncertainty is the extent and severity of the current recession in the OECD and slowdown in other major emerging countries. The importance of taking policy measures to bolster demand worldwide has somewhat over-shadowed concerns over a possible disorderly unwinding of the large current account imbalances in the global economy. In fact, the slowdown itself, and the collapse of oil prices have been contributing to their gradual unwinding.

The assessment of progress on the Millennium Development Goals (MDGs) in this year's *AEO* – based on an updated methodology - confirms the diagnosis of last year's *AEO*; on recent trends, only a handful are likely to meet the income poverty target of halving the share of the population living on less than one dollar a day by 2015.

The need to promote good governance is as important as ever. The AU/NEPAD African Peer Review Mechanism has begun to provide a candid assessment of African countries and, thus, to foster progress in governance. Algeria, Benin, Burkina Faso, Ghana, Kenya, Nigeria, Rwanda, South Africa and Uganda have already been reviewed, while Egypt, Gabon, Lesotho, Mauritius and Mozambique will launch reviews in 2009. The *Outlook* notes that progress towards democracy has stalled recently. Conflicts in some countries have started to subside, but they have flared up in others. Despite progress in macroeconomic management and the regulatory environment, more needs to be done to ensure an environment conducive to private-sector development especially in further reducing corruption. However, the deterioration of the economic environment could jeopardize some of the advances made in Africa toward greater democracy and better governance.

Innovation and Information and Communication Technologies (ICT) in Africa

Following the special focus on energy supply and poverty on 2004, transport infrastructure in 2006 and access to drinking water and sanitation in 2007, Chapter 2 of this edition of the *AEO* continues the analysis of network infrastructure by surveying the Information and Communication Technology (ICT) infrastructure sector and its related applications within the overall context of development in Africa.

Africa has the lowest internet penetration rate in the world. In Sub-Saharan African countries, for internet users the penetration rate is below 7; for broadband subscribers the penetration rate is below 1. North African countries are relatively better-off than their Sub-Saharan neighbours (and, indeed other developing regions) with an internet penetration rate of 40.4 per cent. However, even in North Africa the penetration rate for broadband subscribers is only 2 per cent. International backbone infrastructure to connect Africa to the world is being built and will soon be operational. Governments should play a more active role in attracting inland backbone investment and in regulating prices in order to reach more users and increase usage in Africa, since improved international connectivity will not be sufficient by itself.

Despite the low penetration rates, innovative applications of ICT have been proliferating: e-banking, e-payments, e-agriculture, e-trade, e-government, e-education, capacity building programmes for developing ICT skills and, more generically, for driving innovation. Innovative business models have also been gradually expanding the customer base to include significant numbers of low-income households.

Providing appropriate regulation is the most important function of government in the ICT sector since most of the investment required can be mobilised by the private sector. In spite of the financial crisis, telecommunications in Africa remains an attractive business. Governments should be more ambitious in their liberalisation strategies. Regulatory systems have been slowly evolving towards international good practice, but there is considerable need for further improvement.

Governments and regulators should do more to attract private capital to the fixed-line segment. Governments should privatise the remaining state-owned fixed-line incumbents since private investors can bring the technological know-how necessary to upgrade their networks, and more regulators should adopt convergent licensing regimes and symmetric regulation of termination charges to create favourable conditions for fixed-line investments.

13

Part One

Overview

This Overview chapter begins with a section on the international environment facing African countries including prospects for growth in the world economy, international and regional trade, exchange rates, commodity prices, official development assistance, and foreign direct investment. This prepares the way for a section discussing the macroeconomic performance of African countries including prospects for GDP growth, inflation, fiscal balances, and current account balances; detail is provided on five sub-regions and on net oil exporters compared to net oil importers. This is followed by sections on progress in achieving the millennium development goals, governance and political issues, and economic governance.

International Environment

Growth in the World Economy

World GDP grew at 2.2 per cent in 2008, down from 3.8 per cent in 2007, with growth in OECD countries substantially slower than growth elsewhere. GDP growth in OECD countries slowed to 0.9 per cent in 2008, down from 2.7 per cent in 2007. The slowdown began earlier and was more pronounced in the United States than elsewhere due to the fallout from the sub-prime housing loan crisis. By and large, the OECD countries weathered relatively well a series of shocks in the form of financial market turmoil, declines in housing markets, and higher fuel and food prices in the first half of 2008, but the situation deteriorated rapidly towards the end of the year, rapidly spread to the rest of the world and has now taken on the proportions of a global recession. In December, prospects were for GDP in the OECD area to fall by 0.4 per cent in 2009 and for growth to be a weak 1.4 per cent in 2010, but they have worsened since then. At end March, the OECD revised its forecast for OECD growth in 2009 to -4.3 per cent and for growth to be near zero in 2010.

In the United States, household consumption began to fall during the second half of 2008, with a particularly sharp decline in spending on durables; fixed investment has been falling as well. Continued declines in real disposable income, and in housing prices are indicators of future weakness in demand that is likely to persist throughout at least the first half of 2009. Moreover, the sub-prime market crisis has turned into a fully fledged financial crisis that severely affected the US financial sector. Large US financial institutions had to be rescued by the US authorities and credit to the US economy was drastically curtailed. Since late 2008, the effects of the financial crisis have impacted the real economy and have exacerbated the economic slowdown. The contribution to GDP growth of net exports increased in 2008, due largely to contraction of US absorption and a fall in imports. Economic growth in the Euro zone declined in each of the final three quarters of 2008, and GDP contracted in the fourth quarter. Private consumption growth has been anaemic and business investment fell, reflecting greater uncertainty and tighter lending conditions. At the end of 2008, the financial crisis that originated in the United States reached several European countries and pushed governments to bail out major financial institutions. Demand from emerging market economies weakened, reducing the contribution of net exports to growth. In Japan economic activity contracted in the second quarter and again in the fourth quarter. As export growth slowed, reflecting the slowdown in global demand, knock-on effects reduced business investment. Unlike the situation in the United States and the Euro zone, however, residential investment has continued to pick up, as the sector recovered from the effects of regulatory changes introduced in 2007.

In the United States and the Euro zone a significant output gap emerged in the course of 2008 thus reducing inflationary pressure which had been building in 2007. The stance of monetary policy has remained extremely accommodating in response to the turmoil in financial markets in 2007, but became especially expansive in

Figure 1 - Growth in OECD Countries

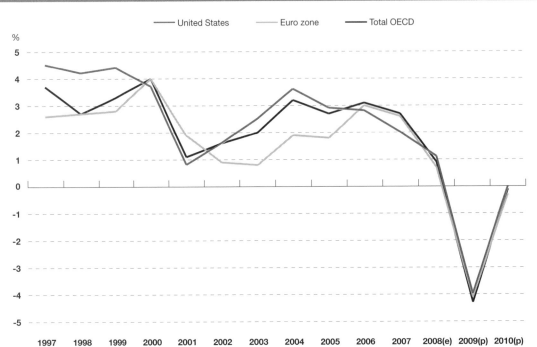

United States — Euro zone — Total OECD

Source: OECD (2008), OECD *Interim Economic Outlook*, 31 March 2009.

StatLink http://dx.doi.org/10.1787/568153762345

the United States and then in Europe in the course of 2008 as the financial turmoil worsened and aggregate demand began to fall. Monetary policy is expected to revert towards neutral once growth momentum is restored in the second half of 2009. Despite the increase in fuel and food prices during the first half of 2008, core inflation had remained stable at about 2 per cent. Inflation as measured by the GDP deflator registered a somewhat higher rate of 2.6 per cent in 2008, up from 2.4 per cent in 2007, and the OECD-wide private consumption deflator registered a somewhat higher 3.3 per cent in 2008. Prospects in 2009 and 2010 are for the OECD-wide private consumption deflator to fall well below 2 per cent in both years.

Outside the OECD area growth also slowed but remained strong, even in Asia, with China exhibiting GDP growth of 9.5 per cent, down from 11.4 per cent in 2007, and India around 7 per cent. Brazil and Russia also registered strong GDP growth in 2008, 5.3 per cent and 6.5 per cent, respectively. In all four countries growth is expected to slow further in 2009 and then

regain momentum in 2010, reflecting an expected moderate recovery in world demand for their exports.

International and Regional Trade

World trade grew at 2.5 per cent in 2008, down from 7 per cent in 2007, and was forecast by the OECD at end March 2009 to contract by 3.1 per cent in 2009 – the first decline in world trade in 60 years. In 2010, growth in world trade is expected to exhibit positive growth of 3.2 per cent as recovery in economic activity gets underway in the countries of the OECD. These figures are subject to considerable downside risk, however. A factor depressing trade beyond the impact of slowing demand has been the sharp contraction in trade credit in OECD countries, along with the freezing of bank lending in general. Progress in the Doha round of trade negotiations has stalled, but efforts to revive them may, at the very least, keep protectionist sentiment – which has been strengthening along with the deepening of the global recession – at bay (See Box 1 for implications for Africa).

The slower growth in the OECD and several large emerging economies in 2008 was reflected in the demand for African exports, which exhibited real growth of 7.9 per cent in 2007, but was estimated at only about 5 per cent in 2008. Nonetheless, the value of exports was sustained by the high prices for oil and many other primary commodities that persisted for most of 2008. Growth in import demand in OECD countries and in Asia is expected to slow dramatically in 2009 and to remain weak in 2010. Export growth is expected to receive an off-setting boost from the Economic Partnership Agreement (EPA) between African countries and the EU, interim agreements' having been signed by most countries. However, little progress in these negotiations was registered in 2008 (See Box 2).

Trends in Intra-African trade

Merchandise exports grew by 17.5 per cent in 2007 to reach USD 424.14 billion in 2007 compared to USD 360.9 billion in 2006. Intra-African merchandise trade was only 9.5 per cent of the total. Manufactured products accounted for 42.5 per cent of intra-Africa trade, fuels and mining products 35.4 per cent and agricultural products 17.1 per cent. North America and EU remained the major trading partners of Africa in 2007 with a cumulative share of exports of over 61 per cent. Asia is

Box 1 - Developments in the Doha Round: Food for Thought for African Countries

A history of missed deadlines: The Doha Round of trade negotiations is now in its 9th year. The main areas under negotiation include but are not limited to: agriculture (including cotton); non-agricultural market access (NAMA); services; TRIPS; WTO rules; special and differential treatment; trade facilitation; and LDCs; among others. The negotiations were supposed to have been concluded by 1 January 2005. Modalities for agriculture and NAMA were to have been agreed by March 2003. This deadline was missed. Efforts to agree on the modalities in Cancún in September 2003 also failed. Even the framework agreement reached in July 2004 was not enough to facilitate an agreement in full modalities in July 2005. The suspension of the negotiations in July 2006, did not elicit sufficient momentum and commitment that could contribute to an agreement on modalities in agriculture and NAMA, as this has remained elusive since the talks' resumption in February 2007. The expectation to have agreement on the modalities by end of April 2008 was not realised and negotiations collapsed in July 2008 and have not advanced much since then.

Why has there been no agreement? As the chronology of events above indicates, agriculture and NAMA have been the main issues. This is not to say that the other areas of negotiations are unimportant. Under the single-undertaking principle of the negotiations, all the areas have to be agreed before the Round can be concluded. The suspension in July 2006 was because of disagreements in the market access and domestic support pillars of the agriculture negotiations on the one hand, and the tariff reduction levels for industrial goods on the other. While the differences in this triangle appeared to have narrowed, the collapse in July 2008 is still attributed to agriculture and NAMA. But this time, it was the question of how developing countries could use the special safeguard mechanism to protect their agriculture sector against import surges that could not be agreed upon.

What have been the interests of African countries? Like other developing countries, African states had great expectations in the Doha Round. The Round's ambitious agenda in agriculture promised to unlock the continent's potential to expand agricultural exports. In addition to improved market access in agriculture, NAMA and services, African countries have been interested in other developmental issues such as fairer trade through elimination of export subsidies and substantial reduction in trade distorting domestic support, developmental

19

flexibilities to safeguard domestic industries and livelihoods of the poor, non-reciprocal preferences, special and differential treatment, duty-free quota free market access for LDCs and aid for trade.

Modest development package out of Doha so far: The results of the Doha Round from a development point of view are modest at best. It includes the amendment of TRIPS to facilitate access to essential medicines; extension of TRIPS transition period for LDCs for seven-and-a-half years; duty-free quota free market access for LDCs; aid for trade; and enhanced integrated framework. Even if duty-free, quota-free market access for LDCs is achieved, failure to have meaningful and simplified rules of origin implies that its benefits may not be fully reaped.

Moving forward, the realities that Africa should face: It is now generally agreed that the challenge in the Doha Round is no longer technical, but political, meaning that the draft modalities will be the basis for the political decisions. Africa should be ready for a much more scaled-down Doha outcome, compared to the original mandate. For instance, in agriculture, the market access and domestic support elements may not be as ambitious as originally hoped for. In NAMA, the flexibilities provided both for countries to apply the formula and those expected to increase their binding coverage are more limited, compared to what the African countries had indicated would be pro-development, in the context of maintaining current policy space. In the case of rules, particularly with respect to regional trading arrangements, the countries will most likely be dealing with more constrained flexibilities through more stringent disciplines. Moreover, even among the champions of the importance of trade for development, protectionist measures have been enacted to protect jobs. All these circumstances will aggravate the current economic crisis and could threaten the modest development package currently on the table reached in the negotiations.

Source: UNECA.

Box 2 - Economic Partnership Agreements (EPAs) between EU and African Countries

The Economic Partnership Agreement (EPA) negotiations between the European Union and the African, Caribbean and Pacific countries (ACP) began in Brussels on 27 September 2002. Their objective is to contribute to the development of a trade regime that promotes sustainable development and the integration of ACP countries into the global economy through a framework for reciprocity, differentiation, regional integration, and co-ordination of trade and aid.

EPAs were initiated to find a means compatible with WTO rules of prolonging preferential treatments extended to ACP countries under the Cotonou Agreement of June 2000. This new agreement was also meant to promote development by covering issues like services, investment and standards and increasing co-operation on trade issues.

However, it was clear by late 2007 that EPA negotiations in Africa would not conclude on time. Faced with the legal expiry of the Cotonou trade regime and the WTO waiver that covered it, the EU and ACP therefore decided to conclude "interim agreements" that would comply with WTO rules but only cover trade in goods. Due to the tight deadline, several interim agreements were subsequently initialled with individual countries rather than full ACP regions, although the ultimate aim remains to conclude full regional EPAs.

By January 2009[1], only one region, the Forum of the Caribbean ACP States (CARIFORUM), had managed to conclude a comprehensive EPA with the EU as initially envisaged. A large number of ACP countries, including 18 African states, and 2 countries in the Pacific had concluded interim agreements with the EU: Cameroon (Central Africa), Botswana, Lesotho, Swaziland, Mozambique and Namibia (SADC region), Côte d'Ivoire and Ghana (West Africa), Kenya, Uganda, Tanzania, Rwanda and Burundi (East Africa), Comoros, Madagascar, Mauritius, Seychelles and Zambia (ESA region). None of the ACP countries had formally signed a full agreement with the EU. EPA negotiations are still continuing with African and Pacific regional groupings.

All interim agreements have a similar structure, albeit with provisions for differences due to particular interests and integration plans. Some African regions like the South African Development Community (SADC) opted for a more comprehensive agreement. However, in West Africa, Ghana and Côte d'Ivoire preferred more limited agreements so as not to jeopardise the wider regional integration process and risk prejudicing future EPA negotiations.

Despite these developments, a comprehensive review of the EPA negotiations indicated that prior to the 31 December 2007 deadline there had been only limited progress in following the agreed roadmap for negotiations and that significant differences persisted in issues such as product coverage, transition periods, rules of origin, sensitive products and preference erosion in areas such as market access and agriculture. Differences also remained over the scope of development provisions, additionality of resources, and the legally binding nature of EU commitments.

The possible impact of the EPAs on Africa's trade and regional integration and socio-economic development is a contentious issue slowing the pace of negotiations. The EC and ACP negotiators have in most cases not been able to agree on the cornerstones of the new trading arrangement, notably, on the development issues and regionalism[2].

The next revision of the Cotonou Partnership Agreement (CPA), to be negotiated in 2009 and adopted in 2010, will provide a useful opportunity to actualise Title II of the CPA on Economic and Trade Co-operation, and in particular Chapter 2 on new trading arrangements. New issues that could be addressed in a revised CPA include the relationship between EPAs and the CPA.

Source: OECD Development Centre, 2009.

also becoming an increasingly important trading partner for African countries. African exports to Asia grew by nearly 50 per cent in 2005-07, but these exports remain concentrated in fuels and mining products that accounted for 78 per cent of total exports during this period. The low-level of intra-Africa trade illustrates weak continental integration, highlighting the urgency with which the continent should deal with the bottlenecks, both in terms of policy and investments especially in common infrastructure.

1. European Union (2009), *Fact sheet on the interim Economic Partnership Agreements: An Overview Of The Interim Agreements*, Brussels.

2. See ODI-ECDPM 2008, *The new EPAs: comparative analysis of their content and the challenges for 2008.*

Important regional integration measures in 2008

African countries are increasingly realising the advantages of regional co-operation and integration as a strategy to achieve economic growth and collectively to play a more important role in the global economy. Through this process, the continent can pool its capacities, endowments and energies together to transform itself, and thereby help uplift the lives of millions of people. To this end, African countries and governments, through the regional economic communities (RECs)[3] and the African Union (AU), are pursuing an agenda of continental integration along a road map of establishing Free Trade Areas, Customs Union and Common Markets.

Africa's RECs' integration process has focused more on market integration through the design and implementation of various partial trade liberalisation schemes. Full market integration however remains to be fully achieved in African sub-regions and intra-community trade remains impeded by inadequate production of goods and deficient capacities in transport, communications and energy.

RECs experiences with FTAs and Customs Unions

The experience so far shows that progress in the elimination of intra-REC tariffs has been mixed. *Regional Integration in Africa* (ARIA I), a joint publication of the ECA and the AU Commission, indicates that, as part of its Free Trade Arrangements, ECOWAS members began eliminating tariffs on unprocessed goods and traditional handicrafts in 1981 and adopted a scheme for eliminating duties on industrial goods during the 1990s. While trade liberalisation has not been fully implemented in all countries, ECOWAS was still expected to become a customs union by the end of 2008, this deadline has been pushed into 2009.

COMESA members began cutting tariffs in 1994, and by 2000 all tariffs were to have been eliminated. Nine countries out of the 19 members satisfied this requirement by October 2000, when the free trade area was declared in accordance with the terms of the trade protocol. Some of the countries have fully liberalised intra-regional trade; others have done so only partially. Burundi and Rwanda have already cut tariffs by 80 per cent and 90 per cent. Ethiopia has cut tariffs by just 10 per cent, while Seychelles and Swaziland have not cut any. Swaziland has been granted a special derogation, however. COMESA was expected to become a customs union at the end of 2008, but this deadline has slipped somewhat.

EAC members are currently implementing tariff reductions, with cuts of 90 per cent by Kenya and 80 per cent by Tanzania and Uganda. Rwanda and Burundi, which joined EAC in 2007, are expected to eliminate all forms of tariffs in conformity with the trade protocols of the community. Co-ordination and harmonisation of trade policies and programmes in the EAC are to be accomplished in tandem, and so much faster than would have been expected under a free trade area. The community is currently a customs union and negotiations are still under way to transform the community into a common market.

In 2008 SADC became a free trade area. However, the tariff reduction programme for the members of the community reflects the varying capacities of the economies concerned to face competition from other countries in the community. Mauritius agreed to allow 65 per cent of goods imports from South Africa to enter its economy duty free in 2000. But Tanzania could offer only 9 per cent that year, and the removal of its tariffs will be staggered—with 88 per cent lifted by 2008 and 100 per cent by 2012. Unlike more formal free trade areas, countries were able to choose which products to reduce duties on as long as the overall goal was attained. South Africa in particular and members

---

3. The eight "pillar" RECs are: Community of Sahel-Saharan States (CEN-SAD), Common Market for Eastern and Southern Africa (COMESA), East African Community (EAC), Economic Community of Central African States (ECCAS/CEEAC), Economic Community of West African States (ECOWAS), Intergovernmental Authority on Development (IGAD), Southern African Development Community (SADC), Arab Maghreb Union (AMU/UMA).

of the Southern African Customs Union (SACU) in general are required to reduce tariffs on intra-SADC trade faster than other members.

UMA had trade liberalisation high on its agenda when the organisation was established in February 1989. In 1991 UMA countries signed a protocol under which goods originating in and traded among member states were to benefit from the elimination of tariffs and non-tariff barriers. Tariff elimination has yet to be fully implemented. Members trade more through bilateral arrangements than through the UMA trade protocol.

Challenges

Despite African countries' determination to dismantle trade restrictions in order to create a common market within the framework of regional and sub-regional agreements, barriers to intra-community trade development are numerous. These barriers are mostly the consequences of the economic structure of the countries; their institutional policies and weak infrastructures; their weak financial and capital markets; and their failure to implement trade protocols. The economic structures of African countries, which are broadly similar, include low-capacity manufacturing sectors, lack of diversified production, and their production and marketing policies lack co-ordination and harmonisation. The weak infrastructure and institutional policies of many of the countries are partly responsible for poor intra-African trade. Furthermore, the numerous roadblocks and checkpoints on African highways contribute immensely to increasing the delays in the delivery of goods and to raising transport costs.

African customs administrations are generally inefficient, contributing to barriers to trade within and outside the continent. Customs regulations require excessive documentation, which must be done manually because the process is not automated and ICTs are absent in most of the custom offices. Furthermore, customs procedures are outdated and lack transparency, predictability and consistency. These inefficiencies result in delays in which tend to raise transaction costs. In addition to the barriers to intra-African trade, payment and insurance systems are also not well

developed. Foreign trade financing, export credit facilities and export insurance systems are also not available in most African countries. There is no inter-convertibility of African currencies because monetary and financial regulations are not harmonised at the regional, sub-regional and national levels. There is a gap between the needs of exporters and the insurance services and products offered.

Proposed COMESA-EAC-SADC Free Trade Area

In October 2008 the three RECs in Eastern and Southern Africa, COMESA, EAC and the SADC agreed to form a free trade area. Should it be achieved such an FTA would deepen intra-African trade by involving 26 countries (almost half of the continent), with a combined population of 527 million people and a combined GDP of USD 624 billion.

One of the main challenges facing the partners is overlapping membership. Of the 26 countries, 17 (almost two-thirds) are either already in a customs union or negotiating another customs union, or are negotiating two separate customs unions. Hence the agreement to initiate an FTA to minimise and eventually eliminate the contradictions brought about by overlapping membership.

The priority areas for policy harmonisation and co-ordination amongst EAC, COMESA and SADC under the FTA include, among others, a common tariff regime, standard rules of origin, simplified customs procedures and documentation, harmonisation of product standards, identification, removal and monitoring of non-tariff barriers, establishment of one-stop border posts, as well as safeguard measures and dispute settlement mechanism.

Exchange Rates

The size of global imbalances has decreased somewhat with the US current account deficit falling from a peak of 6.5 per cent of GDP in 2006 to 5.5 per cent in 2007, and to 4.9 per cent in 2008. In part, the improvement reflects the heightened competitiveness of US exports *vis-à-vis* the Euro zone and Japan as the

Box 3 - Macroeconomic convergence among members of the RECs

Following the framework of the European Monetary Union, the RECs have established targets for selected key macroeconomic variables that must be met by member states. A sizeable number of the RECs are doing their best to achieve these targets while some are struggling with it. Most of the RECs are yet to achieve their monetary and financial integration objectives.

Progress on monetary co-operation arrangements in Africa

In recent years, some RECs have produced blueprints for the establishment of monetary unions. For example ECOWAS is working hard to have a common currency. It hopes to start with a common currency zone for Nigeria, Ghana, Gambia, Guinea and Sierra Leone, which would be merged with the UEMOA franc zone at a later date to create an ECOWAS currency. SADC, COMESA and EAC all have plans of establishing common currencies.

The primary and secondary convergence criteria established by the RECs include agreed targets for macroeconomic variables such as budgetary balance, inflation and public debt. Although the principles are the same, there are some variations in the criteria from REC to REC.

A report from the ECA and the AU Commission, *Assessing Regional Integration in Africa: Towards Monetary and Financial Integration* (UNECA-AU 2008), shows that, although there are some successes, African countries are experiencing enormous difficulties in achieving the desired macroeconomic convergence criteria set by the regional economic communities to which they belong. That is, whereas, some members states, particularly those that belong to monetary unions (WAEMU and WAMU) have done well in maintaining relatively low, single-digit inflation, most countries are posting double-digit inflation and consequently struggling to achieve their targets. Most of the countries have failed to achieve the fiscal targets. Some of the reasons for the weak performance include, among others, negative external shocks, large budget deficits, lack of reliable statistics and poor growth performance.

The Way Forward

• The success of regional integration hinges critically on member countries' pursuing convergent macroeconomic policies. Misalignments of key macroeconomic variables could hamper the regional integration process. It is therefore imperative that the process of strengthening regional integration includes guidelines for the convergence of the macroeconomic and trade policies of the entire regional space so as to strengthen the overall regional integration agenda. In fact, WAEMU and WAMU already have strict convergence criteria for several key indicators, including: (i) fiscal receipts, budget balance, public debt, trade and current account balances, all as percentages of GDP; (ii) inflation; and (iii) public sector wages and public investment financed from domestic resources, both as a percentage of fiscal receipts

• However, for the co-ordination of macroeconomic policies in the RECs to succeed African countries should have a clear sense of their own development objectives and strategies and be fully committed to the pursuit of these goals. Member states of the AU should muster the political will to mainstream regional monetary and macroeconomic objectives into their national development strategies.

Source: UNECA and African Union (2008), *Assessing Regional Integration in Africa III,* Addis Ababa.

dollar weakened between 2002 and 2004, and, after stabilising during 2005, weakened further in 2006 and 2007. Thus, in January 2008, one EUR purchased 55 per cent more USD than in January 2001. However, in the course of 2008 (especially at the end of the year with the spread of the crisis to the Euro zone and Japan) the USD strengthened against the EUR and nearly all other currencies, reflecting its status as a reserve currency and the attractiveness of the highly liquid market for US Treasury bonds during times of uncertainty. Even if the fundamentals driving the current account suggest a substantial depreciation of the USD, its predominance as an international reserve currency limits the chances for a substantial fall of the USD *vis-á-vis* other major currencies (e.g. EUR, GBP or JPY) in the near future.

The unwinding of global imbalances in late 2008 has also affected "carry trade" currencies such as the Japanese Yen (JPY) which have depreciated substantially against the dollar since late 2008. The counterparts to the sizeable current account deficit of the United States continue to be principally in East Asia and in oil-exporting economies. Surpluses in these areas are projected to fall over the next two years. Exchange-rate adjustments have so far been orderly and expectations are that this situation will continue. In the present circumstances, however, any boost to global demand is highly welcomed, and concerns about global imbalances are not likely to rise to the top of the policy agenda until recovery in the global economy is firmly underway.

Figure 2 - **USD per EUR and per Rand** (base 100 in January 2000)

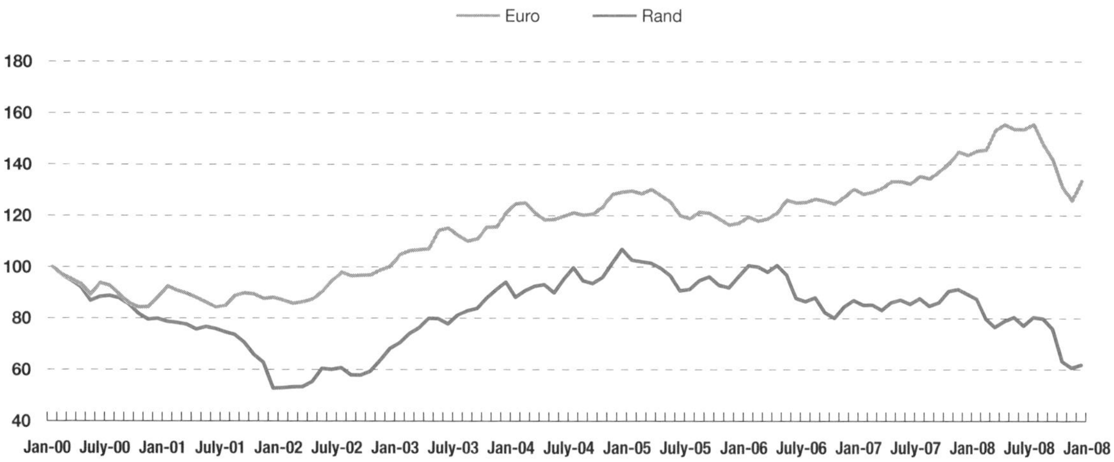

Source: www.x-rates.com.

StatLink http://dx.doi.org/10.1787/568153861631

Raw Material Prices

Commodity prices continued to exhibit considerable strength throughout 2008 even as the world economic expansion continued, possibly magnified by speculative buying which may have pushed prices for many commodities above levels justified by the fundamentals. However, the increases were much greater for oil and metals than for most tropical beverages. A sharp rise in food prices occurred in 2007 and continued in 2008, driven by increases in the prices of fats and oils (102 per cent over two years), and grains (88 per cent). The

increased use of bio fuels has played an important role in driving up grain prices. In 2006, bio fuels accounted for between 5 and 10 per cent of the global production of bio fuel feed-stocks, such as maize in the United States, sugar cane in Brazil, and vegetable oils, mainly rape seed, in the European Union.

The sustained rise in commodity prices improved the export earnings of most African countries in 2008. However, increases in fuel and food prices have hurt most oil importers. Countries that have benefited the most have generally been exporters of petroleum and minerals. For many other countries, gains from higher-priced commodities have been roughly equivalent to losses from higher priced fuel and food.

Oil

Crude oil prices continued to trend upward through mid 2008 and to exhibit high volatility, with the monthly average (Brent) peaking at USD 147 per barrel in July. They then declined sharply, with the average monthly price falling to USD/barrel 41.6, but the average for 2008 was USD/barrel 97.6, 34 per cent higher than the average price in 2007. This followed an increase to USD/72.7 in 2007 from USD/barrel 65.4 in 2006. The assumption of this report (fixed in mid-February) is that the price will average USD/barrel 50 in 2009 and 55 in 2010, an assumption slightly lower than the average of USD 60 per barrel used as a technical assumption in the *OECD Economic Outlook 84* published in December 2008. These lower oil prices are expected to contribute marginally to mitigating the severity of the global recession on oil-importing countries.

Metals

Metal prices reached a peak in the second quarter of 2008 when they were 271 per cent higher than average prices in 2000, in large part because of high demand by emerging Asian economies, especially China. For the year as a whole, prices were only 3.7 per cent higher than in 2007. Moreover, the average price in December was 37 per cent lower than the average price for the year as a whole as metal prices declined sharply along with the global slowdown. The average price in 2009 is expected to be about 50 per cent lower than in 2008, but to recover by more than 10 per cent in 2010.

The price of gold has escalated since mid-2001, sustained by liquid financial markets, low interest rates, the greater demand from booming emerging markets in Asia, and – since late 2008 – the heightened uncertainty in equity markets and the global economy. The price of gold peaked in the first quarter of 2008, but the average price in December of USD 816 per troy ounce (toz) was still 17 per cent higher than the average price in 2007. It is expected to remain high in 2009 (gold has appreciated more than 15 per cent from December 2008-February 2009) and 2010 as investors are reluctant to move strongly into equities and are preferring gold as a safe haven. Another factor influencing gold prices was a decline in output by an estimated 14 per cent in South Africa, the largest producer of gold in the world, contributing to a drop in global mine production of 3.6 per cent. The

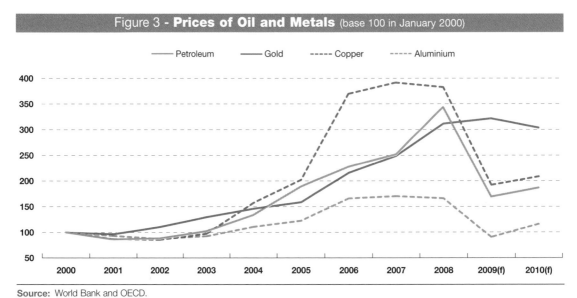

Figure 3 - **Prices of Oil and Metals** (base 100 in January 2000)

Source: World Bank and OECD.

StatLink http://dx.doi.org/10.1787/568200684581

shortfalls in South Africa were due to power supply constraints, an industry-wide skills shortage and an upgrading of mine safety procedures. The higher prices have benefited South Africa and other African gold producers, such as Ghana and Mali, and mitigated to some extent the fall in production in South Africa. However, the price increases did not match those of fuel imports.

Prices of other metals which had risen substantially in 2006 and 2007, had reached a peak by the second quarter of 2008. Copper prices fell by 2 per cent in 2008 with the softening of the global economy. The average price for December was 56 per cent lower than the average for the year as a whole, and copper prices are expected to remain soft in 2009 and 2010. Prices of aluminium have increased at a slower rhythm than other metals, but in 2006 the increase was substantial (35 per cent) on the strength of demand from China. However, they increased by only about 3 per cent in 2007 and fell by a similar amount in 2008. In December 2008 the average price was 42 per cent lower than the average for the year as a whole, and they are expected to remain depressed until the world economy begins to recover. Zambia (for copper) and Mozambique, Ghana, Cameroon and Guinea benefited the most from the increases in metal prices through 2008.

Agricultural Products

Prices of agricultural products were 25 per cent off their peaks by the end of 2008, much less of a decline than in the case of minerals. Most of the products are foodstuffs, which are less sensitive to fluctuations in global economic output.

Prices of tropical commodities have had a mixed performance (Figure 4). Unlike most other commodity prices, cocoa prices moved sharply upwards through the third quarter of 2008, continued to show strength in December, and registered an increase of about 32 per cent for the year as a whole. The price surge appears to be driven by a shortfall of production in Côte d'Ivoire, the world's largest cocoa producer and exporter, estimated to be about 35 per cent lower in 2008 than in 2007. The shortfalls are due to high fertiliser prices and relatively high levels of taxation which have reduced incentives to farmers to replant, instead shifting their efforts to other crops. Cocoa prices had been fluctuating around a narrow range during the period 2004-06, substantially lower than in previous years, but they moved up in 2007 in response to strong demand. The price increases are expected to benefit Ghana, Nigeria, and Cameron where production has been increasing.

27

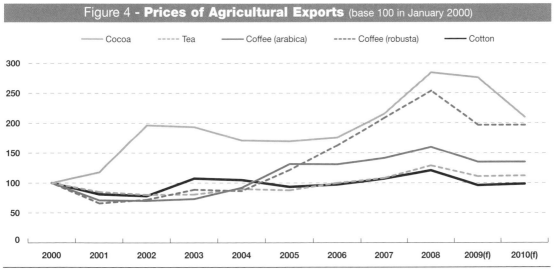

Figure 4 - **Prices of Agricultural Exports** (base 100 in January 2000)

Source: World Bank.

StatLink http://dx.doi.org/10.1787/568201354877

The prices of coffee, a key export for many African countries, continued to rise in 2008 (by 13 and 22 per cent for Robusta and Arabica varieties, respectively). This followed increases in both 2006 and 2007, especially for Robusta, mainly because of a production shortfall in Viet Nam (which has become a large coffee exporter). Unlike metals, coffee prices continued to rise in the third quarter of 2008 before falling back in the fourth quarter, suggesting that commodity traders may have been pushing prices higher than warranted by the fundamentals. Prices for the month of December 2008 were markedly lower than for the year as a whole, down 15 and 22 per cent for Arabica and Robusta, respectively. In the case of the latter the December price was 5 per cent lower than the average price in 2007 due to a recovery of production in Viet Nam. Little change in their current levels is expected in 2009 and 2010 with growth in production likely only slightly to exceed growth in consumption.

Tea prices increased by 18.9 per cent in 2008 compared to 2007. Prices peaked in the third quarter of 2008. By December, the average price was 21 per cent lower than the average price for the year as a whole and 5.6 per cent lower than the average for 2007. Prices are expected to remain at about the same levels in 2009 and 2010. The outlook is not favourable, since continued growth in output continually threatens to outpace growth in demand.

Cotton prices rose by 12.8 per cent in 2008 following an increase of about 10 per cent in 2007 largely due to greater global demand and a fall in US cotton production. However, after reaching their peak in the third quarter, the average price in December 2008 was 22 per cent lower than the average price for the year as a whole and 3 per cent lower than the average price for 2006, thus completely reversing the gains of the past two years (Figure 4). This deterioration of prices is particularly worrisome for countries like Mali, Benin and Burkina Faso which had experienced lower export earnings in 2006 and 2007.

While the recent boom in commodity prices has been good for exporters, food-price inflation has become a problem for many food-importing developing countries in Africa and elsewhere. In 2008, food prices in nominal terms reached an average level 147 per cent higher than the low levels of 2000. Partly, this was a result of the increased use of food crops for bio fuels, but also of higher fertiliser prices (linked to high petroleum prices but also to capacity constraints in fertiliser production), and low stocks in the face of buoyant demand. In some cases, drought has played a temporary role. The World Bank[4]

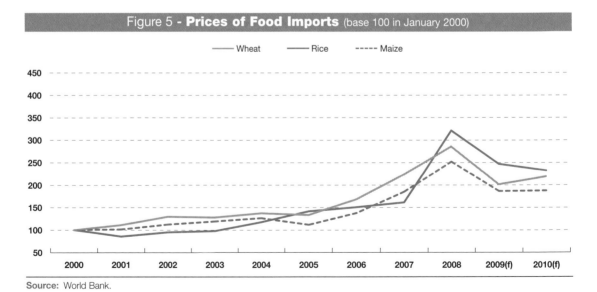

Figure 5 - **Prices of Food Imports** (base 100 in January 2000)

Source: World Bank.

StatLink http://dx.doi.org/10.1787/568210655700

4. World Bank (2008), *Global Economic Prospects 2008* Washington, DC.

has estimated that price increases for vegetable oils and grains between 2004 and 2007 had inflicted a terms-of-trade loss equivalent to 0.5 per cent of GDP for low-income countries on average, but as much as 1 per cent for 29 countries. These high prices have begun to fall back and are expected to be about 26 per cent lower in 2009 compared with the average level in 2008. One reason for this was a reduction in bio fuels production as the price of oil fell sharply thus reducing incentives to substitute bio fuels for petrol and diesel.

Official Development Assistance (ODA)

Excluding debt relief operations, total Official Development Assistance (ODA) continued to increase in 2007. The net increase in ODA from DAC members rose slightly by 2 per cent over the 2006 figure[5]. Estimations show that the positive trend continued in 2008, with an increase of 10.2 per cent in real terms of total ODA from DAC members, this time including debt relief operations. Despite the improvement this trend remains much too slow if donors are to meet the targets for increases in aid by 2010 in line with the commitments taken in Gleneagles in 2005.

The total net ODA from members of the OECD Development Assistance Committee (DAC) was USD 103.5 billion in 2007. This figure represents a decline of 8.5 per cent in real terms[6], and when expressed as a percentage of their combined gross national income, it represents a drop from 0.31 per cent of their combined gross national income in 2006 to 0.28 per cent in 2007. ODA had been exceptionally high in 2005 (USD 107.1 billion) and 2006 (USD 104.4 billion), due to large Paris Club debt relief operations for Iraq and Nigeria.

In 2007, debt relief amounted to USD 9 billion, considerably less than in 2006 and 2007, when it was USD 20 billion and USD 25 billion, respectively[7].

The largest donors in 2007, by volume, were the United States, followed by Germany, France, the United Kingdom and Japan. Five countries exceeded the United Nations target of 0.7 per cent of GNI: Denmark, Luxembourg, the Netherlands, Norway and Sweden. (See DAC 2009 Report Annex A, Table 1 and Chart 1). Japan's net ODA was USD 7.7 billion, representing 0.17 per cent of GNI, a fall of 29.8 per cent in real terms that was in part due to a decrease in debt relief operations, which were exceptionally high in 2005 and 2006, and to a decrease in contributions to international financial institutions. Japan's ODA has been on a downward trend since 2000, except for an increase in 2005 and 2006 mainly due to debt relief.

The combined ODA of the 15 DAC member countries that are also EU members – which represents nearly 60 per cent of all DAC ODA – fell by 6.6 per cent in real terms to USD 61.5 billion, representing 0.39 per cent of their combined GNI. Again, the fall was mainly due to a decrease in debt relief grants. Excluding debt relief, net ODA from DAC EU members rose by 7.7 per cent.

Aid rose in real terms in ten DAC EU countries as follows: Germany (+6.1 per cent), reflecting increases in both bilateral aid and contributions to international organisations; Luxembourg (+15.0 per cent), due to the general scaling up of its aid; Spain (+19.7 per cent), mainly due to a rise in its multilateral contributions, within a planned process of scaling-up of its aid. Austria (+8.3 per cent), Denmark (+2.9 per cent), Finland (+6.4 per cent), Greece (+5.3 per cent), the Netherlands (+3.2 per cent), and Portugal (+5.9 per cent) also increased their aid. Finally, Ireland (+4.8 per cent), raised its ODA/GNI ratio to 0.55 per cent.

Aid from other DAC EU countries fell in real terms, due mainly to decreased debt relief: Belgium (-11.2 per cent), France (-16.4 per cent), Italy (-2.6 per cent),

29

---

5. OECD DAC (2009), *Development Co-operation Report 2009*, Paris.

6. OECD DAC (2009), *op. cit.*

7. *AEO* 2008, p.25.

Sweden (-2.5 per cent) and the United Kingdom (-29.6 per cent). Excluding debt relief, aid rose in these countries with the exception of the United Kingdom, where net ODA decreased slightly due to sales of equity investments.

Net ODA by the European Commission rose by 3.1 per cent to USD 11.8 billion mainly due to increased programme and project aid. Humanitarian aid also increased, and the EC's disbursement capacity continued to improve.

The largest recipient of net bilateral ODA in 2007 was Iraq, which received USD 9 billion, of which USD 4.8 billion were net debt forgiveness grants. Afghanistan was the next largest recipient receiving USD 3 billion,

followed by Tanzania (USD 1.8 billion), Cameroon and Sudan (USD 1.7 billion each).

At the time of the Gleneagles G8 and UN Millennium +5 summits in 2005, donors committed to increase their aid. These commitments were expected to raise ODA by USD 50 billion in 2010 compared with 2004 (at 2004 prices and exchange rates). Excluding debt relief and humanitarian aid, which are expected to return to their historical levels by 2010, the annual average growth rate required to reach the target was is 11 per cent. In particular, at the Gleneagles G8 Summit, donors made specific individual commitments[8]. The "Gleneagles commitment" from Annex II of the Gleneagles G8 Communiqué on Africa stipulated:

Box 4 - What Will Happen to Aid Flows to Africa?

An OECD Development Centre Working Paper explores the evidence on the impact of economic cycles in the donor countries on the scale of aid disbursements. Broadly speaking, the evidence is ambiguous. To cite a few examples, during their economic downturns, between 1991 and 1993 Finland cut bilateral ODA by more than 40 per cent and between 1990 and 1996 Japan cut its aid by 12 per cent. But in the United States, while aid dropped sharply during the recession of 1990-91, during the 2000-01 recession aid increased. Nor does it seem that there is much clear-cut evidence about the relationship between aid disbursement and fiscal balance in donor countries. Again, in the case of the United States, there has been no statistical relationship between net bilateral ODA and either tax receipts, deficits or total government expenditures.

It is therefore impossible to say with any certainty whether fiscally-challenged governments will cut ODA. The only thing we do know is that the global financial crisis is so widespread and so serious that the choices facing donor governments are likely to be stark ones; perhaps much more so than they have been in the recent past. It does not bode well that several donors have already announced major cuts in their aid budgets.

Nevertheless, the financial crisis could (or should) give a new impetus to governments' efforts to improve aid effectiveness, as expressed in the Paris Declaration and the Accra Agenda for Action. Even in the face of the possible stagnation of aid budgets, there might be a pay off if donors react in a way that is pro-poor and more flexible. Indeed, a hard-budget constraint may even help reduce some of the inefficiencies that have become inherent in the international aid system. Now, more than ever, policy makers need to protect aid volumes and allocate them in a way that is pro-poor.

Source: Mold, A., S. Paulo and A. Prizzon (2009), "Taking Stock of the Credit Crunch: Implications for Development Finance and Global Financial Crisis", *Working Paper* No 177, OECD Development Centre, Paris.

8. Annex B *(Progress by G8 Donors on their Gleneagles ODA Commitments)* in DAC 2009 report, presents key statements made by each DAC donor at the G8 Summit and indicates the trajectories now needed to attain the levels promised.

"The EU has pledged to reach 0.7 per cent ODA/GNI by 2015 with a new interim collective target of 0.56 per cent ODA/GNI by 2010. The EU will nearly double its ODA between 2004 and 2010 from 34.5 billion EUR to 67 billion EUR."

While the DAC Secretariat's assessment of donors' stated spending plans through 2010 indicate that a sizeable increase in total ODA and in ODA for Africa will occur, the expected increases will not be enough to meet the Gleneagles commitments in Figure 6.

An OECD survey[9] of donors' forward spending plans showed that, at country or regional levels, donors have already programmed an additional USD 17 billion by 2010 compared to 2004 levels. Record replenishments of IDA and the African and Asian Development Banks will add about another USD 4 billion to this figure in 2010. Thus, about USD 21 billion of the USD 50 billion promised by 2010 has already been delivered or has been planned. This leaves nearly an additional USD 30 billion in 2004 dollars - about USD 34 billion in 2007 dollars - to be programmed into donors' aid budgets if their aid commitments for 2010 are to be achieved[10]. The severity of the economic crisis in major donor countries reinforces doubts on whether aid commitments will be respected. The World Bank and the IMF[11] recently estimated that the current aid gap for Low Income Countries (LICs) is between USD 20 to USD 25 billion taking into account the impact of the global financial crisis.

Figure 6 - DAC Members' Net ODA 1990 - 2007 and DAC Secretariat Simulations of net ODA to 2008 and 2010

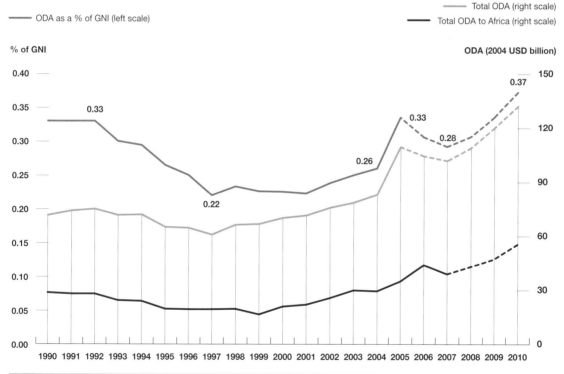

Source: DAC OECD Development Co-operation Report, 2009.

StatLink http://dx.doi.org/10.1787/568220660120

9. See *www.oecd.org/dac/scalingup*.

10. See OECD DAC (2009), *op. cit.*

11. IMF (2009), *The implications of the Global Financial Crisis for Low-Income Countries*, Washington, DC.

Concerning other donors, China is playing an increasing role though, according to the IMF, there are few available data on the growing Chinese presence in Africa in terms of aid, debt and direct investment flows. Aid and direct investment from the Gulf countries have also risen in 2007 especially in infrastructure, hotels, and real estate in West Africa.

Bilateral development projects and programmes which slightly dipped in 2006 started to rise again in 2007. Donors have also been making some progress in gradual scaling up core aid programmes in order to reduce fragmentation, which continues to be a major concern both donors and partners: *a)* for donors managing programmes in many countries (Canada, EC, France, Germany, Japan, and the United States give aid to over 100 countries; Portugal to 19 and New Zealand to 21[12]); and *b)* for partners having to deal with a large number of small donors (37 countries have more than 24 DAC and major multilateral donors; in two thirds of these more than 15 of those donors account for just 10 per cent of their aid)[13].

To address the global challenges of poverty reduction and achieve the MDGs, aid is also reported to be increasingly poverty-focused[14]. Indeed, total net ODA to the Least Developed Countries (LDCs) has nearly doubled in real terms over the last 10 years, to reach USD 32.5 billion in 2007, representing about a third of total aid[15].

Looking at countries in terms of their relative development, the DAC report shows that country programmable aid (CPA) increased by about USD 3.8 billion between 2005 and 2010 for least-developed countries (LDCs) and nearly USD 3 billion for other low-income countries (other LICs).

Regarding scaling up by country, the survey data for individual developing countries indicate that scaling up has been planned in two-thirds of them between 2005 and 2010. The survey suggests an increase in CPA of about USD 10.3 billion in 102 countries, of which 39 are in Africa, with an increase of some USD 6.1 billion. Many of the countries with the largest increases in CPA are priority partners for several DAC members and thus reflect scaling up firmly rooted in donors' country strategies.

Excluding debt relief, net ODA disbursements to fragile states[16] have risen steadily since 2000[17]. However, only five countries among which four in Africa – Afghanistan, Cameroon, Democratic Republic of Congo, Nigeria and Sudan – have received more than half of total ODA to the group in recent years (with a peak in 2006 –74 per cent – due mainly to debt relief for Nigeria). Most of this aid is provided in the form of debt relief or humanitarian relief, leaving some countries marginalised and with limited programmable aid. In these circumstances the unpredictability of aid flows is a major impediment to attaining the aid effectiveness objectives of the Paris declaration[18]. *The DAC Principles for Good International Engagement in Fragile States and Situations* focus on state building as the central objective. Aid for government and civil society (which includes aid for peace, security conflict prevention and resolution) has increased by over 155 per cent in real terms between 2000/01 and 2005/06[19].

---

12. Global Forum on Development, DAC/DCD December 2007

13. OECD DAC (2009), *op. cit.*

14. OECD DAC (2009), *op. cit.*

15. See OECD DAC (2009), *op. cit.*, Annex A, Chart 2

16. Fragile states, a group of 38 countries affected by conflict or burdened with a legacy of weak governance refers also to countries where the Millennium Development Goals (MDGs) are hardest to attain. For a list of fragile states, refer to bottom of Chart 4 in Annex A. (OECD DAC, 2009, *op. cit.*)

17. See Annex A, Charts 3 and 4 of OECD DAC (2009), *op. cit.*

18. Refer to the part on *"Progress in making aid more effective"*

19. OECD DAC (2009), *op. cit.*

Growth of Aid to Africa

Net ODA to Africa amounted to USD 38.7 billion in 2007, representing 37 per cent of total aid. This corresponds to a fall of 18 per cent in real terms, mostly due to the end of exceptional debt relief operations. In 2007, debt relief grants returned to their levels prior to 2005. Excluding debt relief grants, ODA to Africa rose by 12 per cent in real terms. Net ODA to sub-Saharan Africa was USD 34.2 billion, of which USD 21.5 billion was bilateral aid from DAC donors[20]. The largest recipient of net bilateral ODA in 2007 in Africa was Tanzania which received (USD 1.8 billion), followed by Cameroon and Sudan (USD 1.7 billion each)[21]. Donors continued to focus on countries which have historically benefited from large aid flows: Egypt and Morocco in North Africa; and Tanzania, Ethiopia, Sudan, Nigeria, Cameroon, Mozambique, Uganda, Kenya, and DRC in sub-Saharan Africa, these 9 countries accounting for more than 53 per cent of total ODA to SSA in 2007[22].

The Gleneagles G8 summit estimated also that, should donors meet their commitments, total ODA to Africa would *"increase (…)by USD 25 billion a year by 2010, more than doubling aid to Africa compared to 2004."* Final figures on ODA to Africa in 2004 were not known at the time of Gleneagles. The final total was in fact USD 29.5 billion. International organisations are interpreting the Gleneagles estimate as implying an increase in ODA of USD 25 billion at 2004 prices and exchange rates, so that for the promise to be fulfilled, ODA to Africa would need to be at least $54.5 billion in 2010, at 2004 prices and exchange rates[23]. To achieve this target, donors would need to

boost their aid to Africa between 2007 and 2010 by over 17 per cent annually (See 2009 DAC OECD Report's Annex A, Chart 5).

Based on their performance in 2007, several G8 countries would need sharp increases in their aid to meet their commitments. US ODA was USD 5.86 billion in 2007, and is projected to reach USD 6.54 and USD 7.53 billion in 2008 and 2009, respectively[24].

Non-DAC donors, have increased their ODA to the continent. On the basis of the available information, it appears that China has played a variety of roles in Africa: trading partner, donor, financier and investor, contractor and builder. The data also show that trade, investment, and other commercial activities combined have outpaced official development assistance (ODA) and become dominant in financial terms[25].

Chinese aid flows were equal to about 20 per cent of the value of trade with China in the early 1990s. That ratio declined to 3-4 per cent in 2004-05, even though China has stepped up its ODA to Africa since the first China-Africa Co-operation Forum was held in 2000[26]. Indeed, in dollar terms, annual ODA flows from China to Africa increased from about USD310 million in 1989–92 to an estimated USD1-1.5 billion in 2004–05[27]. However, there are major difficulties in estimating Chinese aid disbursements because of a lack of official time series and problems in valuing Chinese technical assistance and in-kind aid according to the IMF's quarterly magazine. Moreover, the IMF reported that incomplete data make it hard to compare the terms on which China provided debt relief on terms

33

---

20. OECD DAC (2009), *op. cit.*

21. OECD DAC (2009), *op. cit.*

22. Data from DAC OECD statistical annex for 2007 ODA.

23. OECD DAC (2009), *op. cit.*

24. OECD DAC (2009), *op. cit.*, P. 17-18.

25. IMF, Finance & Development, March 2008, Volume 45, Number 1 *Maximizing the benefits of China's increasing economic engagement with Africa*

26. *Ibid.*

27. Wang, 2007; Taylor, 1998.

comparable to the terms of the Heavily Indebted Poor Countries Initiative (HIPC).

The 2009 DAC report also shows a small increase in total humanitarian aid. The recent food crises, which have caused riots and troubles in several Sub-Saharan African countries, provoked a slight increase in humanitarian emergency aid for the sub-region. This increase comes from DAC and non-DAC member countries, as well as from World Food Program, other UN agencies, and nongovernmental organisations (NGOs). However, the general picture shows that much humanitarian aid globally continued to be concentrated on Iraq and Afghanistan, as a consequence of US increased ODA to Afghanistan by 5 per cent, to USD 1.5 billion, and USD 3.7 billion for Iraq. Humanitarian aid, like debt relief from bilateral donors, decreased for Africa, while other sources of ODA rose. (See Figure 7)

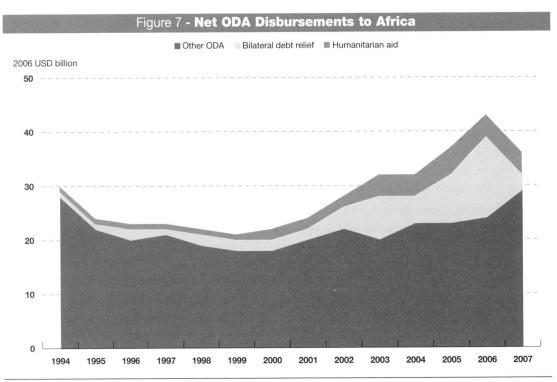

Figure 7 - **Net ODA Disbursements to Africa**

Source: DAC OECD Development Co-operation Report, 2009.

StatLink http://dx.doi.org/10.1787/568234823152

In 2008, as in 2007, the largest African aid recipients included several among the 28 which have achieved their HIPC[28] completion point or are in the process of doing so. As of March 2009, 20 African countries had reached their completion points and 8 more had reached the decision point under the enhanced HIPC Initiative; 5 others are potentially eligible[29]. The challenge of the HIPC initiative, and of the Multilateral Debt Relief Initiative (MDRI), is to ensure that the resources that are freed from debt repayment are channelled to expenditures on health, education and other social services[30].

The concern expressed in *AEO 2007/08* over debt sustainability is still relevant. The immediate problem, however, is the drying up of trade credits with the contraction of the secondary market in commercial paper, prompting the IMF and the World Bank to

28. The HIPC initiative, started in 1996, is a comprehensive approach to debt reduction for heavily indebted poor countries pursuing IMF and World Bank supported adjustment and reform programmes.

29. IMF (January, 2009), "Fact Sheet: Debt Relief Under the Heavily Indebted Poor Countries (HIPC) Initiative".

30. *Ibid.*

enter the market as a supplier of trade finance. This problem has been exacerbated by the global financial crisis that started in late 2008. To be sure, many African countries have continued to contract credits with emerging donors who are not members of the DAC and are not obliged to implement the Paris Declaration and other tools for better management and aid effectiveness. China has continued to lend important amounts of money to several Sub-Saharan African countries, but due to the incomplete data on China's aid and credits to Africa, it is difficult to estimate such flows. Thus, even after debt relief under the HIPC and MDRI initiatives is fully implemented, maintaining a sustainable level of debt service, while seeking additional financing needed to make progress towards the MDGs, will still be a challenge[31].

To address the concern among developing countries in Africa and elsewhere that the current crisis may result in reductions in aid budgets instead of the further increases that have been pledged[32], the OECD's Secretary-General, Angel Gurría, and the Chair of the DAC, Eckhard Deutscher, have issued a statement calling upon the world's major donor countries to stand by their development pledges in order to prevent the "… financial crisis from generating an aid crisis", which would have a serious impact on developing countries, especially in Sub-Saharan Africa, already struggling with the global food crisis and rising oil prices. Their "Aid Pledge" urges DAC members to "… reaffirm their aid commitments and refrain from any budgetary action that is inconsistent with such commitments."[33]

As a positive sign, preliminary figures for 2008 released by the DAC at the end of March 2009 indicate that net bilateral ODA from DAC donors to Africa and Sub-Saharan Africa totalled USD 26 billion, of which USD 22.5 billion went to Sub-Saharan Africa. This

corresponds to real growth rates of 10.6 and 10 per cent for Africa and for Sub-Saharan region, excluding debt relief grants. If debt relief operations are included, the estimated growth rates were of 1.2 and 0.4 per cent respectively.

Progress in making aid more effective

Since the G20 meeting of November 2006 in Melbourne, donors renewed their commitments to increase aid effectiveness during the Accra High Level Forum in 2008. It was generally agreed that the Paris Declaration can expand development goals by strengthening cross-sectoral issues such as gender equality, respect for human rights, and environmental sustainability. Each principle of the Paris Declaration was redefined with a view to integrating these values. Concrete illustrations of the possibility of integrating these concepts and values were further shared[34].

Although the aid effectiveness agenda remains unchanged, indicators to measure the progress made in the field are evolving. The Accra High Level Forum 2008 set new priorities[35] to increase aid effectiveness into the Paris Declaration's principles which effectively means:

- increasing development actors' delivery capacity,
- finding methods of including civil society in the delivery process;
- improving transparency and accountability on both donors and governments' parts so as to account for the inclusion of such values;
- adapting the evaluation and monitoring criteria accordingly.

Untying aid continues to increase[36]. Not only was the 2001 DAC Recommendation complied with, but

31. See AEO 2008 report.

32. OECD DAC (2009), *op. cit.*

33. The full statement can be seen at: *www.oecd.org/document/2/0,3343,en_2649_201185_41601282_1_1_1_1,00.html*

34. OECD DAC (2009), *op. cit.,* pp. 89-99.

35. For more information, OECD DAC (2009), *op. cit.,* pp. 92-93.

36. See Aid Effectiveness: Progress Report, p.12.

also in May 2008 DAC members agreed to expand the coverage of the recommendations to eight heavily indebted poor countries (HIPCs) that are not LDCs.

However, progress towards ownership seems to be uneven among partners and donors and often remains narrowly based within partner countries. National governments appear to encounter difficulties in making their strategies operational, especially when it comes to allocating budgets for specific results.

Progress made towards alignment is reflected in the gradually increasing and selective use of public financial management (PFM) and national public procurement systems (PP). In both cases, although progress is recorded, it seems to be insufficient to meet the 2010 goals. The use of PFM appears to be linked to budget support and the best results for the use of national systems of PP are found where the partner government is itself results-focused[37].

Harmonisation is progressing, thanks to the multiple efforts conducted by donor countries through the adoption of joint programming and assistance strategies, the pooling of funds and the use of country systems when feasible. More specifically, efforts have been seen in Tanzania, where joint assistance led to integrating a gender-focused approach to a sectoral, co-operative division of labour[38]. Overall consensus building seems to be the key to generating more harmonisation.

Managing for results still proves difficult to implement due to the lengthy process it involves. Most partner countries are still in the midst of devising monitoring frameworks with results-oriented strategies, which are difficult to organise without help from donor countries to plan, budget, manage and account for the results of policies and programmes.

For this reason, most donors provide some form of capacity building aid focusing on the particular needs of each country[39]. In Uganda, where gender inequalities are deemed to be a major issue, the government, together with civil society and academic institutions, was helped to create budgetary incentives for local governments to focus on poor women and children[40]. In Africa, Tanzania, Mozambique and Uganda are the countries making the most progress towards the attainment of results-oriented frameworks according to the World Bank.

Through the lessons learnt at the Accra High Level Forum, the development community realised that although the Paris Declaration improves aid effectiveness, much better delivery and monitoring are needed on the ground in order to achieve the Millennium Development Goals by 2015.

The Progress Report on implementing the Paris Declaration highlights several areas for possible improvement on the part of both partners and donors. Among these, the most striking are: leadership issues to spur the Paris Declaration's implementation process as well as broadening the base of stakeholders involved in the process; the necessity to change the incentive structure further to encourage donors and partners; and coherence issues between aid policies and trade, migration and environment[41]. Other areas of concern have been identified in the 2008 monitoring survey and the World Bank's Review, *Results-Based National Development Strategies: Assessment and Challenges Ahead*. They point out "definitional clarity, accelerated construction of monitoring frameworks, and greater agreement on how to strengthen systems" as being essential to reach the 2010 target of reducing by one-third the proportion of countries without transparent and verifiable performance assessment frameworks[42].

---

37. See progress report on Aid effectiveness, pp. 11-12.

38. See OECD DAC (2009), *op. cit.,* pp. 95.

39. See report on Aid effectiveness p.13.

40. OECD DAC (2009), *op. cit.,* pp. 96-97.

41. OECD DAC (2009), *op. cit.,* p. 10.

42. Aid effectiveness, p.86.

Box 5 - How Does Africa Fare in Making Aid More Effective?

How far from the 2010 targets?	Key factors for aid effectiveness	How does Africa fare?
Progress on track	Significant improvements in providing technical co-operation in a co-ordinated and aligned manner	For indicator 4, the 2008 survey shows that globally, the target has already been exceeded from 48 per cent in 2005 to 60 per cent in 2007. Figures for Africa show also a similar upward trend, improving from 39 per cent in 2005 to 56 per cent in 2007.
	Encouraging improvements in the quality of country PFM systems	The objective of indicator 2a is to measure and encourage improvements in developing-country systems for managing public funds. At the global level, 36 per cent (10 countries) have improved the quality of PFM systems. Six out of these ten countries are from Africa (Zambia, Rwanda, Burundi, Ethiopia, Ghana and Mauritania), improving the score for the quality of PFM systems by at least one measure.
	Improvements in untying aid both globally and in Africa	For indicator 8, global figures show increase in untying aid from 75 per cent in 2005 to 88 per cent in 2006. In Africa, it improved from 78 per cent in 2005 to 88 per cent in 2006.
Targets requiring efforts but within reach	Accountability of aid has improved both globally and in Africa	The objective of indicator 3 is to improve transparency and accountability of aid by encouraging partner countries and donors to accurately record aid in the national budget. Globally, on average, the realism of the country's budget improved from 42 per cent in 2005 to 48 per cent in 2007 African countries have improved budget realism by 6 per cent from 45 per cent in 2005 to 51 per cent in 2007.
	Aid predictability has improved both globally and in Africa	For Indicator 7, there has been modest improvement in donors disbursing aid within the scheduled year. Globally, on average, the proportion of aid disbursed within the fiscal year for which it is scheduled for has improved slightly from 41 per cent in 2005 to 46 per cent in 2007. In Africa, the figure has improved from 44 per cent in 2005 to 48 per cent in 2007.
	Use of programme-based approaches decreased slightly in Africa	Globally, donors increased the use of co-ordinated mechanisms for aid delivery by channelling more aid through PBAs, from 43 per cent in 2005 to 47 per cent in 2007. In Africa, the use of PBAs has decreased slightly from 48 per cent in 2005 to 46 per cent in 2007, reflecting, in part, more stringent definitions used in the survey.
	The number of parallel project implementation units decreased in Africa – yet there is a long way to go	The objective of indicator 6 is to encourage donors to make increasing use of country systems to avoid using parallel project implementation units (PIUs), Globally, the stock of parallel PIUs reduced from 1817 in 2005 to 1601 in 2007. In Africa, the number of parallel PIUs reduced from 960 in 2005 to 902 in 2007, still a far cry from the target of two-thirds reduction of the stock of parallel PIUs.

37

Box 5 - How Does Africa Fare in Making Aid More Effective?

Making country development strategies operational remains a challenge for Africa

Indicator 1 assesses the degree in which partner countries design development strategies that are operational and effective in achieving their own development goals. Progress has been slow – globally, countries with sound operational strategies have increased from 17 per cent in 2005 to 24 per cent in 2007, but far from the target of 75 per cent. Compared to 2005, seven African countries obtained a rating of B for the quality of a country's national development strategies, four of which had increased the score from C to B between 2005 and 2007 (Burkina Faso, Ethiopia, Ghana and Zambia).

Sound frameworks for monitoring development results remains a challenge

Significant challenges remain in establishing sound frameworks for results-based monitoring. Globally, the share of countries that have sound quality frameworks has improved slightly from 7 per cent in 2005 to 9 per cent in 2007. The challenge is shared in Africa, with only two countries obtaining a score of B in 2005 and three countries obtaining a B in 2007 (Mozambique, Tanzania and Uganda).

Targets requiring special efforts

Global improvement in the use of country systems, but decline in Africa

Indicator 5a and 5b measure, respectively, the degree in which donors use in-country public financial management and procurement systems. Globally, the percentage has risen modestly from 40 per cent in 2005 to 45 per cent in 2007 for the use of domestic PFM systems and 39 per cent in 2005 to 43 per cent in 2007. However, in Africa, the use of domestic PFM systems has declined from 40 per cent to 38 per cent and from 43 per cent to 41 per cent for country procurement systems. The survey results show little evidence to suggest that donors make more use of national systems if they are of sound quality.

Significant challenges remain in co-ordinating donor missions and country analytical work.

One of the most frequent complaints made by partner country authorities is that too much time is spent meeting with donors. Indicator 10a shows that the number of co-ordinated missions has not increased. Globally, the proportion of donor missions that are co-ordinated rose from 18 per cent in 2005 to 21 per cent in 2007, and in Africa, from 19 per cent to 22 per cent. The total number of donor missions remains high, with 7 500 missions in Africa.

Mechanisms for establishing mutual accountability mechanisms at country level has largely stalled, both at the global level and in Africa

Indicator 12 records whether countries have mechanisms for mutual reviews. Globally, only 14 out of 55 countries have such mechanisms. In Africa, only Burundi, Ethiopia, Ghana, Malawi, Mozambique, Senegal and Tanzania have such mechanisms.

Source: DAC Secretariat.

Both the 2006 Baseline Survey and the 2008 Survey on Monitoring the Paris Declaration featured 19 African countries[43] representing a broad spectrum of geographic, linguistic and situational differences. The Box below provides an overview of how African countries fare in improving the quality of aid vis-à-vis the global pool of countries which took part in the 2008 Survey on Monitoring the Paris Declaration.

---

43. The 19 African countries that took part in two rounds of surveys are: Benin, Burkina Faso, Burundi, Cape Verde, Democratic Republic of Congo, Egypt, Ethiopia, Ghana, Kenya, Malawi, Mali, Mauritania, Mozambique, Niger, Rwanda, Senegal, Tanzania, Uganda and Zambia. In addition 12 new Africa countries took part in the 2008 Survey to establish a baseline. They are: Cameroon, Central African Republic, Chad, Ivory Coast, Gabon, Liberia, Madagascar, Morocco, Nigeria, Sierra Leone, Sudan and Togo.

Efforts are already underway to respond to some of these challenges. Several donors and partners have started work on designing verifiable indicators that both could use leading up to the next high-level forum in 2011. The DAC Network on Development Evaluation is also working to improve the quality of evaluation systems by producing and distributing evaluation quality standards, glossaries and guidance.

Finally, it should be mentioned that the proliferation of aid channels has been combined with fragmented aid. ODA fragmentation can be damaging to the effectiveness of ODA, particularly in recipient countries with low institutional capacity, as it may increase the transaction costs of aid. Fragmentation is manifested in different forms, such as the number of donor-funded activities, the financial size of aid commitments and the dispersion of small-scale free-standing technical assistance as a modality (instrument) of aid delivery. The 2007 EU Code of Conduct on Complementarity and Division of Labour, for instance, links efforts to reduce aid fragmentation to enhanced donor coordination and harmonisation[44].

Foreign Direct Investment

FDI has been one of the principal beneficiaries of the liberalisation of capital flows over recent decades and now constitutes the major form of capital inflow for many SSA countries, including some low-income ones like Chad, Mauritania, Sudan and Zambia. Economies are often considered less vulnerable to external financing difficulties when current account deficits are financed largely by FDI inflows, rather than debt-creating capital flows. For instance, in South Africa in 2007, FDI covered the whole of the current account deficit. There is no denying the importance of FDI inflows both for their contribution to sustaining current account imbalances in countries and for their contribution to broader economic

growth, through technological spillovers and competition effects.

Prior to the financial crisis, foreign direct investment (FDI) inflows to Africa had been rising strongly since 2002, reaching USD 53 billion over 2007, a 47.2 per cent increase on 2006 and their highest historical level. In 2007, USD 22.4 billion was directed to North Africa and USD 30.6 billion to Sub-Saharan Africa. Africa's share of global FDI flows registered a significant decline to 2.9 per cent of global FDI in 2007, down from 3.2 per cent in 2006. Even according to recent estimates[45], while global FDI may have fallen by up to 20 per cent in 2008; flows to Africa have remained resilient, growing by 16.8 per cent to USD 61.9 billion over 2008, despite the slowdown. The rate of return of FDI in Africa has been, increasing since 2004 and, at 12.1 per cent, was the highest among developing host regions in 2007. Mergers and acquisitions (M&As) in Africa rose by an estimated 157 per cent to USD 26 billion in 2008.

Behind a large share of the rise in FDI lies surging prices for raw materials, particularly oil, which fuelled a boom in commodity-related investment. High raw-material prices also helped maintain outward FDI flows from Africa, which remained stable at USD 6.5 billion in 2007. As a percentage of gross fixed capital formation, inflows stabilised at 21 per cent. Nevertheless, with the advent of the crisis, lower world demand and depressed prices for Africa's commodity exports are expected to affect investment levels, with particularly negative short-term effects for the resource-exporting countries in the region.

Attracting FDI into diversified and higher value-added sectors remains difficult in many countries. According to UNCTAD data, the primary sector remained the main focus of foreign investment. However, foreign interest in communications, manufacturing and infrastructure investments also

39

44. http://europa.eu/scadplus/leg/en/lvb/r13003.htm

45. UNCTAD "Assessing the impact of the current financial and economic crisis on global FDI flows", January 2009.

increased. Service-sector investment rose in North Africa, but remained negligible in Sub-Saharan Africa, barring financial institution buy-ins. Notably, some commodity-exporting countries have been making significant efforts to move up the value chain by, for example, expanding their refinery activities (Côte d'Ivoire, Egypt, Nigeria), though higher labour costs than other developing countries still hobble the potential for FDI in manufacturing.

FDI increased in 36 countries, and declined in 18. Top FDI destinations for 2007 were: Nigeria (USD 12.5 billion) Egypt (USD 11.6 billion) and South Africa (USD 5.7 billion) followed by Morocco, Libya, and Sudan. South Africa shifted back to a positive balance after having found itself a net exporter of investment capital in 2006, according to preliminary estimates, South African inflows more than doubled over 2008 to USD 12 billion. The most attractive countries for investment tend to hold significant natural resource endowments, active privatisation programmes, liberalised FDI policies and active investment promotion activities.

FDI levels and prospects still vary widely by region, sector and country. North Africa's sustained privatisation programmes and investment-friendly policies continued to attract large FDI inflows, reaching USD 22 billion in 2007, a 15 per cent increase on 2006. FDI investments in North Africa were the continent's most diversified, with projects in textiles, oil and chemicals and the production of generic pharmaceuticals. Inflows to Egypt remained substantial, reaching USD 11.6 billion. Privatisations also boosted FDI to the sub-region (for example the privatisation of the Crédit Populaire d'Algérie and the USD 5.4 billion foreign entry into Libya's state-owned Tamoil). West Africa continued to benefit from the commodity boom and ambitious privatisation schemes, leading to inflows of USD 15.6 billion in 2007. Nigeria still accounted for 80 per cent of total West African investment, mostly reflecting oil industry expansion projects.

Central African inflows grew by 28 per cent to USD 4.1 billion. East Africa, still the lowest recipient

of FDI on the continent, saw a 65 per cent increase in FDI flows in 2007, from USD 2.3 billion to USD 3.8 billion, thanks to new prospects in the primary sector and through projects in Madagascar[46] and privatisations in Kenya.

In Southern Africa, Angola remained a net capital exporter in 2007. South Africa, the continent's most diversified economy after having become a net exporter of capital in 2006, once again registered positive net inflows of USD 5.7 billion. Preliminary estimates suggest a further boost of inflows over 2008, reaching USD 12 billion at year's end. South Africa's stock of FDI at work in the country remains the highest in the continent by far at USD 93 billion, nearly a quarter of total FDI stock in Africa (standing USD 393.4 billion at end 2007). In 2007, FDI to the LDCs increased to USD 10 billion, from USD 9.6 billion the previous years.

Ten African countries introduced policy measures to improve the investment climate in 2007, most notably improving regulations pertaining to FDI and transnational company involvement in the economy. Regional entities also introduced FDI-promoting measures in 2007, including the COMESA Common Investment Area, which ambitions to establish a free investment area by 2010 and help its members, most of which are too small to attract sufficient investment to support national development and regional integration projects. ECOWAS created a department to promote cross-border investment and joint ventures so as to promote investment and promote public-private partnerships and is working to deepen the financial integration of the sub-region through its Finance and Investment Protocol. The SADC is also undertaking a joint investment promotion programme with the EU. In May 2008, the AfDB signed a memorandum of understanding with the Export-Import Bank of China, with provisions for co-financing and guarantees for public and possibly private sector projects.

FDI outflows from Africa remained strong in 2007 at USD 6 billion, though short of the peak of

---

46. UNCTAD classifies Madagascar in East Africa.

USD 8 billion of 2006. This performance was due to expanding operations of trans-national corporations, particularly from South Africa but also from countries that had been benefiting from high commodity prices. Top contributors to outward FDI were South Africa, Egypt, Morocco, Liberia, Angola, Algeria and Nigeria, mostly investing in natural resources exploitation and the services sector. South African firms invested heavily in banking, ICT and infrastructure. South African TNCs accounted for 80 per cent of total African outflows in 2007, with Morocco, Liberia and Nigeria accounting for a further 12 per cent. Though African FDI outflows remained centred on extraction, African TNCs also engaged in telecommunications and retail-sector investments.

While the boom in commodity markets contributed to maintaining growth in foreign investment through 2008, lower demand and depressed raw material prices brought on by the crisis have made disinvestment a looming prospect. This is echoed by the latest UNCTAD survey findings, stating that only 20 per cent of investors plan to increase investment in Africa between 2007-09 (against 80 per cent for Asia), illustrating foreign investors' narrow perspective on African investments.

The composition of non-FDI capital flows shows persistent variations between country groupings: ODA and bank lending predominate in Low Income Countries (LIC); equity flows are largely restricted to South Africa; bond financing is making inroads into middle-income countries, even though Nigeria had to cancel its first global Naira-denominated bond issue in early 2009 due to bad market conditions. South Africa is also developing into a source of external financing for other African countries.

The value of cross-border mergers and acquisitions (M&A) activity fell sharply in 2007 to USD 10.2 billion from USD 19.8 billion in 2006, partly due to fewer

extractive and exploration projects for sale. Nevertheless, preliminary estimates for 2008 show sharp swing back of 157 per cent to USD 26.3 billion[47], thanks to a massive jump in M&A activity in Egypt to USD 15.9 billion.

China expanded its support to Chinese investments in Africa, building on its general investment policy on Africa adopted in 2006. In 2007 the Export-Import Bank of China financed over 300 projects in the region, constituting almost 40 per cent of the Bank's loan book. The Industrial Bank of China (ICBC) made a large investment in the Standard Bank Group of South Africa. Japan announced in May 2008 its decision to set up a USD 2.5 billion investment fund (the Facility for African Investment, managed by JBIC) to help Japanese firms do more business in Africa, as part of its target to double Japanese private-sector investment on the continent to USD 3.4 billion by 2012.

Sovereign Wealth Funds and national investors are also investing more in Africa's infrastructure and have become, through their sheer size (predicted to reach at least USD 5 trillion by 2012[48]), important potential sources of FDI. Also increasing importance are investors from the Middle East, especially, but not limited to, North African projects.

While Africa was recently being hailed as an exciting financial frontier, even barring the crisis, local equity markets remain small, and local currency debt markets often too illiquid to exert a significant growth impact. Though the number of functioning stock markets has risen from five in 1989 to sixteen in 2007, in effect, the majority of African exchanges list only a handful of companies and are highly illiquid. There was for example no trading on the Maputo Stock exchange for the whole of 2004. Excluding South Africa's Johannesburg Stock exchange (JSE, with 401 listed companies in 2006), the average number of domestic companies listed per exchange was only 43 in 2006.

41

---

47. From an alternative source: total value of the top ten M&A deals to the end of October 2008 was USD 6.4 billion, compared with USD 14.9 billion for the top ten deals of 2007, with three of 2008's deals being refinancing rather than new projects.

48. JP Morgan *Sovereign Wealth Funds: A Bottom-up Primer* May, 2008.

In response to perennial size and liquidity problems, two exchange operators are attempting to create centralised, continent-wide exchanges[49]. The Johannesburg Stock Exchange (JSE), the largest on the continent, is attempting to bring the largest African firms to make secondary listings in South Africa. The second initiative involves Financial Technologies, the operator of India's commodity exchange, which is seeking to establish a pan-African commodity bourse. Based in Botswana, Bourse Africa could facilitate trades across the continent.

The African Union has also been looking to develop a pan-African Stock exchange[50], but the project remains in early stages. Widespread exchange controls, incompatible regulatory regimes and national resistance remain formidable hurdles to any pan-African exchange project.

As of March 2009, the Johannesburg Stock Exchange (JSE) had lost 45 per cent from its peak in May 2008[51]. This is not a bad performance, relative to that of many mature markets, but the rapid currency depreciation following the repatriation of foreign capital has exacerbated the impact of the fall.

Private equity fund raising, static at USD 2.3 billion in 2006 and 2007, increased to USD 3.2 billion for 2008, bringing the total funds invested through private equity funds to USD 7.6 billion for 2008. South Africa's private equity industry reached ZAR 86.6 billion in funds under management at end-2007, an increase of 46 per cent over 2006, and with funds under management representing 2.8 per cent of GDP, up from 1.7 per cent in 2006. Sixty-four per cent of funds raised over 2007 were from US sources, up from 39 per cent in 2006. Private equity investment activity reached 5 per cent of total South African M&A activity (measured in terms of deal size i.e. debt and equity) in 2007. South African private equity investment activity reached 11th place in 2007 global rankings, its highest ever position.

Nevertheless, knock-on effects of the downturn are starting to be felt through the suspension of projects. A USD 3.3 billion Nigerian-Chinese deal to build cement plants throughout the continent was suspended[52]. A USD 9 billion agreement between China and the Democratic Republic of Congo for mineral resources in exchange for infrastructure has also stalled, in part due to unwillingness from Western creditors to write off the country's significant outstanding debt as it contracts new debt[53].

The Institute of International Finance forecast in January 2009 that net private sector capital flows to emerging markets would fall to about USD165 billion in 2009 from the USD466 billion recorded in 2008, and warned that capital flows to emerging markets are in danger of collapse as the financial crisis in developed economies chokes off the supply of credit to developing economies. According to the IIF, commercial banks are expected to make a net withdrawal of about USD61 billion from emerging markets in 2009. Remittance inflows to Africa, estimated at USD 10 billion for 2007, are also set to fall by up to a third as the economic situation of migrants in developed host countries deteriorates.

While the small size and isolation of Africa's financial markets initially appeared to provide effective protection in the first stages of the financial crisis, it has quickly become clear that the continent, dependent on external factors such as the Asia-driven commodity boom for its outstanding growth run of recent years, is very much in the front line for the second-round effects of a global recession.

---

49. *Financial Times*, Initiatives beat drum for African capital markets, 8 February 2009.

50. http://www.afriquejet.com/news/africa-news/african-experts-agree-on-pan per cent11african-stock-exchange-2009011219374.html
http://www.afrimap.org/newsarticle.php?id=1265

51. Source: Datastream, FTSE/JSE index.

52. *Financial Times*, "China trade with Africa hit by deal rethink", 17 December 2008.

53. *Financial Times*, China in the Congo, 9 February 2009.

Africa's access to external finance is likely to be severely constrained, creating uncertainty as to how it will secure the substantial foreign investment it requires to fund projects, create jobs, finance current account deficits and continue to develop. With global banks pulling back capital from all emerging markets, African banks, while not initially affected by the crisis and little exposed to toxic instruments, will find themselves with much tighter credit conditions limiting the availability of trade finance and constraining their own lending.

There is however the possibility that South-South investments could help take up some the slack. Two recent examples are noteworthy. First, the Liberian government has recently signed a USD 2.6 billion agreement with a Chinese company, China Union, to excavate iron ore, in what constitutes one of the largest ever FDI projects in the continent[54]. Secondly, the Brazilian company Petrobras has announced a massive expenditure plan for the period 2009-2013, reaching USD 174 billion, of which 2 billion are planned for Nigeria and 800 million for Angola[55]. Over the medium to long term, as commodity prices recover investor interest can be expected to return. These new forms of co-operation are not without risks, however (See Box 6).

Box 6 - China's Financial Co-operation with the Democratic Republic of the Congo

China is an attractive investment partner for some African countries. The Democratic Republic of Congo (DRC) authorities base their development strategies on the president's five-point plan and aim to maintain high levels of spending in the approach of the 2011 presidential elections. This has made them reluctant to take on the conditions associated with the HIPC debt relief process. There is no doubt that the country has large financial needs, especially for reconstruction and pacification in the East of the country. Moreover, DRC faces a serious economic downturn due to macroeconomic instability, a heavy debt burden, poor governance and the current global financial crisis.

In 2007, China signed a deal with the DRC including USD 9.2 billion in loans focused on infrastructure in the transport, energy, housing, health and education sectors. In return, the DRC agreed to cede rights in a joint venture to develop copper and cobalt concessions with prospects for strong growth in revenues. This deal represents the most important commitment made by China in Africa. It has often been praised by the Chinese as win-win co-operation. Although it may seem beneficial to both countries, several challenges to this deal have risen particularly within the context of the global economic slowdown.

A major challenge is the DRC debt's sustainability. The IMF and the traditional donors have suspended their assistance and the debt relief process through the HIPC initiative, which was supposed to write off about USD 9 billion, because of the unfavourable terms of the Congo-China deal. Other problems are the lack of clarity in the Congolese commitments and the current slowdown in the mining sector which has already resulted in the closing of several copper smelters and severe job losses especially in Katanga. DRC had based its growth prospects and financial resource mobilisation strategies to repay the debt around the performance of the mining sector. The sharp declines in the prices of copper and cobalt have thus slowed down the implementation of the Congo-China deal which is now exposed to higher risks of default on loan repayment obligations Therefore, it may be necessary for both parties to renegotiate the deal in order to adjust the terms in a way that would allow the DRC to return to the HIPC debt relief process.

Source: UNECA.

54. http://www.voanews.com/english/Africa/2009-01-23-voa8.cfm.

55. "Bresil: La crise, quelle crise?", *Jeune Afrique* No. 2508, From 1 to 7 February 2009, page 58.

43

Nevertheless, the impact of tighter credit conditions on African small and medium businesses is likely to be limited. Most companies have always had very limited access to bank credit, which accounts for example for only 10 per cent of the capital lent to Nigeria's manufacturing sector.

As private sources of capital dry up, so development finance institutions, such as the IFC, will have a critical role to play. The African Development Bank's plans to triple lending for African infrastructure schemes in an effort to salvage key projects are an indication of the increasingly important role multilaterals, development banks and DFIs may be led to play should downside risks materialise fully.

The AU has established the African Investment Bank, which while not yet functional, appears to be making some progress, with a proposed launch set for 2011. To be based in Tripoli, Libya, and wholly-owned by African actors, the bank is designed to serve finance private sector development and development initiatives, notably infrastructure.

A possible positive outcome for the crisis may be that African banks develop innovative means to tap the continent's domestic savings, which remain underutilised. To replace ebbing revenue sources, African banks could very well develop consumer businesses and domestic loans.

Macroeconomic Performance in Africa

Economic Growth

In 2008 GDP growth in Africa was 5.7 per cent; it was 6.1 per cent in 2007. This was, thus, the fifth consecutive year when growth exceeded 5.5 per cent. However, the impact of the global economic crisis is expected to slash growth rates to 2.8 per cent in 2009, less than half of the average growth rate achieved during the past five years. The IMF[56] found that over the last 30 years a 1 per cent slowdown in the rest of the world has led to a fall of 0.5 per cent in Sub-Saharan Africa, therefore any further worsening of international economic conditions could well reduce the growth prospects for Africa in 2009 and 2010 even further. The steady process of integration of the continent into the global economy that occurred during the last 15 years, has increased the vulnerability of Africa to drastic falls in financial flows, such as foreign direct investment, trade credit and remittances and to reductions in export earnings. A greater-than-expected fall in these flows will certainly have negative consequences for African growth. On the other hand, the impact of these negative effects could – at least partially – be offset by the prudent macroeconomic management (See Box 7) of most African countries during the last decade, as well as increased trade links with China, India and other emerging economies. Moreover, more than 60 per cent of the population live in rural areas, are dependent on domestic food production, and are thus somewhat less vulnerable to external shocks.

In 2008, growth was driven by the commodity-price boom, which peaked at mid-year and had clearly collapsed by the end of the year, accompanied by strong growth in private investment. Growing conditions in the agricultural sector were also generally favourable. Countries were beginning to have problems with controlling inflation, but, by and large, were continuing to reap the benefits of sound macroeconomic policies (See Box 7). As in previous years, oil exporters fared better than oil importers. All countries had to cope with higher prices of food and fertilisers. Thus, the gap in GDP growth rates between the two groups of countries widened to two percentage points. Growth would have been somewhat higher for the oil importing countries were it not for the energy crisis in South Africa and the post-election civil unrest in Kenya.

---

56. Op cit. IMF (2009).

Table 1 - Average Growth Rates of African Regions (annual percentage change)

Region	2000-05	2006	2007	2008(e)	2009(p)	2010(p)
Central	5.7	3.4	4.0	5.0	2.8	3.6
East	4.9	7.6	8.8	7.3	5.5	5.7
North	4.1	5.6	5.3	5.8	3.3	4.1
South	4.1	6.8	7.0	5.2	0.2	4.6
West	7.1	5.1	5.4	5.4	4.2	4.6
Africa	**4.8**	**6.0**	**6.1**	**5.7**	**2.8**	**4.5**
Memorandum items						
North Africa (including Sudan)	*4.2*	*6.1*	*5.7*	*6.0*	*3.5*	*4.2*
Sub-Saharan Africa	*5.2*	*5.9*	*6.4*	*5.5*	*2.4*	*4.7*
Oil-exporting countries	*5.4*	*6.1*	*6.8*	*6.6*	*2.4*	*4.5*
Oil importing countries	*4.1*	*5.8*	*5.4*	*4.6*	*3.3*	*4.5*

Source: Various domestic authorities; IMF *World Economic Outlook* and authors' estimates (e) and projections (p).

StatLink http://dx.doi.org/10.1787/574313086568

Box 7 - Macroeconomic Policies for Growth and Stability in Africa

In many African countries, good macroeconomic policies have helped promote investment, facilitate sustainable economic expansion, and maintain macroeconomic stability. Economic recovery was underpinned by domestic factors such as the improvement in macroeconomic management and the business environment, as well as key external factors such as strong global demand and debt relief. Further issues need to be addressed.

Monetary policy, inflation management and growth

Countries across the continent share the common goal of reducing inflation to low single digits. Strategies differ from country to country, but most seek to reduce the growth rate of the money supply. Demand-pull inflation, resulting from a process of economic expansion, will be positively associated with growth as long as the inflation rate remains moderate. Where inflation comes from excessive profit taking by business, supply shocks, or exchange-rate volatility, accommodating some of this inflationary pressure by allowing the money supply to expand may be appropriate.

Monetary policy instruments and targets

Many countries in Africa target the growth rate of monetary aggregates. However, pro-cyclical monetary management and the tightening of monetary policy in response to a negative economic shock in order to maintain low inflation rates runs the risks of worsening the economic impact of these shocks.

Real economic outcomes – such as growth and employment – represent long-run goals and may not be useful when making short-run monetary policy decisions. Therefore, intermediate targets for short-term real interest rates would be used to conduct monetary policy. These intermediate targets would be set consistent with longer run development objectives. For example, one goal would be to keep real short-term interest rates at a low, but positive, level. Short-term interest rates would replace the growth of monetary aggregates as the operating targets used to formulate monetary policy. Since the emphasis would be on targeting *real* interest rates, the intermediate target would embody the balance between inflation management and supporting economic growth.

45

Exchange rates and capital management

Misaligned real exchange rates can harm economic growth. Therefore, maintaining a competitive real exchange rate may be an important policy tool for raising growth.

African countries also need strategies to reduce exchange-rate volatility associated with capital-market liberalisation and the choice of exchange-rate regimes. As African equity and bond markets become increasingly sophisticated, the relevance of volatile capital flows and related exchange rate uncertainty will grow. South Africa provides a useful example of these issues in the African context.

Fiscal policy and public investment

Macroeconomic policies will only promote growth in Africa if sufficient complementary public investments – in physical infrastructure, basic economic services, and skills and education – are undertaken.

The need for strategic public interventions implies that fiscal policy is an important component of a broader set of economic policies that provides an environment conducive to growth while maintaining stability and managing macroeconomic balances. In African countries, fiscal policies often operate within a policy environment characterised by high external and domestic debt, large inflows of donor-directed overseas development assistance (ODA), and limited capacity to mobilise public resources from domestic sources. These factors limit the discretionary funds available to pursue important growth-supporting policies and call for closer co-ordination of macroeconomic policies. Therefore, spending priorities need to be matched with efforts to mobilise public revenue, particularly from domestic sources.

Collection of taxes from domestic sources, for a given level of income, can be increased in three ways: *i)* increasing the efficiency of tax collection; *ii)* expanding the tax base; or *iii)* raising tax rates or introducing new taxes. In recent years, many countries in Sub-Saharan Africa have improved revenue collection through: preventing the erosion of traditional sources of revenue (e.g. taxes from international trade); improving the efficiency of tax collection; maintaining a diverse set of tax instruments; and exploring ways of raising domestic non-tax revenues (e.g. licensing fees for access to natural resources). Extraction firms as well as informal businesses should be fully incorporated into the tax base.

For most African countries there is a need to raise increased non-debt generating external assistance in the form of debt relief or ODA. Many African countries qualify for debt relief under the HIPC programme. Non-HIPC countries could still apply for debt relief measures, even though they do not fit exactly into the HIPC profile. However, while complete external debt relief would free resources for developmental spending, and higher levels of direct budget support could potentially increase the resources available to foster investment, ODA flows can be uncertain and volatile, undermining the budget-planning process.

Overall, a counter-cyclical stance may be essential for fiscal policy to promote sustained growth especially in the context of high dependence on commodity booms. However, the implementation of a counter-cyclical policy requires policy space that is not always available to African countries.

Source: James Heintz and Robert Pollin (2008), "Targeting Employment Expansion, Economic Growth and Development in Sub-Saharan Africa: Outlines of an Alternative Economic Program for the Region", *ECA Policy Research Paper*, March, Addis Ababa, Ethiopia.

In 2008, GDP growth was particularly strong in net oil-exporting countries, at 6.6 per cent, down only slightly from the exceptionally strong 6.8 per cent registered in 2007 largely due to the increase in oil prices and increases in production in a number of countries, together with increased public and private investment. However, the growth differential between these and net oil-importing countries widened from 1.4 percentage points in 2007 to a full two percentages points in 2008 with average GDP growth in the latter of 4.6 per cent in 2008, down considerably from the 5.4 per cent registered in 2007.

The contrast with the growth projected for 2009 is striking. Growth is expected to be markedly lower in both groups. However, the impact of the global crisis is expected to be felt more strongly in the oil-exporting countries (and mineral exporters) than in more diversified economies and in those exporting certain agricultural commodities such as beverages. Thus, the net oil importers can expect GDP growth of 3.3 per cent in 2009 compared to 2.4 per cent for the net oil exporters. A major factor accounting for the slowdown of growth in the oil exporters is the assumption that the African members of OPEC (Angola, Algeria, Libya and Nigeria) fully respect the agreement reached within that organisation to reduce production quotas in an attempt to sustain oil prices at levels somewhat above those assumed in this report. Our assumption is that the quota reductions will translate on average into a reduction of production of about 8 per cent for these four countries.

GDP growth is expected to pick up in 2010 when the average real GDP growth rate for the continent as a whole is expected to be 4.5 per cent, with net oil-exporting and net oil-importing countries growing at the same pace.

These forecasts are based on a number of plausible but somewhat optimistic assumptions, suggesting that they are subject to significant downside risk such as a more severe and prolonged international economic recession than expected, and greater than expected falls in aid, remittances, capital and trade flows. Apart from assuming a resumption of moderate growth in

the global economy in 2010, they also assume that oil prices rebound to USD 50 per barrel in 2009 and USD 55 in 2010; that growing conditions in agriculture will be favourable in 2009 and 2010; that oil output of OPEC members will increase by about 3 per cent in 2010; that no new regional conflicts having significant macroeconomic impacts emerge; and that the worsening fiscal balances and current-account balances forecast for many of the net oil-importing countries (and a few net oil-exporting countries) will be fully financed. Thus, the continued implementation of debt-relief agreements for a number of the HIPC countries that began in 2006 will be particularly helpful.

North Africa

Economic growth was 5.8 per cent on average in 2008, up from 5.3 per cent in 2007. It is expected to slow significantly in 2009, to 3.3 per cent before increasing to 4.1 per cent in 2010. The 2008 growth rates reflected strong performances in nearly all the countries of the region. Exceptionally high growth was recorded in Egypt (7.2 per cent), Libya (6.5 per cent), and Morocco (5.7), while growth in Mauritania and Tunisia was slightly above 5 per cent. A sluggish hydrocarbon sector brought GDP growth in Algeriadown to 3.3 per cent. All North African countries will grow more slowly in 2009, with reductions of about 3 percentage points for Algeria and Libya, due to cutbacks in oil production, and in Egypt because of lower tourism, Suez Canal revenues, and income from a range of other exports. Morocco and Tunisia have a pattern of production and exports that is less vulnerable to the reduction in demand resulting from the global crisis, but growth will slow there as well. With a global recovery in 2010, resumption of demand for exports from North African countries is expected to reverse many of the negative factors, leading to better figures for growth of between 3.7 per cent in Algeria and Libya to 5.4 per cent in Morocco.

West Africa

Real GDP growth in the countries of West Africa was 5.4 per cent in 2008, as it was in 2007, and is

47

48

projected to slow by more than one percentage point to 4.2 per cent in 2009, before strengthening to 4.6 per cent in 2010. In the West African Economic and Monetary Union (WAEMU), consisting of Benin, Burkina Faso, Côte d'Ivoire, Guinea-Bissau, Mali, Niger, Senegal and Togo, economic performance improved in five of the eight countries, but slipped back a bit in Niger and Senegal. In Togo, however, GDP growth in 2008 was estimated to have been barely positive, at 0.8 per cent, continuing the pattern of declining growth in per capita income over the past several years, which was worsened by severe flooding in June 2008. Among the factors for the improved growth in most of these countries was the consolidation of political stability in Côte d'Ivoire – the largest economy within WAEMU – which had GDP growth of 2.3 per cent, about one-half percentage point higher than in 2007. Growth slipped back to 3.7 per cent in Senegal, primarily because of weakness in the output of cereals and groundnuts, as well as in industrial output, especially of phosphates and fertiliser. Cotton production also increased, especially in Burkina Faso where it reached record levels in 2008. The major positive development in the WAEMU was the sustained growth in agricultural production in several of them. Mali benefited from high gold prices and reasonably strong growth in food production, and Niger from uranium prices. GDP growth in Mali was 3.6 per cent, up from 3.2 per cent in 2007; in Niger, it was 4.8 per cent, rather less than the 5.7 per cent registered in 2007.

Within the eight non-WAEMU members (Cape Verde, The Gambia, Ghana, Guinea, Liberia, Nigeria, Sierra Leone and São Tomé and Principe), Nigeria – by far the largest economy in West Africa – had GDP growth of 6.1 per cent in 2008, about the same as in 2007, despite reduced oil output of 8 per cent caused by disrupted oil production in the Niger Delta. Projections for 2009 indicate a slowdown of Nigeria's growth rate to 4 per cent, mainly due to the binding constraint of the OPEC quota on oil production and the slowing down of growth in investment. Cape Verde's growth performance remained strong in 2008 (6.1 per cent), compared to 6.9 per cent in 2007. In Liberia post-conflict spending on infrastructure and

the recovery of agricultural production were responsible for exceptionally strong growth of about 7.3 per cent for the third year in a row, while in Ghana and Sierra Leone growth in 2008 was 6.4 per cent and 5.4 per cent, respectively, on the basis of good performance in cocoa production and processing, and strong increases in food production. Forecasts for 2009 are mixed, but, in addition to Nigeria which was mentioned above, most other countries are also expected to exhibit slower growth due mainly to slower growth in public and private investment associated with lower commodity prices and remittances. Unlike other countries in this group, Liberia and Sierra Leone are expected to continue to enjoy high growth levels as output recovers after years of conflict.

Central Africa

In 2008, average GDP growth in the seven countries of Central Africa was 5 per cent, up from 4 per cent in 2007. In 2009, GDP growth is expected to slow sharply, to 2.8 per cent and to increase to a moderate 3.6 per cent in 2010. The strong growth in 2008 was due mainly to a strong rebound of oil production in the Republic of Congo and continued strong growth in Equatorial Guinea (9.9 per cent) and Gabon (5.5 per cent), also net oil exporters. GDP failed to increase significantly in Chad in 2008 for the third consecutive year as a strong increase in agricultural output was offset by a sharp decline in oil production. Growth is projected to strengthen to 7.7 per cent in 2009 (compared to 7 per cent in 2008) in the Republic of Congo due mainly to increased oil production and high international oil prices which underpinned an expansion of public investment. In all other countries growth is expected to remain low or to fall, reflecting mainly the reduction in demand for the oil and minerals as a result of the global economic crisis. In the case of the Democratic Republic of the Congo, the effects of the global crisis have been compounded by renewed civil unrest, leading to a forecast of essentially zero GDP growth in 2009. The projections for Cameroon show some weakening in 2009 and 2010 with GDP growth of about 3 per cent per year, down from 4.1 per cent in 2008.

East Africa

GDP growth in East Africa averaged 7.3 per cent in 2008, down from a very strong 8.8 per cent in 2007, despite the turmoil in Kenya which caused growth to slow to 2.6 per cent, compared to 7 per cent in 2007. This strong growth is expected to slow to 5.5 per cent in 2009 and is projected to be about the same in 2010. In 2008, Ethiopia, Rwanda, Sudan, Tanzania and Uganda continued to be the fastest growing countries within East Africa, growing at 11.6 per cent, 8.5 per cent, 8.4 per cent, 6.8 per cent and 7 per cent, respectively. All five countries are also projected to maintain strong, but lower growth in 2009 and 2010 because demand for their major agricultural and horticultural exports is less sensitive to the effects of the global crisis than minerals and textile fibres; tourism has, however, been heavily impacted, and, these forecasts are subject to considerable uncertainties due to the unstable political situation in some countries. Burundi, Comoros and Seychelles, which have recently been exhibiting slow growth, are expected to continue stagnating, the latter two countries experiencing depressed tourism due to the global recession and, in the case of Comoros, to civil unrest as well. Djibouti, however, which grew by 5.9 per cent in 2008, is expected to experience an acceleration of GDP growth in 2009 and 2010, reaching about 6.6 per cent on average in this period. Kenya is also expected to exhibit strong growth in 2009 (5 per cent) due to recovery of domestic demand following the sharp slowdown in 2008. However, this rate of growth is about 1 percentage point lower than the average rate of growth in 2005-2007, reflecting the continued weakness of demand in the tourism sector.

Southern Africa

Economic growth in Southern Africa was 5.2 per cent, down sharply from the 7 per cent registered in 2007. It is expected to slow dramatically in 2009, to only 0.2 per cent before recovering to 4.6 per cent in 2010. This dramatic slowdown is mainly due to developments in South Africa and in Angola. In South Africa, growth slowed to 3.1 per cent, down from 5.1 per cent in 2007 due mainly to the energy crisis which affected large portions of the economy, a fall in private consumption and less buoyant private investment. The further slowdown to 1.1 per cent projected in 2009 is due mainly to the impact of the global economic crisis on demand for South Africa's mineral exports compounded by a contraction in private consumption and investment. In Angola, growth remained extremely high (15.8 per cent) in 2008, but down from the 21 per cent registered in 2007. However, the economy is expected to contract by 7.2 per cent in 2009 on the assumption that the reduction in quotas by OPEC countries will translate into a reduction of oil production in Angola of about 10 per cent. In Madagascar and Malawi, growth accelerated to reach 7 per cent and 8.4 per cent, respectively due to strong growth in agriculture in both countries and to large investments in the mineral sector in the former. Growth slowed all the other countries in the region, many of them affected by the slowdown in South Africa. In addition, mineral exporters (Mozambique, Namibia, Tanzania and Zambia) began to experience a slowing of investment in the second half of the year. Growth in Mauritius remained high, although it, too, lost some momentum compared to 2007. These trends are expected to intensify in 2009 with a further slowing of growth forecast for all countries. In the case of Madagascar, the situation is expected to be worse because of the impact of the political crisis, particularly on the tourism sector, with GDP growth expected to fall by more than 2 percentage points, to 4.8 per cent. On the assumption of a resumption of moderate growth in the world economy in 2010, these trends are expected to be reversed symmetrically with growth likely to accelerate (or resume, in the case of Angola) in nearly all countries.

Inflation

Inflation in Africa (excluding Zimbabwe) accelerated to the double-digit level of 11.6 per cent in 2008, up sharply from 7.5 per cent in 2007, largely due to the impact of higher energy (mostly hydrocarbons), fertiliser and international food prices. This surge in inflation affected both net oil exporters and net oil importers although, as might be expected, the increase in inflation was larger by about 1 per cent for the latter. This group, (excluding Zimbabwe) experienced an upward surge of

49

inflation from 7.9 per cent in 2007 to 13.5 per cent in 2008. In 2009, inflation in this group of countries is expected to return to about the same level as in 2006, and to fall further in 2010. In oil-exporting countries, inflation, which increased by less, is expected to fall more slowly. The number of African countries (excluding Zimbabwe) with double-digit inflation increased from only 6 in 2007 to 28 in 2008. This number will decline to 11 in 2009 and then to 6 in 2010. Even CFA franc

countries, which have had historically low rates, experienced inflation in the high single digits, thus increasing the differential between them and the Euro zone considerably. The forecasts assume that the authorities will not need to tighten monetary policy significantly since commodity prices have already fallen sharply and domestic demand has weakened along with the deterioration of the economic outlook due to the international financial and economic crisis.

Table 2 - **Weighted Mean CPI Inflation of African Regions** (annual percentage change)						
Region	2000-05	2006	2007	2008(e)	2009(p)	2010(p)
Central	15.8	6.3	2.9	8.8	7.2	6.5
East	5.9	12.0	10.1	17.8	10.1	8.0
North	2.6	3.6	6.8	8.1	7.7	5.3
South	13.8	7.4	9.6	15.2	7.6	6.6
West	10.3	7.4	5.4	10.6	8.6	8.0
Africa	**7.9**	**6.4**	**7.5**	**11.6**	**8.1**	**6.5**
Memorandum items						
North Africa (including Sudan)	*2.9*	*4.5*	*7.0*	*8.6*	*7.7*	*5.5*
Sub-Saharan Africa	*11.6*	*7.7*	*7.9*	*13.8*	*8.3*	*7.2*
Oil-exporting countries	*9.8*	*5.9*	*7.2*	*10.0*	*9.1*	*7.1*
Oil importing countries	*6.0*	*7.0*	*7.9*	*13.5*	*6.9*	*5.8*

Note: All figures exclude Somalia for lack of data and Zimbabwe due it its hyperinflation.
Source: Various domestic authorities; IMF *World Economic Outlook* and authors' estimates (e) and projections (p).

StatLink http://dx.doi.org/10.1787/574318121436

North Africa

Inflation in North Africa accelerated to 8.1 per cent in 2008, up from 6.8 per cent in 2007 as inflation rose to 11.7 per cent in Egypt, to 7.6 per cent in Mauritania and to 11.2 per cent in Libya, increased from 3.1 per cent to 5 per cent in Tunisia, and remained high in Mauritania at 7.4 per cent. Algeria and Morocco managed to keep inflation at around 4 per cent. The average rate of inflation in North Africa is projected to decline in both 2009 and 2010, when it is expected to average 5.3 per cent. However, in Egypt it is expected to increase still further in 2009, to 13 per cent, before falling back to single-digit levels in 2010.

West Africa

In 2008, the average rate of inflation in West Africa was 10.6 per cent, up from 5.4 per cent in 2007. The

WAEMU countries, whose currencies are pegged to the Euro, still have a far lower average inflation rate than the member countries of the West African Monetary Zone (WAMZ)[57], four out of five of which had inflation rates ranging from 11 to 19 per cent. In Guinea, inflation remained high, at 19.3 per cent, but this was a bit lower than in 2007. The rate of inflation in Nigeria accelerated from 5.4 per cent in 2007 to 11 per cent in 2008. In Ghana inflation surged from 10.7 per cent in 2007 to 14.1 per cent in 2008. In São Tomé and Principe inflation increased from 18.5 per cent in 2007 to 25.9 per cent in 2008, reversing the modest improvement it had made in 2007. In Sierra Leone inflation increased from 12.1 in 2007 to 13 per cent in 2008. Inflation in Liberia increased from 11.4 per cent in 2007 to 17.5 per cent in 2008. In Cape Verde, where inflation has generally been much lower than in other West African countries, it increased from 4.3 in 2007 to 6.7 per cent in 2008, and in The Gambia,

---

57. Gambia, Ghana, Guinea, Nigeria and Sierra Leone.

inflation increased from 5.4 per cent in 2007 to 6.4 per cent in 2008. Projections for 2009 and 2010 are for gradual declines in the region as a whole but to remain in the high single digits.

Central Africa

The average rate of inflation in Central Africa accelerated to 8.8 per cent in 2008, up from 2.9 per cent in 2007 due to large increases in Cameroon (5.7 per cent, up from 1.5 per cent), Central African Republic (9.2 per cent, up from 0.9 per cent), Chad (9.2 per cent, up from 9 per cent), and DRC (26.2 per cent, up from 16.7 per cent. Inflation was about 5.5 per cent in Congo Republic, Equatorial Guinea and Gabon in 2008, as well, but the year-to-year increases were much lower. All of these countries are net food importers and depend on imports of refined petroleum products even if some of them are net oil exporters. The projections for 2009 and 2010 are for a gradual reduction in inflation to 6.5 per cent in the latter year. In fact, all but the DRC are expected to have inflation rates of 5 per cent or less, with most countries below that rate, moving closer to the convergence target of 3 per cent accepted by the countries belonging to the Bank of Central African States (BEAC) area (Cameroon, the Central African Republic, the Republic of Congo, Equatorial Guinea and Gabon). Only in the DRC is little progress expected, with inflation expected to remain at about 20 per cent in both 2009 and 2010.

East Africa

In 2008, inflation increased dramatically in East Africa (excluding Somalia), to 17.8 per cent, up from 10.1 per cent in 2007. This was substantially higher than in any other African region. Inflation exceeded 20 per cent in four countries: Burundi (24.5 per cent), Ethiopia (25 per cent), Kenya (25.8 per cent), and Seychelles (37 per cent). It was at least 10 per cent in another 6 countries (Djibouti, Eritrea, Rwanda, Sudan, Tanzania, and Uganda. Only in Comoros did inflation remain at a moderate level (5.9 per cent). The high

inflation in East Africa in 2008 was largely due to the high prices of imported fuel (essentially hydrocarbons), fertilisers and food, which had knock-on effects increasing the cost of domestic food production. However, domestic factors also played a role, particularly in three of countries where inflation exceeded 20 per cent. In Ethiopia, sustained rapid growth added to the upward pressure on prices. In Kenya, the civil unrest which followed the tightly contested elections in the first half of the year, disrupted transportation and agricultural production and, thus, the movement of food from farms to markets pushing prices of agricultural products. In Seychelles, a major devaluation magnified the effect of increases in the international prices of imports. The inflation outlook in East Africa for 2009 and 2010 is for substantial reductions in most countries. In 2009, inflation is expected to be above 20 per cent only in Seychelles because of further depreciation of the currency, and is expected to be in the range of 10 to 15 per cent in only 3 others. In 2010, inflation is projected to be at or below 10 per cent in all 11 countries, although achieving this will be a challenge for monetary policy. Thus, the average rate of inflation in East Africa is expected gradually to fall to 10.1 per cent and 8 per cent in 2009 and 2010, respectively.

Southern Africa

In Southern Africa (excluding Zimbabwe), inflation averaged 15.2 per cent in 2008, but it was already nearly 10 per cent in 2007. The average is dominated by South Africa, where inflation was 11.5 per cent in 2008, up from 7.2 per cent in 2007[58]. In 2008 it ranged from 8.3 per cent in Malawi to 13.2 per cent in Angola, but in all but 3 countries, it was above 10 per cent. The high rates in all countries were caused by the acceleration of international fuel, fertiliser and imported food prices, as in other African regions. However, high rates of government spending and supply constraints in Angola, and the pervasive effects of the electricity crisis in South Africa were aggravating factors. Since most of these factors were transitory, inflation in the region as a whole (excluding Zimbabwe), is expected to decline to 7.6 per

51

---

58. The reference index for South Africa has shifted from the CPIX to the CPI.

cent in 2009 and to 6.6 per cent in 2010. Moreover, inflation in 2010 is projected to be below 10 per cent in all countries, although achieving this in some of them, which have had a history of generally high inflation (Angola, Madagascar), may prove to be a challenge for the monetary authorities.

Public Finances

In 2008 the overall fiscal balance (including grants) of the group of net oil-exporting countries increased to 6.1 per cent in 2008, up from 4 per cent in 2007, mainly because of higher oil prices but also because of increases in production in some of them (but not in Algeria, Libya or Nigeria). The group of net oil-importing countries exhibited an overall deficit equivalent to 1.8 per cent of GDP in 2008, compared to a very small deficit in 2007 (0.3 per cent). The increase in the deficit of the net oil-importing countries reflects increases in fuel, fertiliser, and food subsidies in many countries as they attempted to mitigate the effects of high import prices. The continuation of generally good macroeconomic management and the maintenance of a high level of grants, including a portion provided in the form of debt relief prevented deficits from increasing even further. Projections for 2009 are dramatically different for these two groups of countries. Net oil-importing countries are expected to experience a further widening of their average deficit to 2.7 per cent mainly because of a decline in tax receipts as GDP growth slows. However, for the net oil

exporters, the fiscal surplus in 2008 is expected to give way to a large deficit equivalent to 7.5 per cent of GDP mainly due to declines in oil prices and production (in some countries). Small improvements for both groups of countries are expected in 2010. The forecast for government spending in the oil-exporting countries assume that these large deficits can be financed by drawing on the surpluses accumulated in earlier years. However, it remains important for the oil exporters to continue investing in the types of project that promote diversification of their economies to reduce dependence on their oil sectors. For the poorer oil-importing countries, debt relief and other forms of financial support from international financial institutions and their bilateral development partners will be particularly important as they attempt to maintain positive GDP growth during the current global recession. For countries where inflation has increased to double-digit levels, monetisation of the increase in these projected deficits would be problematic. There is a clear need to improve domestic resource mobilisation in most African countries and the awareness of the importance of this agenda is growing (See Box 8).

North Africa

In North Africa the average fiscal balance was equivalent to a surplus of 5.3 per cent of GDP in 2008, up from 3.6 per cent in 2007. The higher oil prices resulted in substantial increases for the largest oil-exporting countries in the region, Algeria (6.8 per cent

Table 3 - Average Budget Balance to GDP Ratio						
Region	2000-05	2006	2007	2008(e)	2009(p)	2010(p)
Central	2.0	17.5	7.4	11.6	3.3	4.2
East	-2.2	-3.9	-3.6	-2.2	-4.8	-5.2
North	-1.1	6.5	3.6	5.3	-5.6	-5.1
South	-2.5	3.2	2.3	1.9	-4.6	-3.6
West	-0.5	6.4	-0.4	-0.3	-8.6	-9.2
Africa	**-1.4**	**5.0**	**1.9**	**2.8**	**-5.4**	**-5.0**
Memorandum items						
North Africa (including Sudan)	*-1.0*	*5.5*	*2.8*	*4.9*	*-6.0*	*-5.6*
Sub-Saharan Africa	*-1.7*	*4.7*	*1.4*	*1.5*	*-4.9*	*-4.6*
Oil-exporting countries	*0.3*	*8.6*	*4.0*	*6.1*	*-7.5*	*-7.1*
Oil importing countries	*-2.9*	*1.1*	*-0.3*	*-1.8*	*-2.7*	*-2.3*

Note: Due to lack of data, these aggregates do not include Somalia or Zimbabwe.
Source: Various domestic authorities; IMF *World Economic Outlook* and authors' estimates (e) and projections (p).

StatLink http://dx.doi.org/10.1787/574335241357

Box 8 - Taxation, Mobilising Domestic Resources, and Strengthening Public Financial Management: The African Tax Administration Forum

In August 2008, Commissioners and Senior Tax Administrators from 39 countries, together with representatives from development partners, including the OECD's Centre for Tax Policy and Administration and the Development Co-ordination Directorate, met in Pretoria, South Africa.

The meeting discussed taxation, state building and capacity development in Africa and took stock of the progress made, challenges faced and a possible new direction for African tax policy and administration in the 21st Century. The focus of the gathering was on:

i) The importance of taxation in state building;

ii) The changing environment of taxation in Africa; and

iii) An African initiative: Strengthening African Tax Administrations

The goal was to lay a strong basis for a new approach to taxation, state building and capacity development of African Tax Administrations and the launch of an African Tax Administration Forum.

The Commissioners agreed that

i) The Importance of Taxation in State Building

Capable and responsible states are key actors in confronting and overcoming today's global developmental challenges.

Governments around the world recognise that revenue mobilisation is central to this goal and their ambitions to achieve the Millennium Development Goals (MDGs). More effective tax systems can:

1. Mobilise the domestic tax base as a key mechanism for developing countries to escape aid or single-resource dependency.
2. Reinforce government legitimacy through promoting accountability of governments to tax-paying citizens, effective state administration and good public financial management; and
3. Promote economic growth, reduce extreme inequalities, and thereby significantly improve the lives of our citizens;
4. Achieve a fairer sharing of the costs and benefits of globalisation;

ii) The Changing Environment of Taxation in Africa

Developed and developing economies, NGOs, private investors and international organisations should work together to promote fair and efficient tax systems and administrations that will ensure each country receives the fruits of its own economic achievement and improves its overall governance.

One of the most pressing issues facing Africa is to free African countries from their dependence on foreign assistance and indebtedness. An indispensable condition of this is the strengthening of our capacity to mobilise domestic resources. Domestic revenue should be one of the main sources for fiscal space expansion because of its sustainability, thereby reducing dependence on donor assistance.

53

Billions of USD per year left the African continent between 1991 and 2004. These outflows are estimated at 7.6 per cent of the annual GDP of the region and, in effect, make African countries net creditors of donor countries. They also undermine African countries' tax bases. Action by the international community is required to ensure that the potential tax base of developing countries is not undermined.

Overall revenue yields and voluntary compliance are low in many African countries; the tax bases often remain narrow, while the informal sector continues to grow; the taxation of international transactions, in particular transfer pricing, has become increasingly difficult; the overall tax gap remains unquantified.

Over the coming decade, African countries will need to enlarge their sources of tax revenue and broaden the tax base considerably in order to compensate for the move away from trade taxes resulting from WTO obligations and from regional trade agreements.

iii) An African initiative: Strengthening African Tax Administrations

A key component of a capable state is the existence of efficient and effective tax administrations. Improving revenue performance will require a major improvement in tax administration through better service delivery, and taxpayer education, effective use of automated systems, better co-operation between tax administrations to counter tax evasion and aggressive tax planning, and strengthening audit and human resource management capability.

Donors can do more to support revenue-raising efforts in partner countries. Of the USD 7.1 billion spent in 2005 on bilateral aid for government administration, economic policy and public-sector financial management, only 1.7 per cent was directed to tax-related assistance.

It is in this context that to explore the feasibility of launching a new initiative that would primarily focus on capacity building in African tax administrations and which will help our governments meet their Monterrey commitments.

The senior African Tax Administrators participating in this meeting mandated a Steering Group of African Commissioners which will be the voice of African Tax Commissioners and provide a vital opportunity to develop joint strategies and programmes to develop this initiative on their behalf. This will be an African programme reflecting African needs and African strategies. African countries will drive and manage the programme priorities, supported by donors, other tax administrations and development partners. This initiative is an opportunity for Africa to say what Africa wants in the tax area; for African based processes and institutions to take the lead on the continent.

The new African Tax Administration Forum will act as a focal point for exchanging experiences on good practices, benchmarking performance, improving co-operation between, and setting the strategic direction for African Tax Administrations. The Forum will conduct research work on taxation on the African continent, develop specific diagnostic tools for African revenue bodies and develop a capacity building programme. An integrated part of the programme will also be to build on the work of the OECD's Forum on Tax Administration and the work of the WCO, IMF, the African Development Bank and of bilateral donors.

Taking forward this initiative

To take forward this initiative, the Steering Group of African Commissioners from Botswana, Cameroon Ghana, Nigeria, Rwanda, South Africa and Uganda, met again in Cape Town in February 2009 to develop ATAF's action plan. That meeting with interested development partners agreed the adoption of a roadmap and to set up an interim Secretariat. The roadmap anticipates a formal launch in late 2009 and in the meantime, will commence work on researching tax systems in Africa; developing and delivering a technical support programme for African officials (beginning with an event in Kigali in April 2009); and constructing a framework for diagnostic studies.

Source: Centre for Tax Policy and Administration, OECD.

of GDP, up from 4.8 per cent) and Libya (34.5 per cent of GDP, up from 26.2 per cent). In Egypt the deficit widened to 6.8 per cent of GDP in 2008, up from 5.6 per cent in 2007. Mauritania and Tunisia, on the other hand, experienced little change in their fiscal deficits in 2008 compared with 2007, while Morocco continued to show a small surplus. In 2009, fiscal balances are projected to deteriorate for all countries in the region, dramatically in the case of the oil exporters. In Algeria, the surplus of 2008 is expected to give way to a deficit of 11.5 per cent in 2009, while in Libya the large 2008 surplus will disappear in 2009. Few changes are expected in fiscal balances in 2010 for any of these countries.

West Africa

In 2008, fiscal balances (including grants) deteriorated in most West African countries. However, as a percentage of GDP only four countries registered deficits of 4.5 per cent of GDP or more: Burkina Faso (6.4 per cent), Ghana (10.0 per cent), Mali (5.4 per cent) and Senegal (4.5 per cent). Guinea-Bissau which had a large deficit in 2007 (10.3 per cent of GDP), momentarily moved into surplus due to debt relief. In 2009 all five countries are expected to continue to have large deficits, most showing little change. The small Nigerian surpluses in 2007 and 2008 will give way to a deficit of 11.1 per cent in 2009. Fiscal balances are projected to remain about the same in 2010. Apart from Nigeria, which has large surpluses to draw upon, the large deficits projected for the five countries

mentioned above may prove difficult to finance. This suggests that the GDP outlook for these countries as presented in this AEO is subject to considerable downside risk should funding difficulties translate into reductions in projected government spending,

Central Africa

In 2008, five of the seven countries in Central Africa, most of whom are oil exporters, registered surpluses which were larger than in 2007. The exceptions were the Central African Republic, whose small surplus fell slightly, and the Democratic Republic of Congo. The fiscal balance of the DRC, in fact, moved from a small surplus in 2007 to a deficit of 5.8 per cent in 2008. Projections for 2009 and 2010 are for further reductions in the surpluses of Cameroon, Central African Republic, Chad, Congo Republic, Equatorial Guinea and Gabon. The already substantial deficit of DRC is projected to increase still further. Since the inflation outlook in that country is already quite poor, this deficit would need to be financed from external sources. This suggests that there is considerable downside risk associated with the (poor) outlook for GDP growth in this report.

East Africa

In 2008 the combined fiscal deficit (including grants) in East Africa (excluding Somalia) improved, falling from 3.6 per cent of GDP in 2007 to 2.2 per cent in 2008 due to strong growth, increases in export earnings and improved resource mobilisation. However, there were considerable differences among the 11 countries. Deficits fell substantially or remained low in 8 countries. However, deficits as a percentage of GDP worsened or remained high in three others: Burundi (8.9, up from 3 in 2007), Eritrea (8.5, down slightly from 10 in 2007), and Kenya (6.1, up from 1.1 in 2007). The reasons for the differences in performance varied widely. In Kenya the deterioration was linked to the decline in economic activity in several sectors in the first half of 2008. Improvement in the Seychelles was due to the implementation of an economic austerity and reform programme. In Sudan and Tanzania the improvements were due to increase in the value of their export earnings. Since many of these factors were transitory, prospects for 2009 are rather different. The small surplus exhibited by Sudan in 2008 is expected to give way to a deficit of 10.6 per cent of GDP in 2009. On the other hand, Burundi is projected to benefit from sizeable debt relief and, thus, to exhibit a large surplus in 2009. The high deficit in Kenya is expected to return to a more moderate 3 per cent. However, the large deficit in Eritrea is projected to persist. Relatively little change in these fiscal positions are expected for 2010. Thus, the overall deficit for the region is expected to worsen to 4.8 per cent of GDP in 2009 and 5.2 per cent in 2010.

Southern Africa

The average fiscal surplus of the countries in Southern Africa fell slightly from 2.3 per cent in 2007 to 1.9 per cent in 2008. However, surpluses fell or deficits increased in 9 of the 11 countries. Only in Mauritius and Zambia did fiscal balances improve with reductions in the deficits of both countries of about 1 percentage point of GDP. The projections for 2009 are dominated by changes in two countries. In Angola, the surplus of 10.8 per cent of GDP registered in 2008 is expected to be transformed into a deficit of 8.7 per cent in 2009 due to the fall in oil prices and the reduction in production required to respect the quota reductions agreed within OPEC. In South Africa the deficit is expected to widen substantially, from 1 per cent of GDP in 2008 to 3.7 per cent in 2009 due to the effects on government revenue of the economic slowdown and the decision of the government to

implement a counter-cyclical fiscal stimulus in the face of the global crisis. Some improvement in budget balances is generally expected in nearly all countries in 2010 along with improved rates of economic growth. Thus, the combined fiscal deficits of the region as a whole in 2009 and 2010 are expected to be 4.6 and 3.6 per cent of GDP, respectively.

Balance of Payments

In 2008, Africa's average current account balance exhibited a surplus equivalent to 3.3 per cent of GDP, up from 2.2 per cent in 2007. This overall figure, however, masks large differences among countries. On the one hand, net oil-exporting countries recorded a current account surplus of 10.7 per cent in 2008 (up slightly from 8.9 per cent in 2007); on the other hand, the group of net oil-importing countries experienced a large average current account deficit of 7.1 per cent of GDP in 2008 (up from 5.4 per cent in 2007) compared with an average of 1.6 per cent in the period 2000 to 2005. Among the net oil importers, only 7 countries out of 40 improved their current account balances significantly (Burundi, Cameroon, Chad, Guinea, Liberia, Mali and Swaziland). The surplus in the current account balances of net oil-exporting countries is projected to give way to deficits of 3.5 and 2.4 per cent of GDP in 2009 and 2010, respectively, due to declines in oil prices and production (among the African OPEC countries). Meanwhile the average current account deficit of the net oil-importing countries is expected to improve in 2009 with reductions in the international prices of their imports exceeding reductions in the prices of their exports, but then to worsen slightly in 2010 as imports pick up along with economic growth.

In recent years, Africa's overall balance of payments has benefited from increased foreign direct investment flows and significantly reduced debt service payments in many heavily indebted poor countries (HIPCs) (see details in previous section). However, the rapidly rising current account deficits associated with the global recession is rapidly eroding international reserves, with African countries increasingly turning to the IMF for support in order to avoid exchange rate crises.

56

Table 4 - Average Ratio of Current Account Balance to GDP

Région	2000-05	2006	2007	2008(e)	2009(p)	2010(p)
Central	-4.1	1.9	-0.5	9.0	-5.4	-3.0
East	-5.5	-9.3	-9.3	-6.3	-7.6	-8.3
North	5.6	14.9	12.1	11.5	0.7	1.1
South	-1.1	-1.1	-3.3	-2.0	-6.8	-7.4
West	-2.4	4.4	-0.2	0.0	-8.4	-7.0
Africa	**0.6**	**4.8**	**2.2**	**3.3**	**-4.4**	**-4.1**
Memorandum items						
North Africa (including Sudan)	*4.5*	*12.2*	*9.6*	*10.1*	*-0.6*	*-0.5*
Sub-Saharan Africa	*-2.0*	*0.4*	*-2.4*	*-1.0*	*-6.9*	*-6.5*
Oil-exporting countries	*3.0*	*13.1*	*8.9*	*10.7*	*-3.5*	*-2.4*
Oil importing countries	*-1.6*	*-4.2*	*-5.4*	*-7.1*	*-5.5*	*-6.4*

Note: Due to lack of data, these aggregates do not include Somalia.
Source: Various domestic authorities; IMF *World Economic Outlook* and authors' estimates (e) and projections (p).

StatLink http://dx.doi.org/10.1787/574406724248

North Africa

In 2008, northern African countries continued to display large differences in their current account balances. Algeria and Libya continue to exhibit large current account surpluses of about 25 per cent and 32 per cent of GDP, respectively in 2008, similar in size to those of 2007, despite little growth in exports of hydrocarbons, as improvements in terms of trade offset strong growth in import volumes. Egypt registered a small surplus, which was slightly lower than in 2007. The deficits of Morocco and Tunisia worsened somewhat, but remained moderate as a percentage of GDP, at 3.7 and 4.2 per cent, respectively. Mauritania's deficit decreased slightly in 2008 to 9.3 per cent, down from 11.3 per cent in 2007. In 2009 and 2010, the surpluses of Algeria and Libya are projected to fall quite sharply due to the collapse of oil prices. Egypt is expected to exhibit a small deficit in 2009, while the deficits of Morocco and Tunisia are expected to fall slightly, whereas the sizeable deficit in Mauritania is expected to worsen. Little change in current account balances is expected in 2010. As a result of the above, North Africa's current account surplus fell from 12.1 per cent of GDP in 2007 to 11.5 per cent in 2008, but is expected to be only about 1 per cent in 2009 and 2010.

West Africa

In 2008, 8 countries out of 16 in West Africa registered current account deficits ranging from about 7 to 14 per cent of GDP. The deficits of three other countries were even higher, ranging from 18 to 34 per cent. Surpluses were registered only in Côte d'Ivoire and Nigeria. The combined current account balance in West Africa is dominated by Nigeria where the current account surplus was 3.2 per cent of GDP in 2008, little changed from 2007. In 2009 many countries are expected to exhibit major changes due to the effect of the global crisis on their terms of trade, and reductions in import volumes in some of them as large investment programmes slow down (Liberia) or balance of payments constraints cause public investment growth to slow. Thus the deficits of Gambia, Guinea, Mali, Senegal and Togo expressed as a percentage of GDP are expected to decline by amounts in the range of 3.8 to 9.5 percentage points, and the deficit of Liberia is expected to decline from 28.8 per cent in 2008 to 5.7 per cent in 2009. In Nigeria, the surplus in 2008 is expected to give way to a deficit of 9.1 per cent in 2009. In 2010 the pattern is for a slight widening of these deficits in most countries. However, under the assumptions of higher oil prices and production in Nigeria, the current account deficit in that country is expect to fall somewhat. Thus for the region of West Africa as a whole, the current account is expected to exhibit deficits of 8.4 per cent of GDP in 2009 and 7 per cent in 2010.

Central Africa

In 2008, the average current account balance in Central Africa was in surplus equivalent to 9 per cent

57

of GDP (compared to -0.5 per cent in 2007), largely due to further large increases in the nominal value of oil exports in Chad, the Republic of Congo, Equatorial Guinea and Gabon. Cameroon and DRC also registered small surpluses which represented improvements in their current account balances compared to 2007. However, the deficit in the Central African Republic increased significantly, to 9.4 per cent of GDP, up from 6.1 per cent in 2007. Because of the lower oil prices for 2009, the surpluses of oil exporters in that year are expected to disappear; and, indeed, the Congo Republic is projected to register a large deficit. In 2010 the pattern on current account balances not expected to change much. Thus, in 2009 and 2010, the countries in Central Africa as a group are expected to register a deficit on their current accounts of 5.4 per cent and 3 per cent, respectively.

East Africa

In 2008 the average current account deficit in East Africa fell slightly to 6.3 per cent of GDP (down from 9.3 per cent in 2007) compared with an average of 5.5 per cent for the period 2000-05. All the countries in East Africa, except for Sudan, are net oil-importing countries and many import fertilisers and food as well. They were thus especially affected by the increases of international prices for these products in 2008. Consequently, all of them experienced a worsening in their current account deficits. In Sudan, the only net oil exporter, however, the current account deficit fell to 3.4 per cent, down from 16.3 per cent in 2007. For 2009 and 2010, the fall in oil prices is expected to nearly reverse this situation with deficits falling or remaining roughly unchanged in the net oil importing countries, but deteriorating in Sudan. Little further change is expected in 2010. Thus, for East Africa as a whole current account deficits in 2009 and 2010 as a percentage of GDP are expected to be 7.6 per cent and 8.3 per cent, respectively. These large deficits have also taken a toll on international reserves, for example, nearly exhausting those of Ethiopia.

Southern Africa

Among the countries in Southern Africa, a worsening of the current account deficits of 9 of the 11 countries

in 2008 was offset by an increase in the surplus of Angola due to the increase in oil prices and, to a much lesser extent, in the current account of Swaziland because of a large increase in net transfers. Among the deficit countries, Madagascar experienced an increase from 13.9 per cent of GDP in 2007 to 25.8 per cent in 2008 due to large increases in imports of investment goods associated with a major mining project. In 2008, South Africa had a current account deficit of 7.8 per cent of GDP due to a fall in exports and an increase of imports due to the implementation of a massive infrastructure modernisation programme. In 2009, South Africa expects to continue with its infrastructure programme requiring large imports of capital goods. The deficit is therefore expected to be around 6.4 per cent of GDP but will depend on export prices and the value of the ZAR. In 2009 in Angola the decline in international oil prices and the reduction in production of oil required to stay within its OPEC quota are expected to result in the current account surplus of 12.9 per cent of GDP realised in 2008 giving way to a deficit of 8.1 per cent in 2009. Not much change in this picture is expected for 2010. Thus, for the region as a whole the overall current account deficit in expected to worsen from about 2 per cent of GDP in 2008 to 6.8 per cent and 7.4 per cent in 2009 and 2010, respectively. In some countries, such as Malawi, international reserves have already declined to critical levels, making support from the IMF essential to avoid compounding the effects of the crisis.

The Millennium Development Goals Progress Report

Just six years from the deadline set by the international community for achieving the Millennium Development Goals (MDGs), world reports indicate that none of the Sub-Saharan African countries is currently on track to attain all of the goals by 2015. This broad statement however, inevitably conceals the variety of the results obtained by each country, and more particularly, the striking progress made by some.

For several years now, the economic and political context in Africa has been developing favourably with good economic performances and a significant drop in the number of countries suffering from civil conflict. Several African countries have conducted strict macroeconomic policies and have launched democratic and growth acceleration reforms. However, rising world prices for food products combined with the global slowdown in economic growth and the ever-present risk of conflict and long-term climate change are undermining the conditions for growth and attaining the MDGs. The repercussions of the food crisis and climate change on the ability of African countries to eradicate poverty and attain human development goals makes it all the more imperative that MDGs be integrated into national programmes, backed up by a reinforced commitment by political actors and by financing from development aid institutions.

The table *Main Progress Towards Achieving the Millenium Developement Goals* is the outcome of the application of a methodology calculating a measure of progress for each goal. This indicator is obtained by comparing the current rate of growth with the rate of growth necessary to attain the goal by 2015. Four levels of progress have thus been identified: "early achiever" meaning that the goal is already attained or will be by the expected deadline; "on track" meaning that the country is on course to attain the goal; "off-track" if progress is slow, and lastly, "regressing" signalling a reversal in the trend towards the goal. Figure 8 - Distribution of Countries Status by MDGs shows the distribution of African countries according to each country's indicator value.

The measurement of progress towards each goal enables us to take account of the work remaining to be done.

Goal 1 – Eradicate extreme poverty and hunger

Target 1 – Reduce by half, between 1990 and 2015, the proportion of the population whose income is less than 1 USD a day.

Significant progress has been registered in terms of reducing poverty in Sub-Saharan Africa, which went from 58 per cent in 1999 to 50 per cent in 2005. Of the 48 countries for which data is available, alongside the

countries of North Africa, Cameroon, Cape Verde, Mauritania, Senegal, Kenya and Ghana registered the best performances and have every chance of attaining the goal. Likewise, Benin, Republic of Congo, Guinea, Swaziland and Uganda are on target, although these countries exhibit poverty rates that are higher than average.

However, more than half of African countries exhibit either deteriorating poverty or insufficient progress to reverse the indicator's historic trend. This applies mainly to the countries of Western Africa (10 countries) and Southern Africa (9 countries). If trends continue, none of these countries will manage to obtain the goal. Even more alarming, some of these countries have poverty rates that are substantially higher than the average and they risk being completely marginalised. Despite good economic performances and an improved political climate, growth was not sufficient to speed up poverty reduction. Strong initial inequalities combined with demographic growth have prevented growth from adequately reaching the poorest sections of the population.

Furthermore, the ability of African countries to reach this goal is currently compromised by upheavals in the world economy with rising food prices and financial turbulence liable to destroy former progress. In light of these developments and with a high proportion of the poor in rural areas combined with low agricultural productivity, emergency measures to promote a sustainable improvement in agricultural productivity have become imperative.

Target 2 – Reduce by half, between 1990 and 2015, the proportion of the population who suffers from hunger.

In terms of combating hunger, the results are mixed. In Sub-Saharan Africa, the proportion of the population that is under-nourished fell from 32 per cent in 1990 to 28 per cent in 2005 but efforts have been slow and insufficient to guarantee that the goal will be attained by 2015. In Sub-Saharan Africa, one third of the population concentrated in Central and Eastern Africa suffers from hunger. Angola, Chad, Djibouti, Ghana and Mozambique posted significant improvements.

59

The incidence of hunger increased however in Republic of Congo, Burundi, Liberia, Guinea-Bissau and Comoros as well to a lesser extent in Botswana, Swaziland, Tanzania, Gambia, Sierra Leone and Madagascar. Lastly, in the countries of North Africa as well as in Mali, Mauritius, South Africa, Zambia and Zimbabwe progress has been modest.

Food security is facing new threats due to rising food and petrol prices, and an increasing population while a large part of the population resides in rural zones and agricultural productivity remains poor.

Goal 2 – Achieve universal primary education

Target 3 – Between now and 2015, give children everywhere, boys and girls alike, the means to complete a full course of primary schooling.

Net primary enrolment rates

In Sub-Saharan Africa 23 million children attended school in 2006, whilst this figure was 16 million in 1999. In the region, primary enrolment rates increased 14 points between 1999 and 2006, from 56 per cent to 70 per cent. However, the strong rise in the number of primary-school aged children, which should grow by 26 million between now and 2015 necessitates increased efforts. Despite this progress, only 49 per cent of countries reached (18) or are on track to reach (8) the goal by 2015. Madagascar, Malawi, Mauritius, São Tomé and Principe, Seychelles, South Africa and Tanzania join the countries of North Africa that have already achieved the target. Certain countries with rates inferior to or near 50 per cent in 1990 recorded remarkable performances, thus attaining net enrolment rates in excess of 70 per cent in 2006. These include Benin, Ethiopia (with a rate rising from 22 to 71 per cent), Guinea, Malawi, Mauritania, Mozambique and Tanzania. The elimination of enrolment fees and the implementation of school-construction programmes particularly in rural areas doubtlessly explain the results. However, half of the countries in the region will not reach the target. In some, progress is practically inexistent (Central African Republic, Democratic Republic of Congo, Guinea Bissau, Sierra Leone and Somalia) or

has even in some cases declined significantly as in Angola, Botswana, Cape Verde and Liberia.

Proportion of school children beginning the first year of studies in primary education and completing the fifth year

The enrolment of children in primary schooling is clearly a necessary step towards universal primary education, but it is not in itself sufficient. Increasing the completion rate in primary education poses a real challenge for the region. The performances registered in enrolment rates have not been accompanied by a sufficient increase in primary completion rates. In Sub-Saharan Africa, more than 30 per cent of children enrolled in education do not complete the primary cycle (versus 10 per cent in North Africa). While net enrolment rates are close to 100 per cent in North African countries and exceed 85 per cent in 11 Sub-Saharan African countries, they are particularly weak in Burkina Faso, Central African Republic, Eritrea and Niger. Likewise, while the literacy rate has improved since 1990 (from 66.5 per cent in 1990 to 73 per cent in 2006), progress remains wholly inadequate to attain the goal of 100 per cent by 2015. In 2006, save for the countries of North Africa, only 10 countries in which the initial rates were already high recorded rates of between 80 and 90 per cent, while in 8 countries less than 50 per cent of youth are literate.

Goal 3 – Promote gender equality and empower women

The progress in eliminating gender disparities in access to primary education is the most striking. Gender gaps in education are weakest in Eastern Africa, followed by South Africa and North Africa, while Southern Africa exhibits the greatest disparities. Thus, 67.9 per cent of countries have reached or are on course to reach the target by 2015 and more than 80 per cent have a rate superior or close to the average. Gambia, Guinea, Mauritania and Benin have reached parity with gaps closing by more than 30 points since 1990. Some countries (Mauritania, Gambia, Rwanda and Malawi) exhibit moreover an advantage in favour of women. In contrast, disparities remain particularly high and register weak improvements in Somalia, Central African Republic, Guinea Bissau and Chad. Lastly, four countries (Cape Verde, Eritrea, Libya and Swaziland) although close to the average in terms of status, have not progressed. Performances in primary education are to a lesser extent reproduced in secondary education where disparities between countries are correlated to those in primary schooling.

While the eradication of gender disparities in school enrolment represents a major development objective in itself, it is also imperative that women have the opportunity to enter the labour market and participate in political decision making. In this field, progress has been mixed. Thus, the reduction of gender disparities in labour market participation is not significant. On the other hand, representation of women in the political sphere while poor, is improving. Thus, in 12 countries the percentage of national parliamentary seats occupied by women more than doubled between 1990 and 2007. Rwanda exhibited the best performance with a rate of 56 per cent, followed by Mozambique (34.8 per cent) and South Africa (32.8 per cent). In contrast, the already high inequalities in São Tomé and Principe were maintained and they deepened further in Chad and Mali.

Goal 4 – Reduce mortality of children under five

Target 4 – Reduce by two-thirds, between 1990 and 2015, the under-five mortality rate.

Overall, the under-five child mortality rate fell by 12.85 per cent for Africa as a whole between 1992 and 2007, while an annual rate of decline of 8 per cent is needed if the goal is to be attained on time. Child survival presents a real challenge for the region. But this broad trend however, conceals variations between regions and between countries. While the rate receded by 55 per cent in North Africa, this trend was reversed in Central Africa where child mortality increased by 13 per cent. Only 32.7 per cent of countries have attained or are on course to attain the goal by 2015. Besides the North African countries, some countries (Eritrea, Malawi, Mauritania, Namibia, Comoros and

Gabon) with initially high mortality rates made remarkable progress by having already attained the goal (with a more than 45 per cent reduction). Likewise, Gambia, Madagascar, Uganda and Djibouti, all on course, recorded rates of decline of about 40 per cent. However, in 31 countries, performances are distinctly inadequate and four countries (Democratic Republic of Congo, Côte d'Ivoire, Nigeria and Angola) exhibited a deterioration of the indicator. A significant proportion of countries with below-average ranking followed. In addition, there is a strong correlation between the status and performance in Goal 1 and the position achieved in terms of infant mortality. Deaths are attributable to poverty responsible for increasing malnutrition and declining conditions of hygiene thus reducing immune system defences and causing diseases that could have been prevented by immunisation. Measles is the leading cause of death in children in Africa before AIDS, tuberculosis and malaria (World Health Organization, 2008). While vaccination coverage against measles has registered an improvement in Sub-Saharan Africa (56 per cent in 1990 and 72 per cent in 2006), it remains inadequate to effectively ensure children's chances of survival. Beyond the average trends, it appears that the scale of the challenge of child survival varies from one country to the next. A number of countries, even poor ones, have displayed noteworthy performances (Eritrea, Malawi and Namibia) raising the possibility that progress is possible with political will, adequate resources and targeted strategies.

Goal 5 – Improve maternal health

Target 5 – Reduce by three quarters, between 1990 and 2015, the maternal mortality ratio.

The performance of the maternal mortality ratio in Africa signals an urgent need for action in order for goal 5 to be attained. According to a WHO study (2008), almost 265 000 maternal deaths, or half of global maternal deaths were recorded in Sub-Saharan Africa. The number of maternal deaths per 100 000 live births varies from 2 100 in Sierra Leone to 23 in Mauritius, with 8 countries registering rates of over 1 000. With a less than 1 per cent reduction in the ratio between 1990 and 2007, a great deal of ground remains

61

to be covered to reach the target. With the exception of Eastern Africa, which experienced a 49 per cent reduction from relatively high initial rates, in other regions maternal health has stagnated or declined.

Only 26.9 per cent of countries made sufficient efforts to reach the target by 2015. While Mauritius, Cape Verde, Tunisia and South Africa have reached the target from poor starting ratios, Rwanda, Eritrea, and Mozambique have performed remarkably well reducing mortality by more than 50 per cent (or more than 60 per cent for some). With ratios now below 1 000, this progress has enabled these countries to improve their standing in terms of this target. In contrast, in 21 countries, maternal health has deteriorated with increases in the mortality ratio sometimes in excess of 60 or 70 per cent. The situation is particularly worrying in Liberia, Guinea, Mali, Malawi and Central Africa Republic where ratios are near the critical threshold of 1 000 as well as for Sierra Leone and Angola for which the ratio of 1 000 appears increasingly out of reach.

Maternal mortality is linked to complications arising from pregnancy or childbirth. The main causes, in decreasing order of importance, are: haemorrhage; sepsis and infections, including HIV; hypertensive disorders; complications following abortion; and obstructed labour. In Niger the risk of maternal mortality over a lifetime is highest, with a mortality rate linked to pregnancy of 1 in 7, compared with 1 in 3 300 women in Mauritius (1 in 15 women in Mali). Lastly, the number of adolescent pregnancies represents a risk factor. Despite a noticeable decrease since the 1990s (from 121 per 1 000 in 1997 to 103.5 in 2007), adolescent fertility remains particularly high in Southern Africa (185.3) and Western Africa (124.1); with a rate of 218.8, Liberia has the highest level of adolescent births. These causes could be avoided through improved access to and quality of health care for women, universal access to reproductive health services, access to family planning, prevention of unwanted pregnancies and improved education levels of women. In 2007, only 50 per cent of women gave birth under the supervision of a qualified health worker, compared with a rate of 45 per cent in 1990 with strong country differences,

ranging from 10 per cent in Ethiopia to 95 per cent in Algeria. Even when initiatives existed, they could be beyond the reach of the poorest segments of the population. Beyond the challenge of inadequate quality, access to health services can be determined by place of residence in the absence of good communication infrastructure between urban and rural areas, as well as by household wealth or the education level of women.

Goal 6 – Combat HIV/AIDS, malaria and other diseases

Target 6 – Have halted by 2015 and begun to reverse the spread of HIV/AIDS.

The target of halting the spread of HIV/AIDS is beyond the reach of Africa by 2015. In 2007, 22 million adults in Sub-Saharan Africa were living with HIV and 1.5 million deaths were due to AIDS. Although HIV prevalence was stabilising in some countries, the rate went from 2.1 per cent in 1990 to 4.9 per cent in 2009. Southern Africa continues to register the highest rates (higher than 15 per cent, or even more than 20 per cent) contrasted with rates of below 10 per cent in Western, Central and North Africa. Only Ghana, Kenya and Rwanda appear to have reached the target. Likewise, Uganda, which had an initial rate of 13.7 per cent, has achieved sufficient progress to reverse the trend. In contrast, in more than 80 per cent of countries, the HIV infection rate has not sufficiently reduced or, on the contrary, has increased. A defining characteristic of the illness is the speed with which it has spread. In South Africa, Lesotho and Swaziland the infection rate grew from less than 1 per cent to in excess of 20 per cent. Women are those most affected by HIV (59 per cent); infection rates of pregnant women are very high which increases the risk of transmission to children. Furthermore, the increase in the number of AIDS orphans presents a real development challenge in Africa with negative effects on other development objectives. In Southern Africa, more than 70 per cent of orphaned children are due to AIDS. Even in areas where HIV infection rates have stabilised, the number of orphans continues to rise due to the delay between the time a person contracts and dies from the disease. While effective treatments exist, access to them remains unequal from country to country. In Namibia and Botswana, more than one third of those needing antiretroviral treatment receive it, while only 10 per cent in Ethiopia, Lesotho, Mozambique, Nigeria, Tanzania and Zimbabwe receive treatment. An effect of the HIV epidemic has been to increase the number of cases of tuberculosis. Despite existing treatments and an 84 per cent immunization rate, the incidence of tuberculosis has not fallen except in North Africa, Ghana, Mali, Mauritius, São Tomé and Principe, Seychelles and Somalia. The number of cases of tuberculosis is at the highest in Southern Africa with Swaziland leading (1 262 cases per 100 000). Southern Africa also has registered the strongest increase compared with other regions with prevalence increasing by 58 per cent between 1990 and 2005.

Goal 7 – Ensure environmental sustainability

Goal 7 focuses on ensuring environmental sustainability by improving access to clean water and sanitation supply systems. Despite an increase in the coverage rate of the population with access to safe water from 56 per cent in 1990 to 64 per cent in 2006, this progress is insufficient for all African countries to achieve the target by 2015. In terms of status, 14 countries have coverage rates below 55 per cent; Ethiopia registers the lowest rate and Mauritius the highest. In addition, access to clean water is higher in urban areas than in rural ones (85 per cent versus 51 per cent). From the point of view of performance, slightly more than 60 per cent of countries (32 countries) have reached or are on track to reach the goal. Thus, starting from a relatively poor initial rate, Namibia, Liberia, Lesotho and Ghana have achieved significant progress. The trend is equally promising for Angola, Central African Republic, Mauritania and Mali. However, 14 countries appear to have performed poorly exhibiting either inexistent progress (Seychelles) or a reduction in their coverage rate (Algeria, Comoros, Republic of Congo, Equatorial Guinea, Ethiopia, Somalia). The challenge lies in extending coverage to the poorest segments in rural zones and urban slums.

Even more worrying is the situation regarding access to sanitation services. Africa has made little progress on this front, with a sanitation rate of 33 per cent in 1990 rising to just 38 per cent in 2006. Coverage is highest in North Africa and lowest in Western Africa. However, access to sanitation is key for other sectors such as health, the environment and education, but also for attaining gender equity. Demographic growth and the acceleration of urbanisation with increasing growth of slums will inevitably aggravate the situation to the detriment of health and the environment. Lastly, given the demographic growth outlook, the real challenge is not to reduce the gap between those with access to safe water and sanitation to reach the goal, but to make provision for all of those needing services who will be born by 2015.

Goal 8 – Develop a global partnership for development

To fulfil the first seven MDGs, donors must contribute even more aid, make debt relief grants more sustainable and opt for more equitable trade regulations. Yet, as can be noted from the above sections, progress has been largely inadequate except in terms of external debt relief.

References:

- African Development Bank (2008), *Gender, Poverty and Environment Indicators*, volume IX.
- World Health Organization (2008), *Maternal Mortality in 2005: Estimates by WHO, UNICEF, UNFPA and the World Bank.*
- UNAIDS (2008), *Report on the Global Aids Epidemic.*
- UNPD (2007), *Human Development Report 2007/08: Fighting Climate Change.*
- UNESCO (2009), *EFA Global Monitoring Report. Overcoming Inequalities: Why Governance Matters.*
- UNICEF and UNAIDS (2006), *Africa's Orphaned and Vulnerable Generations: Children Affected by AIDS.*
- UNICEF (2007), *The State of the World's Children 2008: Child Survival.*
- UNICEF (2008), *Progress for Children: A Report Card for Maternal Mortality, September.*
- UNICEF and WHO (2008), *Progress on Drinking Water and Sanitation.*

63

64

Table 5 - Main Progress Towards Achieving the Millennium Development Goals

HDI Rank / Indicators / Targets	Goal 1 Eradicate extreme poverty and hunger — Reduce by half population, between 1990 and 2015, the proportion of whose income is less than USD1 a day — Proportion of Population living Below USD1 (PPP) a day	Goal 2 Achieve universal primary education — Ensure that all children can complete primary school — Net primary enrolment ratio (%)	Goal 3 Promote gender equality and empower women — Eliminate gender disparity in all levels of education — Girls to boys ratio (primary school level)	Goal 4 Reduce child mortality — Reduce by 2/3 under-5 mortality rates — Under-five mortality (per 1 000)	Goal 5 Improve maternal health — Reduce maternal mortality by 3/4 — Maternal mortality (per 100 000)	Goal 6 Combat diseases — Combat HIV/AIDS, malaria and other diseases — HIV prevalence rate (%)	Goal 7 Ensure environmental sustainability — Halve the % of people without access to safe water — Population with access to a sustainable water source (%)	Goals for which a country is classified as "early achiever" or "on track"
100 Algeria	early achiever	early achiever	on track	early achiever	regressing	regressing	regressing	4 of 7
157 Angola	off track-slow	regressing	off track-slow	regressing	regressing	regressing	on track	1 of 7
161 Benin	on track	on track	early achiever	off track-slow	early achiever	regressing	off track-slow	4 of 7
126 Botswana	off track-slow	regressing	early achiever	off track-slow	regressing	regressing	early achiever	2 of 7
173 Burkina Faso	off track-slow	off track-slow	on track	off track-slow	off track-slow	off track-slow	early achiever	2 of 7
172 Burundi	off track-slow	on track	off track-slow	off track-slow	on track	regressing	early achiever	3 of 7
150 Cameroon	early achiever	early achiever	off track-slow	off track-slow	regressing	regressing	early achiever	3 of 7
118 Cape Verde	early achiever	regressing	regressing	early achiever	early achiever	...	early achiever	4 of 7
178 Cent. Afr. Rep.	off track-slow	off track-slow	off track-slow	off track-slow	regressing	regressing	on track	1 of 7
170 Chad	regressing	off track-slow	off track-slow	off track-slow	regressing	regressing	early achiever	1 of 7
137 Comoros	off track-slow	off track-slow	on track	early achiever	off track-slow	regressing	regressing	2 of 7
130 Congo	on track	off track-slow	off track-slow	off track-slow	off track-slow	off track-slow	regressing	1 of 7
177 Congo, DRC	regressing	off track-slow	early achiever	regressing	early achiever	off track-slow	off track-slow	2 of 7
166 Côte d'Ivoire	off track-slow	off track-slow	off track-slow	regressing	off track-slow	regressing	early achiever	1 of 7
151 Djibouti	regressing	off track-slow	off track-slow	on track	regressing	regressing	off track-slow	1 of 7
116 Egypt	early achiever	early achiever	on track	early achiever	off track-slow	regressing	early achiever	5 of 7
115 Equat. Guinea	...	off track-slow	early achiever	off track-slow	off track-slow	regressing	regressing	1 of 7
164 Eritrea	regressing	off track-slow	regressing	early achiever	early achiever	regressing	early achiever	3 of 7
169 Ethiopia	early achiever	on track	on track	off track-slow	early achiever	regressing	regressing	4 of 7
107 Gabon	early achiever	early achiever	early achiever	early achiever	regressing	regressing	early achiever	5 of 7
160 Gambia	early achiever	on track	early achiever	on track	on track	early achiever	early achiever	7 of 7
142 Ghana	early achiever	off track-slow	early achiever	off track-slow	off track-slow	regressing	early achiever	3 of 7
167 Guinea	on track	on track	early achiever	off track-slow	regressing	regressing	off track-slow	3 of 7
171 Guinea-Bissau	regressing	off track-slow	early achiever	off track-slow	regressing	regressing	early achiever	1 of 7
144 Kenya	early achiever	off track-slow	early achiever	off track-slow	off track-slow	early achiever	early achiever	4 of 7
155 Lesotho	early achiever	regressing	early achiever	off track-slow	regressing	regressing	early achiever	3 of 7
176 Liberia	regressing	regressing	on track	off track-slow	regressing	regressing	early achiever	2 of 7

52	Libya	...	early achiever	regressing	early achiever	early achiever	regressing	off track-slow	3 of 7
143	Madagascar	off track-slow	early achiever	early achiever	on track	off track-slow	regressing	off track-slow	3 of 7
162	Malawi	off track-slow	early achiever	early achiever	early achiever	regressing	regressing	early achiever	4 of 7
168	Mali	early achiever	on track	on track	off track-slow	regressing	regressing	on track	4 of 7
140	Mauritania	early achiever	on track	early achiever	early achiever	off track-slow	regressing	on track	5 of 7
74	Mauritius	regressing	early achiever	early achiever	early achiever	early achiever	regressing	early achiever	5 of 7
127	Morocco	early achiever	early achiever	on track	on track	on track	regressing	on track	6 of 7
175	Mozambique	off track-slow	off track-slow	off track-slow	off track-slow	early achiever	regressing	off track-slow	2 of 7
129	Namibia	regressing	early achiever	early achiever	early achiever	regressing	regressing	early achiever	4 of 7
174	Niger	regressing	off track-slow	off track-slow	off track-slow	off track-slow	regressing	off track-slow	0 of 7
154	Nigeria	regressing	off track-slow	early achiever	off track-slow	off track-slow	regressing	off track-slow	1 of 7
165	Rwanda	regressing	early achiever	early achiever	on track	on track	early achiever	early achiever	5 of 7
128	São Tomé and Principe	regressing	early achiever	early achiever	off track-slow	regressing	...	early achiever	3 of 7
153	Senegal	early achiever	off track-slow	early achiever	regressing	off track-slow	regressing	early achiever	3 of 7
54	Seychelles	...	early achiever	early achiever	off track-slow	...	...	regressing	2 of 7
179	Sierra Leone	off track-slow	off track-slow	off track-slow	...	off track-slow	regressing	early achiever	2 of 7
...	Somalia	...	...	early achiever	regressing	off track-slow	regressing	regressing	0 of 7
125	South Africa	off track-slow	early achiever	early achiever	off track-slow	early achiever	regressing	off track-slow	3 of 7
146	Sudan	...	regressing	off track-slow	early achiever	off track-slow	regressing	off track-slow	0 of 7
141	Swaziland	on track	regressing	regressing	off track-slow	off track-slow	regressing	early achiever	2 of 7
152	Tanzania	regressing	early achiever	early achiever	regressing	off track-slow	regressing	early achiever	3 of 7
159	Togo	regressing	off track-slow	on track	off track-slow	off track-slow	regressing	off track-slow	1 of 7
95	Tunisia	early achiever	early achiever	early achiever	early achiever	on track	on track	early achiever	6 of 7
156	Uganda	on track	early achiever	early achiever	on track	off track-slow	regressing	early achiever	2 of 7
163	Zambia	regressing	early achiever	early achiever	off track-slow	regressing	regressing	off track-slow	1 of 7
...	Zimbabwe	regressing	off track-slow	early achiever	off track-slow	regressing	regressing	off track-slow	
	Early Achiever	**15**	**18**	**27**	**13**	**9**	**3**	**27**	
	On track	**5**	**8**	**9**	**4**	**5**	**1**	**5**	
	Off track-slow	**12**	**19**	**13**	**31**	**17**	**3**	**14**	
	Regressing	**16**	**7**	**4**	**4**	**21**	**43**	**7**	
	Satisfactory Performance Ratio	**41.7%**	**50.0%**	**67.9%**	**32.7%**	**26.9%**	**8.0%**	**60.4%**	

Sources: African Development Bank.

StatLink ▄▄▄ http://dx.doi.org/10.1787/57420267833

Figure 8 - Distribution of Countries Status by MDGs

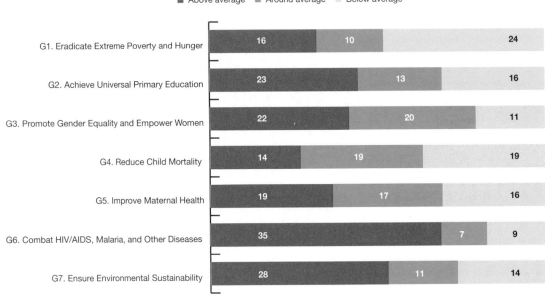

■ Above average ■ Around average ■ Below average

MDG	Above average	Around average	Below average
G1. Eradicate Extreme Poverty and Hunger	16	10	24
G2. Achieve Universal Primary Education	23	13	16
G3. Promote Gender Equality and Empower Women	22	20	11
G4. Reduce Child Mortality	14	19	19
G5. Improve Maternal Health	19	17	16
G6. Combat HIV/AIDS, Malaria, and Other Diseases	35	7	9
G7. Ensure Environmental Sustainability	28	11	14

Source : African Development Bank.

StatLink ⬛⬛ http://dx.doi.org/10.1787/568238566361

66

Governance and Political Issues

On the whole, political and social stabilisation has been generally progressing on the continent, while higher political awareness among the population has obliged governments to become more accountable, as witnessed by the organisation of regular electoral consultations and the implementation of structural reforms in public administration, which have improved governance and increased transparency. However, the administrative capacity of government remains weak, impeding the consolidation of democratic institutions (especially in fragile states); the judicial system still receives little political priority. Gaps in the implementation of regulations are common and, as a result, application of the rule of law remains tenuous.

As noted in *AEO 2007/08*, violence during ordinary demonstrations of democratic dissent, like strikes or demonstrations remains a characteristic of political life in some countries and continued during 2008. Since the end of 2007, when rising living costs triggered a

series of disturbances, political economy considerations have acquired increasing relevance and the authorities have had to strike a careful balance between the need to take some measures to control unrest and the need to avoid a shift to authoritarianism which would limit civil rights, including freedom of the press. With some exceptions, the stance taken by governments faced with these problems turned out to be constructive. The challenge will be to continue on this track, against a background of decreasing public resources, and uncertain donor support.

Conflicts and Political Troubles

Although slow progress towards more stable and democratic regimes continued in many countries, in others the situation generally worsened in 2008 compared to 2007, mainly due to further intensification of long-term conflicts, a resurgence of troubles in countries which had gained stability in the recent past, or new waves of episodic instability in relatively stable countries due to the rising costs of living. (see Table 22 in the Statistical Annex).

Several post-conflict countries have been successful in their struggle to couple macroeconomic normalisation with the promotion of social stability. Angola and Mozambique are good examples of this, with the former holding democratic elections for the first time since the end of the civil conflict, and only the second time since independence. Although insecurity remains a concern, especially in urban areas, stability has improved in Liberia and Sierra Leone, after a decade of particularly destructive conflicts. After 6 years of civil unrest, the situation in Côte d'Ivoire continued to stabilise. Although successful in bringing hostilities to an end and leading to the formation of a national union government, the signing of the Ouagadougou agreement in March 2007 has not yet resulted in elections as originally foreseen. Despite this, violence on the part of both sides of the conflict has decreased dramatically, while the relaxation of the social climate allowed the state to regain control of security in the northern region and resume the delivery of basic services. The Great Lakes region seems to be laying the bases for an improvement in the near future. The conflict in Uganda has lost impetus with the elaboration of a peace agreement in April 2008 (although not yet signed by the rebels), and, after a dramatic intensification of the conflict in DRC, the year closed with the arrest of the chief of one of the rebel groups which had been fuelling violence in the North-Kivu region, thanks to the fruitful co-operation between the governments of Joseph Kabila in DRC and Paul Kagame in Rwanda.

Despite these welcome improvements, there are signs of increasing political tension that cannot be ignored. The year had started on a positive note in DRC, with the organisation of a Peace Conference in Goma in early January. However, violent clashes between the army and several rebel groups poisoned the situation in the north-east part, continuing to fuel instability in the entire region for most of the year. In Chad, the conflict opposing President Deby and the rebellion burst into open warfare when the latter attacked the capital city, N'djamena. With the support of France, the government regained control, although episodic clashes between the army and the rebels continued throughout the year, worsened by ethnic and religious feuding. Neighbouring Sudan and the Horn

of Africa remained restless. The Darfur war continues to kill civilians, while the humanitarian situation risk becoming catastrophic after president Bachir ordered international humanitarian non-governmental organisations out of the country in early 2009 in reaction to an arrest warrant issued by the International Criminal Court bringing charges against him of crimes against humanity. In stateless Somalia the situation remains critical, and the civil war is in its eighteenth year. The signature of a peace deal in June 2008 between the Transitional Federal Government (TFG) and the Alliance for the Re-liberation of Somalia (ARS) did not stop the fighting, and the lack of an effective state threatens the security of the entire region. Besides the on-going battles among rival groups, in 2008 several attacks by pirates on foreign commercial ships spread insecurity along the coast, and weapons which are smuggled into Somalia are also trafficked into other countries in the region. In Central and East Africa, Burundi and the Central African Republic have had trouble in overcoming the effects of past civil conflicts with dramatic episode of violence threatening peace agreements.

An upsurge in the violent activities of a number of rebellion movements can also be observed. Since mid 2007, the Touareg rebellion has acquired new strength in Niger and Mali, intensifying killings and kidnapping of soldiers and foreigners. While the government of Niger has not recognised the existence of a rebellion and refuses to deal with the Touareg, Mali signed a peace agreement with them in April 2008; however, the situation has not yet completely returned to normal. In Nigeria the conflict in the Delta Niger region continued in 2008. Since 2005, it is estimated that Nigeria lost some 20 per cent of its oil production due to these incidents. Despite the creation of a ministry in 2008 to deal with these issues, pacification still seems elusive.

In Kenya, following the contested election of December 2007, some 1 300 people were killed and more than 350 000 were displaced.

In 2008, there were a number of coups d'état. The Mauritania military junta was officially sanctioned by

67

the African Union, which urged it to return to constitutional order after the army overthrew the first ever democratically elected president in August 2008, Mohamed Abdallahi. In December, and after months of social unrest, the army took power in Guinea, taking advantage of the death of the former president, Lasana Conté. The series of coups continued at the beginning of 2009, with the killing of the President Joao Bernardo Vieira of Guinea Bissau by the army, after two failed attempts during 2008. The country had been particularly restless in recent years, due to the increasing presence of Latin American drug dealers using West African coasts as a channel to smuggle drugs in Europe. In early 2009, a harsh political struggle broke out between President Marc Ravalomanana and the mayor of Antananarivo, Andry Rajoelina resulting in violent demonstrations and a number of deaths when the army fired on protesters. After an intervention of the army in support of Rajoelina, President Ravalomanana stepped down, in what was condemned by the African Union and several African leaders as an "unconstitutional transfer of power".

68

Hunger riots began at the end of 2007 and intensified during 2008, triggered by unprecedented increases in food and fuel prices which reduced the real income of households already struggling with harsh living conditions. Burkina Faso, Cameroon, Egypt, Mozambique and Senegal are only a few of the countries which experienced strikes, demonstration and riots. In Cameroon, protests against high prices were coupled with discontent over president Biya's intention to modify the constitution in order to be allowed to run for a third mandate in the presidential elections to be held later in 2011. In South Africa, violent riots with xenophobic connotations in May 2008 caused the death of 62 foreigners and the displacement of several thousand people.

The situation remains tense in some countries and new tensions could explode in the coming months due to the worsening of economic conditions due to the global crisis affecting employment in the mining sector as well as in services, such as construction. Although several governments managed the situation in 2008 by implementing support measures and containing social discontent, the situation is likely to be more

challenging in 2009, in a context of reduced public resources.

The Political Stance

Partly in response to the rising instability, the political stance hardened considerably in 2008 in several countries (see Tables 23 and 24 in the Statistical Annex). In Mali, episodes of harsh reactions to the Touareg rebellion alternated with attempts to push negotiations forward to solve the crisis. In the case of hunger riots, governments generally reacted by increasing the presence of the army and police, and arresting demonstrators.

The rising pressure over state control resulted in government attacks on local and international press. Reporters Sans Frontières expressed worries about the intimidation of journalists, especially in countries of West and North Africa. Episodes of arrests of journalists, withdrawal of licenses and closing of the editorial units of newspapers or magazines occurred in some countries.

North Africa has also been very active in the fight against illegal immigration, as a result of several bilateral agreements signed with European countries, in particular France and Spain. This resulted in the arrest of hundreds of migrants attempting to reach the coasts of Europe illegally on precarious and overcrowded boats. In a desperate attempt to improve their living standards, hundreds of young people die every year.

However, the country that experienced the strongest hardening of the political stance in 2008 was Zimbabwe. Repression of all opposition increased before and after the elections organised in May, which were won, nevertheless, by Morgan Tsvangirai, the opposition party leader. Robert Mugabe, president since Zimbabwe's independence in 1980, refused to accept the result and further intensified repression, despite the disapproval of AU and SADC leaders. A series of bans on political gatherings, curfews and repression of independent media further restricted political and civil liberties. The country further fell into a deep economic and humanitarian crisis, worsened by a cholera outbreak that killed several thousand people and risked affecting neighbouring countries. In February 2009, Mugabe

Table 6 – Freedom in Africa in 2008, countries sub-scores[59]

Country	Political Rights	Civil Liberties	Status	2007
Algeria	6	5	Not Free	=
Angola	6	5	Not Free	=
Benin	2	2	Free	=
Botswana	2	2	Free	=
Burkina Faso	5	3	Partly Free	=
Burundi	4 (worse 1 pt)	5	Partly Free	Worsened
Cameroon	6	6	Not Free	=
Cape Verde	1	1	Free	=
Central African Republic	5	5 (worse 1pt)	Partly Free	Worsened
Chad	7 (worse 1pt)	6 (worse 1pt)	Not Free	Worsened
Comoros	4 (worse 1pt)	4	Partly Free	Worsened
Congo, Rep.	6	5	Not Free	=
Congo, Dem. Rep.	5	6	Not Free	=
Cote d'Ivoire	7 (worse 1pt)	5 (impr 1pt)	Not Free	Mixed
Djibouti	5	5	Partly Free	=
Egypt	6 (impr 1pt)	5 (impr 1pt)	Not Free	Improved
Equatorial Guinea	7	6	Not Free	=
Eritrea	7	6	Not Free	=
Ethiopia	5	5	Partly Free	=
Gabon	6	4	Partly Free	=
Gambia, The	5	4	Partly Free	=
Ghana	1	2	Free	=
Guinea	6	5	Not Free	=
Guinea-Bissau	4	4	Partly Free	=
Kenya	4 (worse 1pt)	3	Partly Free	Worsened
Lesotho	2	3	Free	=
Liberia	3	4	Partly Free	=
Libya	7	7	Not Free	=
Madagascar	4 (worse 1pt)	3	Partly Free	Worsened
Malawi	4	4 (worse 1pt)	Partly Free	Worsened
Mali	2	3 (worse 1pt)	Free	Worsened
Mauritania	4 (impr 1pt)	4	Partly Free	Improved
Mauritius	1	2	Free	=
Morocco	5	4	Partly Free	=
Mozambique	3	3 (impr 1pt)	Partly Free	Improved
Namibia	2	2	Free	=
Niger	3	4 (worse 1pt)	Partly Free	Worsened
Nigeria	4	4	Partly Free	=
Rwanda	6	5	Not Free	=
São Tomé and Principe	2	2	Free	=
Senegal	2	3	Free	=
Seychelles	3	3	Partly Free	=
Sierra Leone	3 (impr 1pt)	3	Partly Free	Improved
Somalia	7	7	Not Free	=
South Africa	2	2	Free	=
Sudan	7	7 (worse1pt)	Not Free	Worsened
Swaziland	7	5	Not Free	=
Tanzania	4	3	Partly Free	=
Togo	5 (impr 1pt)	5	Partly Free	Improved
Tunisia	7 (worse 1pt)	5	Not Free	Worsened
Uganda	5	4	Partly Free	=
Zambia	3 (impr 1pt)	4	Partly Free	Improved
Zimbabwe	7	6	Not Free	=

Source: Political freedom Index, Freedom House (www.freedomhouse.org)

StatLink ⌐⌐ http://dx.doi.org/10.1787/574440506211

59. In parenthesis: changes from 2007 index. Impr: improved; worse: worsened; =: unchanged. The smaller the index, the higher the level of freedom.

finally accepted to constitute a national unity government, giving the position of Prime Minister to Tsvangirai. At the time of writing, the situation is far from being stabilised, however.

As in 2007, the political freedom index (PFI) from Freedom House for 2008 shows a trend in Sub-Saharan Africa towards some setbacks. Eleven countries experienced a worsening of either political or civil rights, only six showed improvement. The PFI is based on measures of several components of political freedom such as: free and fair elections; honest tabulation of ballots; the extent to which citizens are free to organise in different political parties or other political groupings of their choice; whether there is a significant vote for the opposition and a realistic possibility of coming to power through elections; self-determination, and freedom from any kind of domination; reasonable self-determination for cultural, ethnic, religious and other minority groups; and the extent to which political power is decentralised.

Peace and Security

According to the Heidelberg Institute for International Conflict Research[60], the number of conflicts[61] in Africa (Sub-Saharan African and Maghreb, according to the definition) remained stable at 89, mainly driven by conflicts over natural resources and, to a lesser extent, political power at the national and regional levels. However, in 2008, the number of highly violent conflicts rose from 9 to 12[62] reversing a trend towards decreasing intensity of violence in recent years. The deterioration of the situation in Chad resulted in its reclassification as a country at war, alongside conflicts in Darfur and Somalia. In the latter case, the retreat of the Ethiopian troops at the beginning of 2009 did not bring about a significant improvement,

and clashes continue between the Transitional Federal Government (TFG) and groups loyal to the United Islamic Courts (UIC). As a result, while still ranking second in the world for the number of conflicts, after Asia and Oceania, Africa is now the region with the highest number of wars (highly violent conflicts).

As in the past, Sub-Saharan Africa hosted the largest number of UN-led peace operations in 2008 (10 out of 17), including in Burundi, Central Africa Republic/Chad, Côte d'Ivoire, DRC, Ethiopia/Eritrea, Liberia, Sierra Leone, Sudan (South), Sudan (Darfur), and Western Sahara. In 2008, UNMEE, the UN mission to Ethiopia and Eritrea came to an end, despite the increasing tension over border demarcation in 2007. Although no new mission was deployed, the African Union/UN Hybrid Operation in Darfur (UNAMID) approved in December 2007 was effectively implemented in 2008. This initiative represents the realisation of the UN's goal to strengthen co-operation with multilateral and regional organisations. However, peacekeeping operations did not manage to improve the situation significantly. In view of the increasing instability in DRC, the Security Council decided to increase the number of troops by 3 000 units for the mission (MONUC).

After a very active 2007, which saw the launch of a number of new regional initiatives, new interventions by the African Union (AU) in 2008 were limited to the AU mission to Somalia (AMISOM) and the hybrid UN-AU mission in Sudan. Furthermore, AU observers are still deployed along the border between DRC and Rwanda, with observers from the UN and the two parties, as well as in Southern Sudan. AU Liaison Officers, based in Asmara and Addis Ababa, contribute to the monitoring of the Temporary Security Zone between the two countries. The deterioration of the situation in

---

60. Heidelberg Institute for International Conflict Research (2007), *Conflict Barometer* 2007.

61. According to *Conflict Barometer* a conflict is "The clashing of interests (positional differences) over national values of some duration and magnitude between at least two parties (organised groups, states, groups of states, organisations) that are determined to pursue their interests and win their cases. A conflict is considered to be a severe crisis if violent force is repeatedly used in an organised way. A war is a type of violent conflict in which violent force is used with certain continuity in an organised and systematic way. The conflict parties exercise extensive measures, depending on the situation. The extent of destruction is massive and of long duration".

62. Nine severe crises were recorded in Mali, Nigeria, Southern Sudan, DRC, Burundi and Kenya, while other crises were recorded in Niger, Central African Republic and Ethiopia, while involved in the conflict in Somalia). For the full list, please see the 2008 Conflict Barometer at http://www.hiik.de/en/konfliktbarometer/index.html

70

Somalia caused the UN Security Council to extend the AMISOM mandate by six months on February 2008. In March, AU troops supported the Comoros government in its intervention in dissident Anjouan Island to return it to central government control.

Efforts to make the African Peace and Security Architecture (APSA), launched in Durban in 2002, operational are continuing: the Annual Consultation between the Commission of the African Union (AU), members of the AU Peace and Security Council (PSC), the Regional Mechanisms for Conflict Prevention, Management and Resolution, representatives of the G8 member countries, the European Union (EU), the United Nations (UN) and other partners was held in June 2008 in Addis Ababa. Progress and the implementation of the AU peace and security agenda were assessed and the Panel of the Wise was inaugurated in December 2007. At the end of January 2008, a Memorandum of Understanding (MoU) on Co-operation on Peace and Security between the AU and the Regional Mechanisms for Conflict Prevention, Management and Resolution was signed. As part of the capacity building component of the Africa Peace Facility (APF) put in place by the EU at the request of the AU, a number of Regional Mechanisms have already deployed Liaison Officers with the AU in Addis Ababa. Moreover, the EURO RECAMP initiative was launched in November 2008 by the EU and aims to train African military and civilian leaders belonging to the African Stand-by Force (ASF) in order to compensate for the severe capacity shortage. The ASF is expected to be able to provide rapid reaction in emergency situations. The Continental Early Warning System (CEWS) is expected to become operational by 2009.

Electoral processes

Some 36 million Africans were called to express their vote in parliamentary and presidential consultations in 2008 held in 10 countries; 70 per cent of voters participated, compared to 36 per cent in 2007. Elections in Ghana, the biggest country in terms of population that had an election, accounted for much of this result with a turnout of 70 per cent, while in Angola 98 per cent of voters went to the polls. Generally the outcomes

71

Table 7 - Elections in Africa, 2008-09

	2008	2009
Algeria		Presidential (April) and parliamentary (Dec)
Angola	Parliamentary (Sept)	Presidential (no date)
Botswana		Parliamentary (Oct)
Chad		Parliamentary (no date)
Comoros	Autonomous Island Legislative Assembly Elections (March)	Parliamentary (Apr)
Congo	Senatorial (indirect) (Jun)	Presidential (Jul)
Côte d'Ivoire		Presidential (no date)
Djibouti	Parliamentary (8 Feb)	
Equatorial Guinea		Presidential (Dec)
Ghana	Presidential and parliamentary(Dec)	
Malawi		Parliamentary and presidential (19 May)
Mauritania		Presidential (6 June)
Mauritius	Presidential (indirect) (May)	
Mozambique		Presidential and parliamentary (Dec)
Namibia		Presidential and parliamentary (Nov)
Niger		Presidential and parliamentary (Nov)
Rwanda	Parliamentary (Sept)	
South Africa		Parliamentary (22 Apr)
Swaziland	Parliamentary (Oct)	
Tunisia		Presidential and parliamentary (Oct)
Zimbabwe	Presidential and Parliamentary (March)	

Source : www.electionguide.org et http://africanelections.tripod.com/

StatLink http://dx.doi.org/10.1787/574445007801

were positive: Angola held its first democratic elections after the end of the war, and the second after independence. The electoral process was peaceful and international observers did not report any major irregularities. Rwanda, Zambia, Ghana conducted peaceful elections. In Ghana, the opposition leader, John Atta-Mills, of the National Democratic Congress (NDC) won the poll, while, in Rwanda, women took 56 per cent of the total parliamentary seats, making this country's Chamber of Deputies the first in the world to have a female majority. However, post-electoral violence plagued Zimbabwe, where the situation deteriorated leading to state-sanctioned violence directed towards opposition members. Elsewhere, incidents of violence triggered by the 2007 elections in Kenya and Nigeria continued into 2008.

In 2009 15 electoral consultations are expected, including the long-delayed elections in Côte d'Ivoire, and national elections in South Africa, where rising tensions during the electoral campaign resulted in the split of the major party. The first democratic elections for the presidency are also expected in Angola, although a constitutional reform might delay elections to 2010.

Corruption

According to Transparency International data for 2008, corruption remains a serious challenge for the continent and progress in combating it remains mixed. In 2008 the number of countries listed in the world top quartile rose to three (Botswana, Cape Verde and Mauritius) compared to two in 2007 (Botswana and South Africa). There might have been 4 in 2008 had the score for South Africa not slipped below 5. In 2008, 10 countries were in the second quartile (as in 2007), while 22 were in the third and 18 in the lowest, compared to 20 and 20, respectively, in 2007. Although some countries improved their performance, it is clear that transparency and good governance remain elusive, with 36 countries still scoring less than 3, indicating that corruption is perceived as rampant.

The 2008 CPI results show that countries like Benin, Burkina Faso, Mauritius and Nigeria significantly

increased their score. However, the situation deteriorated sharply in Burundi and Somalia, while setbacks were also recorded in Mozambique, Tanzania and Uganda. Generally, worse performing countries saw their position deteriorate; the number of countries with a score below 2 increased from 6 to 13. These countries also represent those in which human development is among the lowest, confirming that there is a link between fighting corruption and improving the quality of public expenditure to reduce poverty.

Cape Verde, Mali, Mozambique, Niger and Tunisia ratified the United Nations Convention against corruption in 2008, bringing to 39 the number of African countries to have done so. In 2008, Cameroon and Sudan signed the African Union Convention on Preventing and Combating Corruption, bringing the number of African countries having signed to 43 since 2003. In addition, two new ratifications occurred, in Seychelles and Sierra Leone. The convention entered into force in 2007.

Despite the trouble spots, the continent's commitment to achieving good governance in all its ramifications is reflected in the African Peer Review Mechanism (APRM) process, launched in July 2002 as the flagship governance programme of the NEPAD. The primary purpose of the APRM is to foster the adoption of policies, standards and practices that lead to political stability, high economic growth, sustainable development and accelerated sub-regional and continental economic integration. As of February 2008, 29 countries had voluntarily acceded to the Mechanism. Mauritania was, however, suspended in November 2008 following a *coup d'état* that ousted its democratically elected president.

For the first time ever, four peer reviews were conducted in 2008: Benin, Uganda, Nigeria and Burkina Faso. This is an achievement when only five peer reviews had been conducted between 2003 and 2007: Ghana, Rwanda, Kenya, South Africa and Algeria. Country Review Missions to Mali, Mozambique, Lesotho and Ethiopia have been scheduled the first half of 2009 and missions to Mauritius and Zambia are expected in the second half of the year. Mozambique,

Table 8 - Corruption Perception Indexes (CPI) for African Countries, 2007 and 2008

Country	Global Rank 2008	CPI 2008	Global Rank 2007	CPI 2007
Botswana	36	5.8	38	5.4
Mauritius	41	5.5	53	4.7
Cape Verde	47	5.1	49	4.9
South Africa	54	4.9	43	5.1
Seychelles	55	4.8	57	4.5
Namibia	61	4.5	57	4.5
Tunisia	62	4.4	61	4.2
Ghana	67	3.9	69	3.7
Swaziland	72	3.6	84	3.3
Morocco	80	3.5	72	3.5
Burkina Faso	80	3.5	105	2.9
Senegal	85	3.4	71	3.6
Madagascar	85	3.4	94	3.2
Lesotho	92	3.2	84	3.3
Algeria	92	3.2	99	3.0
Gabon	96	3.1	84	3.3
Mali	96	3.1	118	2.7
Benin	96	3.1	118	2.7
Tanzania	102	3.0	94	3.2
Rwanda	102	3.0	111	2.8
Djibouti	102	3.0	n.a.	n.a.
Egypt	115	2.8	105	2.9
Malawi	115	2.8	118	2.7
Zambia	115	2.8	123	2.6
Mauritania	115	2.8	123	2.6
Niger	115	2.8	123	2.6
Togo	121	2.7	143	2.3
Nigeria	121	2.7	147	2.2
São Tomé and Principe	121	2.7	n.a.	n.a.
Eritrea	126	2.6	111	2.8
Mozambique	126	2.6	111	2.8
Uganda	126	2.6	111	2.8
Ethiopia	126	2.6	138	2.4
Libya	126	2.6	n.a.	n.a.
Comoros	134	2.5	n.a.	n.a.
Liberia	138	2.4	n.a.	n.a.
Cameroon	141	2.3	138	2.4
Kenya	147	2.1	150	2.1
Côte d'Ivoire	151	2.0	150	2.1
Central African Republic	151	2.0	162	2.0
Burundi	158	1.9	131	2.5
Gambia, The	158	1.9	143	2.3
Guinea Bissau	158	1.9	n.a.	n.a.
Angola	158	1.9	147	2.2
Sierra Leone	158	1.9	150	2.1
Congo, Rep	158	1.9	150	2.1
Zimbabwe	166	1.8	150	2.1
Equatorial Guinea	171	1.7	168	1.9
Congo, Dem Rep	171	1.7	168	1.9
Guinea	173	1.6	168	1.9
Sudan	173	1.6	172	1.8
Chad	173	1.6	172	1.8
Somalia	180	1	n.a	n.a

Source : *Transparency International.*

73

StatLink ᴍᴤᴸ *http://dx.doi.org/10.1787/574462668310*

Table 9 - African Index of Economic Freedom for 2002-09

World Rank	Country	2009 Score	2008 Score	2007 Score	2006 Score	2005 Score	2004 Score	2003 Score	2002 Score
18	Mauritius	74,3	72.3	69.2	67.5	67.2	64.3	64.4	67.7
34	Botswana	69,7	68.6	68.5	69.2	69.6	69.9	68.6	66.2
61	South Africa	63,8	63.2	63.4	63.5	62.7	66.3	67.1	64.0
63	Uganda	63,5	64.4	63.7	64.5	63.5	64.1	60.1	61.0
71	Namibia	62,3	61.0	63.2	60.3	61.0	62.4	67.3	65.1
73	Madagascar	62,2	62.4	61.1	61.1	63.2	60.9	62.8	56.8
77	Cape Verde	61,3	58.4	57.1	59.2	58.3	58.1	56.1	57.6
85	Burkina Faso	59,5	55.6	55.1	55.8	56.5	58.0	58.9	58.8
90	Kenya	58,7	59.6	59.9	60.0	58.2	57.7	58.6	58.2
93	Tanzania	58,4	56.4	56.8	58.5	56.3	60.1	56.9	58.3
96	Ghana	58,1	56.7	57.3	55.3	56.3	59.1	58.2	57.2
97	Egypt	58	59.2	55.1	53.9	56.4	55.5	55.3	54.1
98	Tunisia	58	59.3	59.6	56.8	54.8	58.4	58.1	60.2
101	Morocco	57,7	56.4	57.2	52.3	52.6	56.7	57.8	59.0
107	Algeria	56,6	55.7	55.0	55.3	52.7	58.1	57.7	61.0
108	Zambia	56,6	56.4	57.2	57.6	55.6	54.9	55.3	59.6
110	Senegal	56,3	58.2	58.1	56.2	57.9	58.9	58.1	58.6
112	Gambia, The	55,8	56.6	57.4	57.1	56.3	55.3	56.3	57.7
113	Mozambique	55,7	56.6	55.9	53.1	56.0	57.2	58.6	57.7
114	Mali	55,6	55.5	54.7	54.1	57.3	56.6	58.6	61.1
115	Benin	55,4	55.0	55.0	53.9	52.2	54.6	54.9	57.3
117	Nigeria	55,1	55.5	56.0	48.4	48.2	49.2	49.5	50.9
118	Gabon	55	53.6	54.2	55.5	54.2	57.1	58.7	58.0
119	Côte d'Ivoire	55	54.9	56.0	57.2	57.6	57.8	56.7	57.3
124	Rwanda	54,2	54.1	52.4	52.8	51.6	53.3	47.8	50.4
127	Mauritania	53,9	55.0	53.6	55.6	59.1	61.8	59.0	52.5
128	Niger	53,8	52.7	53.1	52.4	54.0	54.6	54.2	48.2
129	Malawi	53,7	53.8	54.0	56.5	54.7	53.6	53.2	56.9
135	Ethiopia	53	53.2	54.4	51.7	51.9	54.5	48.8	49.8
136	Cameroon	53	54.0	55.4	54.3	52.7	52.3	52.7	52.8
140	Djibouti	51,3	52.3	53.5	54.3	56.4	55.6	55.7	57.8
142	Eq. Guinea	51,3	52.5	54.1	52.4	54.2	53.3	53.1	46.4
144	Guinea	51	52.8	54.5	52.9	57.4	56.1	54.6	52.9
151	Lesotho	49,7	51.9	53.1	54.6	54.1	50.3	52.0	48.9
153	Burundi	48,8	46.3	47.1	48.7	-	-	-	-
154	Togo	48,7	48.8	49.7	47.3	48.1	47.0	46.8	45.2
156	Cent. Afr. Rep.	48,3	48.2	50.3	53.9	56.2	57.5	60.0	59.8
158	Sierra Leone	47,8	48.9	47.6	45.8	45.4	43.6	42.2	-
159	Seychelles	47,8	-	-	-	-	-	-	-
161	Chad	47,5	47.7	50.0	49.8	52.0	53.1	52.6	49.2
162	Angola	47	47.1	45.2	43.9	-	-	-	-
165	Guinea Bissau	45,4	45.1	46.8	47.2	46.7	42.6	43.1	42.3
166	Congo. Rep.	45,4	45.2	44.4	43.7	46.1	45.9	47.7	45.3
171	Libya	43,5	38.7	37.0	33.2	32.8	31.5	34.6	35.4
178	Zimbabwe	22,7	29.8	31.9	33.4	35.1	34.4	36.7	36.7
-	Swaziland	59,1	58	60.6	61.8	59.9	58.6	59.6	60.9
-	Sudan	-	-	-	-	-	-	-	-
Sub-Saharan Africa		**55,6**	**54.4**	**54.8**	**54.5**	**55.3**	**55.4**	**55.3**	**55.3**
North Africa		**54,3**	**54.0**	**52.9**	**51.2**	**51.4**	**53.7**	**53.7**	**53.7**

Source: The Heritage Foundation/the *Wall Street Journal*, 2009 Index of Economic Freedom. http://www.heritage.org/Index/.

StatLink 🔗 http://dx.doi.org/10.1787/574508714062

74

Lesotho and Mali have already received country review missions and will be peer-reviewed in 2009.

Two additional dimensions were recently added to the APRM process. The APRM Forum embarked on the examination of the cross-cutting issues (areas of deficiencies identified in all the reviewed countries to date) at its first Extraordinary Summit which took place in Cotonou, Benin, in November 2008. The areas of focus were: Managing Diversities and Xenophobia; Elections in Africa; and Resource Control and Management: Land; and, Corruption. At the heart of the peer review process is the National Programme of Action (NPOA) designed to address the various challenges identified in the four thematic areas. For the first time in the history of the APRM, the January 2009 summit of the APRM Forum was dedicated to a comprehensive and holistic review of progress in the implementation of the National Programmes of Action by countries that have completed the Review Process. Ghana, Rwanda, Kenya, Algeria, South Africa and Benin presented their progress reports.

Launched in 2002, the Extractive Industries Transparency Initiative (EITI)[63] promotes transparency in payments made by extractive companies and revenues received by governments of countries rich in oil, gas and minerals. Among the 26 candidate countries, 18 are African[64]. Central African Republic (December 2008) and Tanzania (February 2009) were the most recent countries to join the initiative. To date, only 7 countries (Cameroon, Gabon, Ghana, Guinea, Liberia, Mauritania and Nigeria) have published reports on their revenues and payments, and some of the reports are not very informative. Moreover, civil society engagement – imperative to a successful implementation of the initiative – is still very limited in many of these countries. African countries need to strengthen their

commitments to EITI, embed it in broader governance reform processes, including incorporating revenue transparency into domestic legislation (Nigeria and São Tomé and Principe have taken these steps already).

Economic Governance

Among other key factors such as high commodity demand and prices, improved economic governance, including sound macroeconomic and public expenditure management, and institutional reforms to improve the business environment underpinned good economic performance in Africa prior to the current global downturn. This subsection on economic governance focuses on developments in the business environment in Africa in 2008.

Doing business has become easier in Africa in 2008, as many countries have implemented more reforms in 2007/08 than ever before. In 2007/08, 28 economies implemented 58 reforms as compared to 24 economies and 49 reforms in 2006/07. The pace of reforms is gathering momentum with a 70 per cent rise in the number of countries reforming between 2005 and 2008. Consequently, in 2008 Africa's regional ranking on the pace of reform improved to third place after Europe and Central Asia, up from fifth place in 2007. Three African countries (Senegal, Burkina Faso and Botswana) are among the top 10 in doing business reformers in 2007/08.

Top reformers in SSA[65] in 2008 include Senegal, Burkina Faso, Botswana, Liberia, Sierra Leone and Rwanda. Several regulatory reforms were undertaken in these countries that substantially improved their global rankings on overall ease of doing business by 2008 (Table 10). Starting a business and trading across

63. In 2008 the World Bank initiated EITI++, which is an initiative aiming to complement EITI's focus on transparency in revenues only. EITI++ is a worthwhile advance as it takes a holistic approach to the value chain and aims to provide technical assistance to improve the quality of contracts for countries, and to monitor operations and the collection of taxes and royalties. It further aims to improve resource-rich countries' economic decisions on resource extraction and help manage price volatility and investment of revenues more effectively. However, since EITI++ is in its infancy, it is too soon to tell whether this particular initiative will be able to yield useful information.

64. Cameroon, Central African Republic, Congo, Democratic Republic of Congo, Cote d'Ivoire, Equatorial Guinea, Gabon, Ghana, Guinea, Liberia, Madagascar, Mali, Mauritania, Niger, Nigeria, São Tomé and Principe, Sierra Leone.

65. Only SSA is considered due to data limitation. The data comes from the World Bank's *Doing Business 2009*, which groups North Africa with the Middle East.

75

borders are the most popular reforms in the region this year. Senegal has improved its business environment and moved up from 168th (DB2008) to 149th (DB2009) due mainly to major regulatory reforms that made it easier to start a business, register property and trade across borders. Burkina Faso implemented a new labour code; introduced a one-stop shop for construction permits that made transferring property much easier.

Botswana cut the time to start a business through computerisation, facilitated trade by introducing an electronic data interchange system; and strengthened

investor protections. Liberia facilitated firm entry by simplifying its business registration process and licensing reforms. It also eased access to credit by establishing a borrower database/credit information system held by the Central Bank of Liberia. Starting a business has become much easier in Sierra Leone because of the elimination of some registration formalities such as the requirement to pay taxes upfront and to obtain permission from exchange control. Among other things, reduced time and cost to register property as well as introduction of a single application form for location clearance and building permit made doing business easier in Rwanda.

Table 10 - Top Reformers of Africa in 2008

Country	Major areas of reforms	Progress in global rankings on ease of doing business between DB2008 and DB2009	Remarks
Senegal	• Starting a Business • Registering Property • Trading Across Borders	168 to 149	Senegal is world's top reformer in trading across borders
Burkina Faso	• Dealing with Construction Permits • Employing workers • Registering Property • Paying Taxes	164 to 148	Burkina Faso is World's best reformer in Employing Workers
Botswana	• Starting a Business • Protecting Investors • Trading Across Borders • Paying Taxes (simplifying procedures)	52 to 38	
Liberia	• Starting a Business • Dealing with Construction Permits • Getting Credit (Information)	167 to 157	
Sierra Leone	• Starting a Business • Dealing with Construction Permits • Registering Property • Trading Across Borders	163 to 156	
Rwanda	• Dealing with Construction Permits • Registering Property • Trading Across Borders • Enforcing of Contract	148 to 139	

Source: DB 2009 database.

StatLink http://dx.doi.org/10.1787/574541812582

According to the *Doing Business 2009* Report, the best performers in the overall global ranking on ease of doing business in SSA are Mauritius (24) followed by South Africa and Botswana. In fact, Mauritius has joined the top 25 countries in the world in terms of the ease of doing business in 2009. The country has introduced major reforms in starting a business, registering property and getting credit. South Africa implemented two major reforms in the area of business start-up, and paying taxes. Thanks to amendments to the Corporate Act, electronic submission of documents and publications eased business start-up. The government also reduced the tax burden by eliminating the regional establishment levy and regional service levy.

Table 11 - Some Indicators of the Business Environment, Sub-Saharan Africa vs. Other Regions, 2009

Region	East Asia and Pacific	Eastern Europe & Central Asia	Latin America & Caribbean	Middle East & North Africa	OECD High income	South Asia	Sub-Saharan Africa
Starting a business							
Number of procedures	8.6	7.7	9.7	8.4	5.8	7.4	10.2
Duration (days)	44.2	22.6	64.5	23.5	13.4	32.5	47.8
Cost (per cent of GNI per capita)	32.3	8.6	39.1	41	4.9	31.9	111.2
Min. capital (per cent of GNI per capita)	37.3	36	3.4	331.4	19.7	0.6	173.4
Employing workers							
Difficult of Hiring Index	19.2	36.4	34.7	22.5	25.7	22.2	39
Rigidity of Hours Index	19.2	48	33.1	41.1	42.2	15	43.5
Difficult of Firing Index	20	32.4	25.6	31.6	26.3	41.3	41.5
Rigidity of Employment Index	19.5	38.9	31.2	31.7	31.4	26.2	41.3
Firing Costs (weeks of wages)	38.6	26.3	53.9	53.6	25.8	66	68.3
Registering Property							
Number of procedures	5	6	6.8	6.4	4.7	6.4	6.8
Time (days)	99	72.1	71.4	37.4	30.3	106	95.6
Cost (per cent of property per capita)	4.1	1.9	6	5.9	4.7	5.9	10.5
Enforcing Contracts							
Number of procedures	37.2	36.4	39.7	43.7	30.8	43.5	39.4
Time (days)	551	425.2	710.1	688.8	462.7	1053	659.7
Cost (per cent of debt)	48.4	23.4	31.3	23.7	18.9	27.2	48.9

Source: *Doing Business 2009* database of the World Bank (accessed on 3 March 2009).

StatLink http://dx.doi.org/10.1787/574545162873

77

In addition to starting a business, SSA countries also implemented major tax reforms, reflected in reduced corporate income tax rates, a simplified process of paying taxes, elimination of some taxes, revised tax codes, and the time needed to comply with the corporate tax system (DB2009). Four of the 25 world economies that reduced corporate income tax in 2007/08 are from Africa: Burkina Faso, Côte d'Ivoire, Madagascar and Morocco. Mozambique has simplified the process of paying taxes in 2007/08 and along with Morocco and Zambia has joined the group of countries that revised their tax code in the same year. Madagascar and South Africa are among the few world economies that removed some taxes in 2007/08. Cameroon, Congo Republic and Nigeria are among the 10 economies in the world where it takes over 200 hours to comply with the corporate tax system in 2007/08.

Thirteen SSA countries did not undertake major reforms in 2008; six of these countries are landlocked (Burundi, DRC, Ethiopia, Malawi, Uganda and Swaziland), two are islands (Comoros and Seychelles) and one is an oil economy (Sudan). The remaining countries are Guinea-Bissau, Niger, Tanzania and Togo. Some Sub-Saharan African countries are still in the bottom list of the economies where doing business is most difficult: Burundi (177th), Congo, Rep (178th), Guinea-Bissau (179th), CAR (180th) and DRC (181st).

Nevertheless, Africa is still lagging behind in business environment. Despite profound improvements in the pace of reforms to make the business environment more conducive to domestic and foreign investors, the business environment in Africa is still least attractive to firm entry and growth, compared to the rest of the world.

Starting a business in Sub-Saharan Africa is the most difficult in the world. It entails 10.2 procedures that take nearly 49 days to complete with a cost of 111.2 of GNI per capita and a minimum capital requirement of 173.4 per cent of GNI per capita (Table 11). Only Latin America outranks Sub-Saharan Africa in the length of days (65, compared to 49) to complete a business start up, but in Latin America the process costs less and the minimum capital requirements is lower.

Registering property in Sub-Saharan Africa involves more procedures and cost than in other regions. Again, only the Latin America and Caribbean region is comparable. It has the highest "rigidity of employment" index and the highest costs of firing employees, implying that the labour market is highly inflexible. However, it is worth mentioning that some African countries like Burkina Faso have joined the world's top reformers in employing workers in 2008. Access to credit is the most difficult, compared to other regions of the world, mainly because of the lack of credit information and collateral requirements. For instance, Sub-Saharan Africa has the lowest ranking in terms of a credit information index (1.4) that measures the rules affecting the scope, access and quality of credit information. Nevertheless, the sub-region is close to the world average in terms of contract enforcement, duration of bankruptcy procedure and the subsequent recovery rate. Mozambique is the world's top reformer in enforcing contracts in 2008.

Part Two

Innovation and ICT in Africa

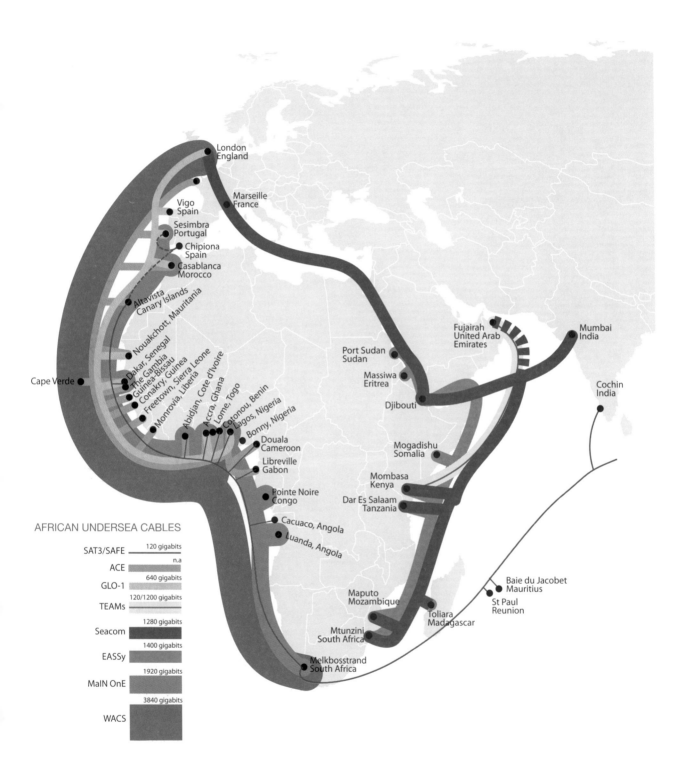

London England
Vigo Spain
Marseille France
Sesimbra Portugal
Chipiona Spain
Casablanca Morocco
Altavista Canary Islands
Nouakchott, Mauritania
Dakar, Senegal
The Gambia
Guinea-Bissau
Conakry, Guinea
Freetown, Sierra Leone
Monrovia, Liberia
Abidjan, Cote d'Ivoire
Accra, Ghana
Lome, Togo
Cotonou, Benin
Lagos, Nigeria
Bonny, Nigeria
Douala Cameroon
Libreville Gabon
Pointe Noire Congo
Cacuaco, Angola
Luanda, Angola
Cape Verde

Port Sudan Sudan
Massiwa Eritrea
Djibouti
Fujairah United Arab Emirates
Mumbai India
Cochin India
Mogadishu Somalia
Mombasa Kenya
Dar Es Salaam Tanzania
Maputo Mozambique
Toliara Madagascar
Baie du Jacobet Mauritius
St Paul Reunion
Mtunzini South Africa
Melkbosstrand South Africa

AFRICAN UNDERSEA CABLES

SAT3/SAFE	120 gigabits
ACE	n.a
GLO-1	640 gigabits
TEAMs	120/1200 gigabits
Seacom	1280 gigabits
EASSy	1400 gigabits
MaIN OnE	1920 gigabits
WACS	3840 gigabits

Africa needs laptops, PCs, fibre optic cables and mobile phones to fuel a communications revolution. It is a revolution that proves no one Information and Communication Technology (ICT) system fits the entire globalised world. Companies and governments are having to adapt to people who want phones that adapt to their often limited resources.

Fixed line telephones have never been a fixture in Africa. The mixture of far-flung villages and scattered cities teeming with low wage families was too much for companies who could easily lay or hang copper wire cables across Europe and North America.

The mobile phone, easy to carry around, and whose infrastructure is cheaper to deploy, has led Africa's revolution. It is the only continent in the world where mobile phone revenues are higher than fixed line. It has the world's fastest growth rate in cellphone usage and governments are reaping the benefit in increased taxes. People in villages and packed cities want to send SMS — Short Message Service — texts and they want to talk, but they want to do it cheaply. So telecoms companies are offering free roaming packages between countries, a world first, and technology to meet the demand. There is e-banking and farmers get market prices on text messages.

So Africa has proved that mobile phones can be acquired and run on limited wages, but the spread of internet has been far slower and general access to ICT services is much lower than the rest of the world and this report will look at the bottlenecks impeding growth. The global economic crisis, lack of connectivity to the rest of the world, inadequate regulation that impedes the spread of the innovative business models and financing all need to be studied. Africa needs to build the skills that drive the innovation behind the African-style e-revolution.

The European Union's Lisbon Strategy has identified Research and Development (R&D) expenditure, structural reforms and labour market de-regulation as the key to rapid uptake of new technology. Improving education to speed up the move to the knowledge economy and boost growth is also crucial to the strategy.

In Africa, it is now believed that knowledge does not just come from R & D, but also interaction between indigenous practices and customs and new technology which can inspire new products and services, such as the e-banking. Liberalisation has helped this trend. Major corporations such as Intel, Microsoft and Nokia have used anthropologists who work with local people to help develop new services.

In line with trends in the Organisation for Economic Development (OECD) and Latin American countries, information and communications technology policies are being integrated into broader science, technology and innovation programmes in Africa. A 2007 African Union (AU) summit adopted a science and technology plan of action. The New Partnership for Africa's Development (NEPAD) is developing a science and technology programme. The AU summit asked the UN Educational, Scientific and Cultural Organisation (UNESCO) to help and talks are now being held between the OECD, UNESCO and the World Bank. UNESCO is supporting a review of science, technology and innovation in 20 countries. It also co-ordinates United Nations (UN) - wide efforts through the UN Science & Technology Cluster - to support NEPAD (see Box 1 for the UN Economic Commission for Africa's (UNECA) contribution). Countries are pushing their own programmes, some with international organisations. Tanzania worked out a science and technology programme with UNESCO and the UN Industrial Development Organisation (UNIDO). Kenya, Mozambique and South Africa also have ambitious programmes while Algeria, Botswana, Mauritius and Rwanda have each set a goal of becoming regional information and communications technology hubs.

Box 1 - Science, Technology and Innovation Can No Longer be Ignored in Africa

Innovation is increasingly becoming an important element in economic growth, and a key driver for the emerging knowledge economy. UNECA is mindful of the fact that for innovation to occur in African countries, scientific collaborative R&D projects need to be strengthened to support technology transfer to Africa and involve African researchers in localising innovation. For example, an ECA-supported ICT R&D project, known as the VarsityNet initiative in partnership with the Department of Computer Science, Addis Ababa University (AAU) in Ethiopia saw the development of an e-government platform based in the Amharic local language for web-based, multilingual and multi-alphabet, customizable document exchange platform to be used by local and central governments in the country. This research initiative led to the growth of the Ethiopian Open Source Community and the creation of the Ethiopia Free and Open Source Network. This environment also saw a marked increase in open source localisation projects in many other Ethiopian colleges, but contributed to the research capacities of the Department in no small measure with respect to software development. Similarly, the AAU also devised a prototype to enable medical practitioners to enter clinical data using mobile devices as well as to access patients' records using the same devices. These serve as an innovation tool for medical institutions, once adopted. This example shows how important innovation is to the African development process and how ICTs can become innovative agents as well. ICTs also offer the power for unleashing and supporting African technological innovation.

ICTs can assist African scientific communities gain better access to scientific knowledge, which would not only be a source of innovation in itself but another way of fostering an innovative environment for scientists. Through ICTs scientists could participate in international projects related to climate change, biodiversity, desertification and other issues of critical importance to Africa. UNECA has launched the "Access to Scientific Knowledge in Africa (ASKIA)" initiative to support and promote access to scientific knowledge by the African scientists, decision makers, students and researchers. It will mainly provide a mechanism for African scientists to tap into global scientific knowledge as well as the production of indigenously owned knowledge that supports economic and industrial growth. Therefore, access to infrastructure, such as broadband access for African universities should become a priority.

According to a recent UNECA report commissioned by the ICT, Science and Technology Division (ISTD), entitled *Promoting Science, Technology and Innovation for Sustainable Development in Africa*, written by Prof. Mohamed Hassan, President of the Third World Academy of Sciences, "Africa does not have the scientific and technological capacity to effectively address the challenges that it confronts. Equally important, it lacks the innovative capacity to devise solutions to overcome these challenges". This is the reason why STI has become an area that Africa cannot continue to ignore any longer, and the rationale for the creation of the ICT, Science and Technology Division of UNECA to address these challenges in African development.

Source: Aida Opoku-Mensah, Director ICT, Science and Technology Division (ISTD), UN Economic Commission for Africa (ECA).

Some science and technology advocates say innovation does not get a high enough priority when donor nations are pressing policies. The UN's Millennium Development Goals do not explicitly mention innovation but do acknowledge its importance by including indicators related to technology access such as the number of fixed-lines, mobile phone subscribers and internet users. Most Poverty Reduction Strategy Papers (PRSPs) for heavily indebted countries do not make full use of innovation and information and communications technology policies unless there is strong local support. In Ghana, for example, with the support of the Kwame Nkrumah University of Science and Technology, innovation was included in the country's PRSP. The 47 countries reviewed in this *AEO* have national ICT policies but they will need support from the donor community and private sector to get them implemented and to help, NEPAD is working on an African Science, Technology and Innovation Indicators Initiative (ASTII).

There are conditions to be taken advantage of and faults to be addressed, however, in the Africa technology debate:

- Science, technology and innovation (STI) policies must be integrated into broader strategies. Innovation and ICT are not effectively integrated into the policy priorities of the donor community. Poverty Reduction Strategy Papers (PRSPs) fail to fully include innovation unless there is strong local support. Development partners must strengthen national ICT policies in Africa.
- Regulatory systems need to improve. Government regulation plays a key role in information and communications technology since most investment comes from the private sector. Regulatory authorities too often favour incumbent fixed-line operators, who have typically problems to make profits, over new entrants and this impedes competition and private investment. However, many countries have introduced better practice to favour incumbent operators through "converged licenses", which allow wider flexibility in choosing technology and through the use of symmetric termination charges. These have created more equality in the regulatory arena between fixed-line and mobile operators.
- Despite the international financial crisis, telecommunications in Africa remains an attractive business. Preliminary evidence suggests that ICT investment in Africa will be less affected by the crisis than other regions, as was the case after the Internet bubble burst in 2000-2001. Several deals were concluded in late 2008 and early 2009. However, the prospects for new deals

are fading and total capital expenditure is falling. Price competition will intensify in coming months and most multinational operators will consolidate their presence.

- New infrastructure connecting Africa to the rest of the world will soon be operational. Many high capacity international backbone network projects are being built to connect Africa to the rest of the world on an open access basis. Wholesale tariffs now at USD 2 000-10 000 for the West coast fibre optic submarine cable, SAT3 and at USD 3 000-5 000 for satellite connection, will start falling to within the range of USD 500-1 000 by late 2009. On the east coast, the first fibre optic submarine cables will be ready in the third quarter of 2009. On the west coast, five fibre optic submarine cable projects and two satellite projects have been announced. Private African capital is behind much of this but there are also public-private partnerships with international investors.
- Improved connectivity will not be enough to reach more users. On top of better international networks, inland backbone trunk networks will be needed and retail prices will have to come down as wholesale tariffs have. Some experts fear that fixed-line operators in Africa will not pass on cost reductions to customers, using them instead to bolster revenues.
- In terms of regional integration, inland regional backbone networks are being built to link major cities in eastern and southern Africa and in landlocked central Africa. Algeria, Botswana, Mauritius and Rwanda are implementing projects to become ICT regional hubs. Pan-African mobile operators are promoting free roaming services, making Africa the first region in the world to offer this innovative service.
- Innovative business models prove it is possible to reach the poor on a commercial basis. Most mobile phone communications in Africa are pre-paid. Micropayments (less than USD 1) to charge mobile accounts are also widespread in Africa. Microfinance business models have been developed in Uganda and Rwanda, and phone sharing is common. SMS messages allow

83

communications for a fraction of ZAR one cent. Advertising-funded services are very successful in South Africa. New and environmentally friendly technology and energy are enabling operators to reach new areas in Africa.

- Governments should privatise the remaining state-owned fixed-line incumbents since private investors can bring the technological know-how necessary to upgrade their networks. This reform has to be coupled with a regulatory environment that is conducive to attracting private investment in order to reverse the fixed-line's tendency to steadily lose business. Innovative good practice in the form of "converged licenses", which are technology neutral, and the symmetric regulation of termination charges, could assist fixed-line operators in their constrained financial situation, while sustaining a level-playing field between fixed and mobile operators.

- International co-operation helps technology and innovation. Telecommunications investment is increasingly dominated by countries such as Kuwait, South Africa and Egypt. China has been providing low cost hardware and credit to under-capitalised state-owned operators, while Indian institutions are building a 53-nation Pan-African E-Network under an African Union initiative. US-style prepaid deals and European SMS messages are extremely popular. E-trade co-operation with the European Union and United States is increasingly important to meeting trade regulations. UK and French companies have also been making large telecommunications investments in Africa. But South-North

Box 2 - Policies on Innovation Science and Technology at Headquarters Must Reach the Field

Sweden has supported research capacity strengthening in developing countries since the 1970s. Tanzania is one of the largest recipients of Swedish aid with a volume of support to research of approximately USD 8 million/year. Since 2007 Sweden has emphasized the importance of science, technology and innovation (STI) in talks with Development Partners (DPs) and the Tanzanian government. Many development partners have programmes that support research in the region and in the country that are usually managed and co-ordinated from headquarters (HQ), but issues concerning STI are seldom raised and streamlined at country level. There are many, though scattered, initiatives to be harmonized and used in a more synergistic and effective way.

As a result of the Paris agenda of aid effectiveness, support through programmes and projects has shifted to general budget support (GBS). However, Tanzania's budget does not have yet a specified line for research which remains an orphan and un-identified sector. Fourteen DPs are providing GBS and, according to Tanzania's Joint Assistance Strategy, have narrowed their field of action to three to four sectors, none of them dedicated to research or ICT exclusively. Although Tanzania's poverty reduction strategy 2005-2010 recognizes the importance of STI for economic growth and the need to increase financing and expand higher education and technological innovation, implementation measures are not well defined and most emphasis is given to promotion of ICT as a cross-cutting issue.

STI is today at the core of many development agendas, the main issue is to move from recognition to implementation and results. A political dialogue is needed to ensure that STI activities are clearly incorporated in poverty reduction strategies and that results can be measured. In the face of immense common challenges a start could be made by providing clear guidelines and building support for field and programme officers.

Source: María Teresa Bejarano, First Secretary, Higher Education and Research, SIDA, Embassy of Sweden, Tanzania.

innovation can also work the other way. Low-cost "classmate computers" which were first sold in Nigeria are now available in Europe and the United States.

- New technology is improving government service efficiency and education quality, and cutting the cost of doing business. Under a NEPAD initiative, all primary and secondary schools are to become e-schools with computers, software and internet access by 2025. E-banking and e-agriculture, both building on indigenous practices, have reduced transaction costs and improved the balance of supply and demand in farmers' markets.

Technology Infrastructure and Services in Africa

The private sector has driven the expansion of information and communications technology in recent years. Figure 1 shows the rapid growth in investment with private participation in African telecommunications from 2000 to 2007. Resource scarce landlocked countries in Sub-Saharan Africa attract the lowest volume of investment. These countries have much lower levels of income, larger rural populations, and lower educational levels than other regions. Oil producer Nigeria has been increasing its dominance, and in 2007 accounted for well over half of total investment in resource rich countries. South Africa's contribution to the resource scarce coastal total has been falling. Between 2000 and 2003, South Africa accounted for 60 per cent of average investment. From 2004 to 2007 this decreased to 22 per cent. North African countries which have higher levels of income and a smaller rural population, accounted on average for 44 per cent of investment in Africa from 2004 to 2007.

Overall investment with private involvement represented an average 1.3 per cent of Africa's Gross Domestic Product (GDP) between 2004 and 2007. In absolute terms, in 2004-2007 Africa attracted on average

85

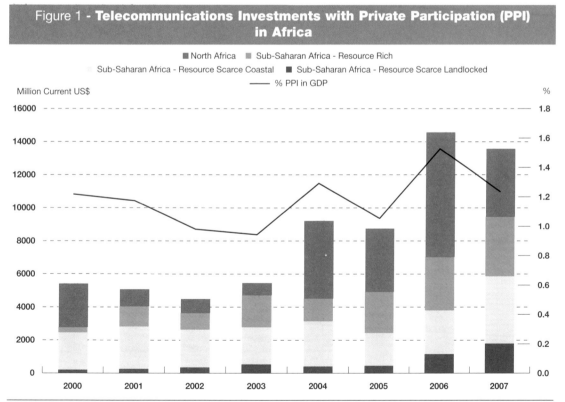

Figure 1 - **Telecommunications Investments with Private Participation (PPI) in Africa**

Source: World Bank PPI Database 2007.

StatLink http://dx.doi.org/10.1787/568243108636

2004-2007 USD 11.5 billion, behind OECD and Central Asia with USD 19 billion and Latin America and Caribbean with USD 13.3 billion, and slightly ahead of South Asia with USD 10.8 billion. East Asia and Pacific countries lagged behind on USD 5.3 billion. Most African countries have extremely low rates of access to ICT services, however, compared to other world regions. According to the Networked Readiness Index 2007-2008 developed by the World Economic Forum and L'Institut Européen d'Administration des Affaires (INSEAD), Sub-Saharan African countries came bottom of the worldwide rankings. North African countries ranked higher, particularly Tunisia with Egypt and Morocco improving their scores. South Africa and Mauritius led the Sub-Saharan rankings.

Access to information technology: Africa in the world rankings

Africa has the lowest internet penetration rate in the world (see Figure 2). In Sub-Saharan African countries, for internet users the penetration rate is below 7 per cent and for broadband it is under 1 per cent. In Latin America and Caribbean, and East Asia and Pacific countries, the figure is around 20 per cent for internet users. North African countries are relatively better-off than Sub-Saharan counterparts with a rate of 40.4 per cent. However, even in North Africa the penetration rate for broadband subscribers is only 2 per cent. In Europe, in contrast broadband penetration is about 15 per cent. In Africa most internet is by low speed dial-up connections which are concentrated in Egypt, Kenya and South Africa. Faster speed broadband connections through Asymmetric Digital Subscriber Lines (ADSL) are found in South Africa, Egypt, Morocco and Algeria.

The penetration of fixed-line services varies significantly. In some North African countries there is a penetration rate of up to 32 per cent, while in Sub-Saharan Africa it can be as low as 3 per cent and this is a major cause of the current difficulties of fixed-line

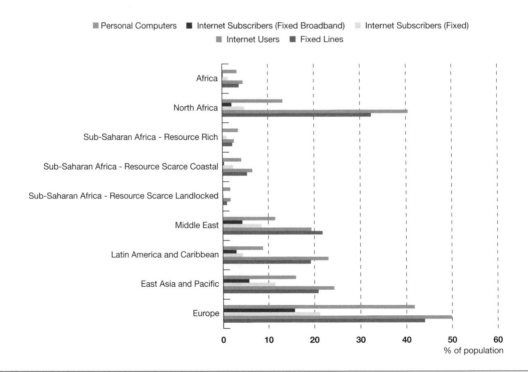

Figure 2 - **Internet in Africa through Fixed-Line**

Source: International Telecommunication Union World Telecommunication/ICT Indicators 2008. Yearly averages for 2005-2007.

StatLink http://dx.doi.org/10.1787/568245266681

Figure 3 - Market Penetration and Growth Rates for Mobile Telephony

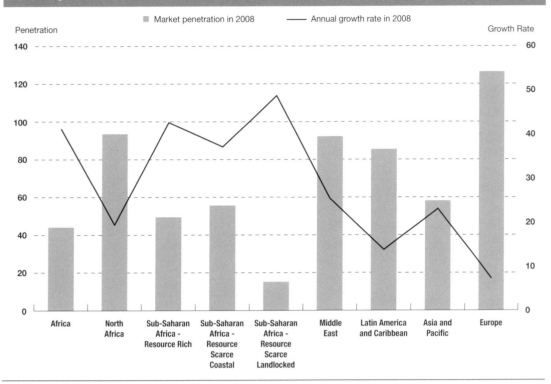

Source: Wireless Intelligence (www.wirelessintelligence.com).

StatLink ⟨⟩ http://dx.doi.org/10.1787/568250253710

operators. In other regions of the world, fixed-line operators had a strong base when mobile penetration arrived. In Africa, the low penetration rate and limited availability of fixed lines made it easier for new mobile entrants to make an impact.

Africa had the world's fastest growth in new mobile phones in 2008. In some Sub-Saharan countries there was growth of about 40 per cent yet overall penetration rates remain low. North African countries, on the other hand, are reaching mature levels with an average penetration rate of 93 per cent, so their average annual growth rate is down to 19 per cent. There are also significant differences between Sub-Saharan countries, with penetration rates in resource rich and resource scarce coastal countries at about 50 per cent, compared to 15 per cent in resource scarce landlocked countries.

Among the big coastal African nations, Nigeria (60 million), South Africa (47 million), Egypt

(37 million), Algeria (31 million) and Morocco (24 million) had the biggest number of subscribers in 2008. Among the landlocked countries, Sudan, Congo and Uganda share the first three places with 10, 8 and 7 million subscribers respectively. With Tunisia's market of 9 million subscribers, four North African countries are among the largest mobile markets in Africa.

But when using market penetration as the measure, Libya, Cape Verde and Comoros have the highest coverage among coastal countries, having reached levels above 100 per cent in 2008. Similar levels have also been reached by Gabon, Algeria and Tunisia. In contrast, in the landlocked countries, the three best performing nations, Lesotho, Sudan and Mali, barely average penetration rates of 25 per cent. At the other end of the scale, Ethiopia, Eritrea and Somalia with a combined population of 92 million people have a penetration rate of just 3.4 per cent. Burundi, Central African Republic and Rwanda have between 5 and 10 per cent.

Box 3 - South-South Co-operation: Large Scale Broadband Wireless Network in Libya

To give customers a wide range of easy-to-use wireless broadband services, Libya's state-owned internet service provider is launching a large scale wireless network. ZTE Corporation of China announced in January 2008 its agreement with Libya Telecom to help build a commercial Worldwide Interoperability for Microwave Access (WiMAX) network. ZTE is one of China's largest manufacturers of telecommunications equipment and is quickly becoming one of the largest suppliers of WiMAX equipment. ZTE provides Internet Protocol (IP) WiMAX product solutions including compact and high-capacity base stations, access gateway, network management system, Multiprotocol Label Switching (MPLS) and IP Multimedia System (IMS).

The network is expected to cover 18 cities. By early 2009, it provided access to 300 000 business and residential subscribers. There are 51 000 broadband subscribers in Libya and about 170 000 consumers that depend on slow dial-up connections. The new service is expected to increase broadband take-up, though the USD 30 per month cost is twice current tariffs. These prices should fall as more customers join the service.

Source: Author.

Operators have concentrated investment on second generation networks in Africa and they will now probably recover this money before getting into third generation high speed networks, even if licences are being granted. As of early 2009 there were only 5 million subscribers — 2.3 per cent of the total subscribers in Africa — for services with Wideband Code Division Multiple Access (WCDMA) and WCDMA High Speed Packet Access (HSPA). The heaviest investment has been in South Africa. The country has three WCDMA and two WCDMA HSPA networks that in 2008 accounted for 45 per cent of third generation network connections in Africa. South Africa, Libya (see Box 3) and Egypt make up to 82 per cent of third generation connections in Africa.

Second generation Global System for Mobile (GSM) communications account for 96 per cent of subscriptions. Code Division Multiple Access (CDMA) technology is only used by 1.5 per cent, but some operators such as Expresso in Sudan have adopted CDMA because it requires less capital investments.

Connecting Africa to the World

Sub-Saharan Africa has the highest internet prices in the world. According to International Telecommunication Union (ITU) and World Bank estimates, the average price of a broadband connection in Sub-Saharan Africa is about USD 110 for 100 kilobit per second. In Europe and Central Asia the price was USD 20 while in Latin America and the Caribbean it was USD 7. Middle East and North African countries also pay below USD 30.

But there is huge potential demand. A 2006-2007 study of 16 Sub-Saharan countries found that in Cameroon, Kenya, Nigeria, Senegal and South Africa more than 10 per cent of the surveyed population use internet. There is a large potential for growth since internet awareness remains very low. In Burkina Faso, Tanzania, Ethiopia, Rwanda, Uganda and Mozambique, less than 10 per cent of the surveyed population knew what internet is. In Namibia, Ghana, Botswana, Benin and Côte d'Ivoire, less than 30 per cent knew what internet is. The telecommunications industry is investing in international bandwidth to meet this potential demand and has currently reached annual growth rates of 96 per cent, compared to a global average of 51 per cent, according to the Telegeography 2008 survey.

The low internet penetration rates and high tariffs stem mainly from a lack of high-capacity international networks (see Figure 4). This allows operators to charge prices far above the marginal cost of the service. There is currently only one submarine fibre optic cable off the West Africa coast, SAT-3, that provides a high quality international service and access is limited to members of the consortium which built the link in 2002. Since mid-2007 operators can purchase capacity at tariffs that have been as high as USD 25 000 per mega bit per second (MBPS) each month and now range between USD 2 000 and USD 10 000 MBPS per month as the cable operators anticipate new competition. Depending on the volume of traffic, South Africa´s wholesale prices are lower while Cameroon and Gabon pay the highest tariffs. Except for Ghana and Benin, it is often impossible to buy a link to SAT-3 and so it has unused capacity.

Figure 4 - International Internet Bandwidth

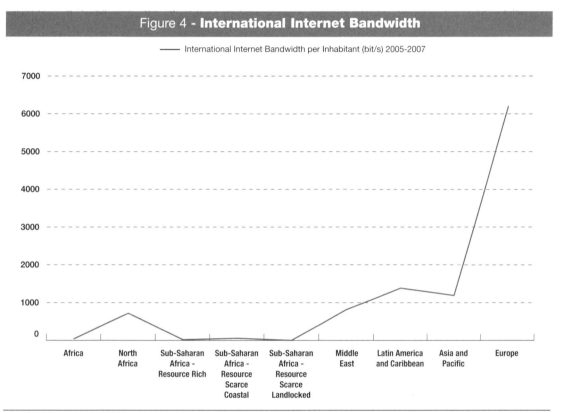

International Internet Bandwidth per Inhabitant (bit/s) 2005-2007

Source: International Telecommunication Union World Telecommunication/ICT Indicators 2008. Yearly averages.

StatLink http://dx.doi.org/10.1787/568251231514

Africa relies on satellites and Very Small Aperture Terminal (VSAT) earth stations for most of its connectivity. This results in high prices — though tariffs often of USD 3 000 – USD 5 000 are often lower than SAT-3 — and the applications are slow compared to other technologies. A web page request can take up to 16 seconds to complete. Intelsat, the world's largest commercial satellite service provider, provides full coverage in Africa. Thuraya, which has Middle East and North African telecommunications and investment companies as shareholders, gives coverage to North and Central Africa.

Moves are being made in west, east and southern Africa to increase the international networks (see Figure 5). But for now, East and Southern Africa relies on satellites and has just 0.07 per cent of the world's international bandwidth capacity. The 10 000 kilometer long East Africa Submarine Cable System (EASSy) was to connect 21 countries from South Africa to Sudan by 2008. Prices were expected to fall to USD 500 - USD 1 500 per Mbps/month under an open-access scheme where every service provider could purchase at the same price, whether or not they were investors. The USD 263 million project has suffered delays largely

Figure 5 - Sub-Saharan Africa Undersea Cables Projected for 2011

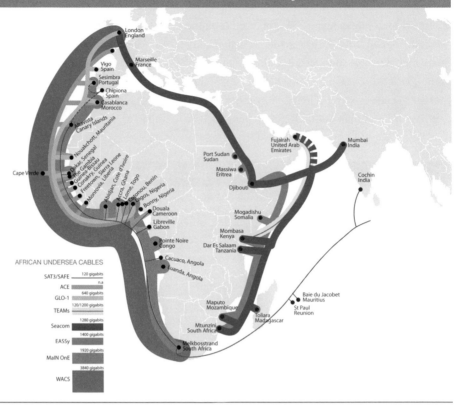

Source: Steven Song www.manypossibilities.net

StatLink http://dx.doi.org/10.1787/568260638546

due to disagreements over management of the consortium.

While EASSy has been delayed, other projects have advanced. Seacom is a 17 000 kilometer submarine fibre optic cable costing USD 650 million scheduled to launch in June 2009 and link South Africa with Mumbai in India, Marseille in France and London via Kenya, Tanzania, Mozambique and Madagascar (see Box 4). Kenya is also working with Etisalat to connect its coastal city of Mombasa to Fujairah in the United Arab Emirates. Alcatel-Lucent has been awarded USD 82 million to lay the 4 500 km fibre-optic cable for the East African Marine System (TEAMS). SEACOM and TEAMS will begin operations in Kenya in the second quarter of 2009 with an open access policy and prices of USD 500 -USD 1 000 per MBPS/month.

The World Bank has allotted USD 424 million to boosting regional networks in eastern and southern

Africa under the Regional Communications Infrastructure Programme (RCIP) which it hopes will increase traffic by at least 36 per cent a year and cut bandwidth costs by one tenth. Kenya, Burundi and Madagascar are involved in the first phase of RCIP, involving USD 164.5 million. By the end of the programme, it is expected that all capitals and major cities in eastern and southern Africa would be linked to competitively priced high bandwidth. The RCIP accounts for more than 10 per cent of total World Bank support to Africa. The African Development Bank (AfDB) is also helping infrastructure development (see Box 6).

On the West coast, Ghana, Nigeria and Senegal have the most significant potential demand for international capacity. Up to seven investment groups have said they would add international capacity in the region but only a few will succeed. Globacom, the second oldest operator in Nigeria, is expected to lay a 9 500 km fibre

Box 4 - SEACOM: Private African Investment Running Ahead of Donor Funded Initiatives

SEACOM is a 1.28 Tbps capacity undersea cable linking South and East Africa to Europe and Asia via the Red Sea, Egypt and the Mediterranean. The EASSy undersea fibre optic cable project in comparison goes from South and East Africa to Sudan. SEACOM plans to deliver open access to capacity and landing infrastructure which is expected to drive international backbone prices down by 90 per cent. The main difference between these systems is that EASSy is a consortium structure for carriers and is funded by International Finance Corporation and other Development Financial Institutions and well as 20 telecommunications operators, while SEACOM is fully privately owned with a 76.25 per cent African ownership. SEACOM's African shareholders (Industrial Promotion Services, Venfin, Convergence Partners and Shanduka) are not telecommunications operators but have sector knowledge and relationships. Their international partner, Herakles Telecom has management expertise. Project finance is provided by Nedbank capital and Investec Bank. While EASSy has suffered from several delays in implementation due to the lack of consensus among parties, SEACOM's deployment is already underway with ships laying cable and cable stations under construction in January 2009. The Ready for Service date is the 27 June 2009.

Source: Author from SEACOM and EASSy Status Reports in December 2008 and January 2009.

Box 5 - Regional Integration in Landlocked Countries

If communication costs remain high, the price of financing trade and ultimately of goods is likely to remain high as well. Broadband networks support regional integration by stimulating cross-border trade and investment among neighbour countries and by strengthening institutional relationships. The World Bank and the AfDB are in the process of committing about USD 300 million for the establishment of a regional backbone project in Central Africa (10 countries involved), the Central African Backbone (CAB), which is expected to decrease the prohibitively high telecommunications costs in landlocked countries.

Source: Yann Burtin, Senior Operations Officer, Information and Communication Technologies Department, The World Bank Group.

Box 6 - AfDB's Support to ICT: African Capitals Connected by Fibre Optic in 2012

The potential contribution of ICTs to poverty reduction, economic growth, productivity and efficiency of public services is well recognized. However, Africa lags behind other regions in ICT penetration and according to the ITU (2009) their rankings on the national ICT Development Index (IDI) are still among the lowest in the world. Accordingly, between 1995 and 2005, the Bank invested USD 440 million in telecommunications infrastructure in Africa and USD 120 million on e-applications such as education, health, agriculture and rural development in order to help close the gap.

Subsequently, the Bank in the past two years has made significant steps towards getting more actively engaged in African ICT. Most notable are the commitment to realizing the Connect Africa Summit goals from Africa Head of State meeting that took place in Kigali in October 2007. The goals included the interconnection of African capitals through broadband links by year 2012 and promoting adequate policy and regulatory environments in order to encourage new ICT infrastructure investment. The Bank also contributes, alongside the AU and Regional Economic Communities, and through supporting efforts in policy harmonisation and infrastructure development, to the realisation of other regional and global initiatives. In this respect AfDB is one of the main actors in the implementation of the ICT policy and regulatory harmonisation framework that was endorsed by African ministers responsible for ICTs at a meeting held in Cairo in May 2008.

In order that the Bank strengthens its current position to deliver its commitments and make a valuable contribution towards the continental economic objectives, a focused ICT Operational Strategy was developed in 2008 and became operational in October 2008 after its approval by the Bank's Board of Directors. The objective of the ICT operations strategy is to make an important contribution to poverty reduction and economic growth of Regional Member Countries (RMCs) by increasing the Bank's role in extending access to ICT infrastructure, stimulating private sector investment and ultimately enhancing good governance through the efficient delivery of public services. The Strategy in the short run (first 24 months), would concentrate on two pillars – direct finance of broadband infrastructure and support to Africa's efforts to attract private financing flows through improvements of the policy and regulatory frameworks. The Bank has recently agreed a USD 14.5 million loan for the fibre optic submarine cable EASSy in the east coast and a USD 50 million loan for the satellite project RASCOM. The Bank is also financing feasibility studies for regional broadband networks. In the medium term, the Bank plans to work towards stimulation of the demand for ICT networks and services by promoting e-government and connectivity to schools, universities, health institutions and through customized response to the needs of Fragile States, Low and Middle Income Countries.

Source: African Development Bank ICT Operation Strategy.

optic link to Lagos in 2009 later going to Accra, Ghana and Dakar, Senegal. The GL01 project, costing USD 150 million, is risky as the operator's current traffic volume in Nigeria, Benin and Ghana does not justify the investment. MaIN One is another Nigerian project implemented by Mainstreet Technologies to link Portugal with Lagos and Accra by May 2010 with USD 200 MBPS/month wholesale prices. The link is ultimately expected to go on to South Africa and cost USD 865 million. The West African Cable System (WACS) is supported by the largest operators in South Africa, MTN, Neotel, Telkom and Vodacom, which have traffic along the West coast. Only landing stations in Lagos and Accra are planned.

The Africa Coast to Europe (ACE) project supported by France Telecom and 14 African operators is expected to connect France to Gabon by 2011. The cable will be built by a France Telecom-managed consortium. The Other Three billion (O3b) satellite, costing USD 750 million, is expected to be in service by 2010 with prices around USD 700 MBPS/month.

It will be able to download web pages in 4 seconds (see Box 7). NEPAD's Uhurunet plan for an undersea fibre optic link around Africa does not have much support. Finally, Thales Alenia Space is constructing the first pan-African telecommunications satellite, Rascom. Originally planned for the 1990s, it is now only expected to provide services after 2010. The West African Festoon System (WAFS) aims to connect countries along the west coast from Nigeria to Namibia. It is expected to have the same governance structure as the SAT-3 cable and also be managed by Telkom SA so WAFS might not offer open access.

Some alternative networks operate with mixed success. More than six electricity companies have received a licence to sell capacity directly or through another company. A 2 000 km fibre optic cable is owned by Société Nationale d'Electricité (SNEL) in Democratic Republic of Congo. These have been badly hit by the country's war. The World Bank is spending USD 315 million in Democratic Republic of Congo, including USD 33 million on a fibre-optic cable

Box 7 - Connecting the Other 3 billion

For network operators in emerging markets, providing a user-friendly, cost-affordable internet service can be very challenging. The founder of O3b Networks, Greg Wyler, learned first-hand as he set out to build Terracom, and Internet Service Provider, in Rwanda in the 2003.

As Mr. Wyler quickly learned, "there was no shortage of last mile solutions available. The challenge was addressing the 'first five thousand miles' ". Located in Central Africa, Rwanda is landlocked and has no immediate access to the undersea fibre cable. For most other developing countries, they are simply bypassed.

Recognizing the lack of affordable connectivity options available for emerging market operators, Mr. Wyler formed O3b Networks placing a constellation of satellites in 2010 in a Medium Earth Orbit (MEO) at approximately 8 000km above the earth unlike a traditional GEO stationary satellite orbit which is located some 35 000km above the earth. Being in a MEO orbit means that travel delay round trip from an O3b satellite will be 130 ms which complies with the ITU standards for a voice grade network whereas a GEO orbit would induce a 400 ms delay. In terms of affordability, in October of 2008, O3b Networks announced services at USD 700 per Mbps/month whereas using GEO stationary satellite capacity had traditionally been in the USD 3 000 - USD 5 000 per Mbps/month price range.

Beyond providing a trunking solution to the global fibre infrastructure, the O3b network can also be used to help operators expand their wireless networks into remote regions. By providing cellular backhaul capacity, O3b allows operators the ability to make the internet and IP services ubiquitous throughout their service region.

Source: Mike Serrano, Director of Marketing, O3b Network.

network. This could be expanded to other members of a proposed Southern African Energy Pool. Escom in Malawi will soon have fibre-optic cable links to Mozambique and the Tanzania Electric Supply Company (Tanesco) says it will build a new national grid with spare capacity used for telecommunications.

Africa telecoms attract investors despite the financial crisis

The financial crisis is likely to speed up consolidation of telecommunications markets in Africa. While small operators struggle to finance network expansion, large cash-flush operators such as South Africa's MTN, Egypt's Orascom Telecom, Kuwait's Zain, France's Orange and UK's Vodafone will be able to move in to African markets. Zain has increased its capital by USD 4.49 billion and says it will spend up to USD 4 billion in Africa before 2010. Business is still

being done despite the crisis such as the sale of Ghana Telecom in August 2008, ONATEL in Burkina Faso in December 2008 and SOTELMA in Mali in January 2009. Millicom's new licence in Rwanda was awarded in November 2008; Orange's new licence in Togo in November 2008 and in Uganda in October 2008, and Orascom Telecom purchased Cell One Namibia in January 2009.

Prospects for the future are uncertain however. The share price of mobile operators in Africa has fallen heavily: MTN by 20 per cent this year and Millicom by 66 per cent. With growth slowing for the past three years, price competition will increase, reducing the high profits that have sustained capital investment. This means third generation networks will be probably delayed.

Foreign Direct Investment (FDI) inflows into African telecommunications were not greatly affected by the

93

Figure 6 - Connection Growth Rates for Mobile Telephony in Africa

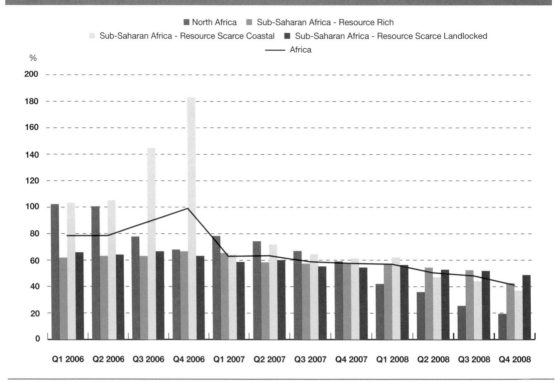

■ North Africa ■ Sub-Saharan Africa - Resource Rich
■ Sub-Saharan Africa - Resource Scarce Coastal ■ Sub-Saharan Africa - Resource Scarce Landlocked
—— Africa

Source: Wireless Intelligence (www.wirelessintelligence.com). Q = quarter

StatLink ⌨ http://dx.doi.org/10.1787/568284004572

Box 8 - Mobile Telephones in Africa: The Impact of the Crisis

Africa is the fastest growing cellular market in the world. It represents around 10 per cent of the total cellular connections worldwide with 450 million connections expected by end of 2009. However, despite the tremendous growth that most mobile operators are reporting in the region, the African telecom sector is not immune to the global economic downturn.

The majority of the fastest growing markets are located in Northern and Western Africa which represent altogether 63 per cent of the total connections in the region. Most of the highly competitive markets are in Nigeria, Zambia, Tanzania, Congo (Kinshasa), Kenya, Algeria, Tunisia, Ghana and South Africa. Those markets have been generating most of the growth and value in the region and are likely to be impacted by the global economic crisis.

The future of mobile operators in most markets depends on their ability to maintain capital (Capex) and operating expenditure (Opex) levels to meet their long term goals. Operators have to expand second generation GSM and third generation WCDMA network coverage, meet their marketing expenses and increase the number of points of sale and retailers. In most fast growing and highly competitive markets, capital expenditure can represent up to 50 per cent of total revenues generated by mobile operators and any sudden decrease in Capex will impact operators' competitive positioning in the long term. The same applies to operating expenditures in markets where operators need to launch innovative product offerings and tariffs including high-speed services.

Africa has attracted a high level of interest from overseas investors who are looking at the high growth potential in Africa to offset their slowing earnings growth in their saturated home markets. Last year, France Telecom-owned Orange launched an effort to become a mobile superpower in Africa. The majority of the African markets are now being contested between Vodafone, Orange, Zain and MTN - groups that benefit from larger economies of scale and substantial liquidity, enabling them to face short term challenges. Local operators are likely to face stronger cash flow pressures leading to more challenges from declining domestic consumption, currency fluctuations and inflation.

Between 2009 and 2010, some heavyweight players might consider expanding their overseas operations and acquire distressed assets in emerging markets. However, it seems that at present, major operator groups are aiming at maximizing profits from their existing operations, putting overseas expansion projects on hold. In Northern and Western African markets, mobile operators are estimated to have generated operating profit (EBITDA) margins in the range of 35-40 per cent in 2008. Although these look like healthy margins, the high level of capital expenditure is shrinking net incomes to around 10-15 per cent of total revenues. In most of those markets, GDP per capita is set on average around USD 1500 and mobile penetration rarely above 50 per cent. Despite the uncertainty behind the impact of the economic downturn, Africa is still likely to remain the fastest growing cellular region in the world.

95

Source: Joss Gillet, Senior Analyst, Wireless Intelligence (www.wirelessintelligence.com or e-mail: info@wirelessintelligence.com).

internet bubble burst in 2000-2001, though only a small number of firms account for a large share of investment. Between 1996 and 2006 France's Vivendi injected USD 6.1 billon, France Telecom USD 4.9 billion and Vodafone of the UK USD 3.4 billion. South-South investments came from Kuwait's Mobile Telecommunications Co. with USD 4.9 billion, South Africa's MTN with USD 4.5 billion and Egypt's Orascom with USD 3.7 billion. More recently, China has offered soft loans to state-owned telecommunications operators. Chinese equipments suppliers such as Huawei and ZTE are probably going to increase their presence in Africa.

The current crisis will probably have less impact on FDI for telecommunications because of Africa's large potential market and the relatively low impact of the crisis on consumers.

The Policy, Legal & Regulatory Lessons

African regulators need more muscle

Telecoms regulators who watch over market structure and the proliferation of new technology are now a fact of life around the world. In Africa, the number of countries with an ICT regulatory agency has grown from 26 in 2000, to 44 in 2007. As most investment comes from the private sector, governments should set the basic goals of telecommunications policy, the regulatory agency should implement and enforce them, and the courts should review them rather than other government branches. According to the International Telecommunication Union (ITU), 60 per cent of regulatory agencies in Africa have been granted autonomy from the executive and become 'independent'.

Some experts say Africa's regulatory agencies should have attracted more private investment. In Latin America and the Caribbean, private investment in telecommunications rose from USD 13.7 billion in 1991 to USD 47.1 billion in 1998 and then shrunk during nine years to USD 15.1 billion in 2007. While private investment in Africa has progressively risen from USD 5.4 billion in 2000 to USD 13.5 billion in 2007, some experts say this could have been higher with more appropriate regulatory frameworks.

There are a large number of cases where private participation in telecommunications in Africa has been affected by discriminatory regulatory decisions. Some agencies which claim to the ITU to be 'independent' of third parties do not act this way. In Mozambique, tariff regulation is essentially set by the fixed-line traditional operator. In South Africa, under the regulatory agency's policy, the fixed-line competitor to the established Telkom became operational only three years after Telkom's monopoly ended, and with only a limited range of services. In Kenya, Rwanda and Namibia, traditional fixed-line operators are protected by the agencies in line with government preferences.

On top of independence and good governance, accountability of political institutions is also needed to enhance the predictability of regulatory processes. All of this increases the incentive for investment. But political accountability is a bigger challenge in Africa than OECD countries.

The World Bank has normally included provisions in loan conditions to provide support for regulators against political interference. However, often the political environment has not supported the development of such institutions. As soon as a World Bank loan was closed, most regulators did not get support from governments, were side-lined or fell under the control of businesses they were meant to regulate. International development partners also have to work harder to improve political accountability as well as the training of regulators.

See Boxes 9 and 10 to find out more about the problem.

Box 9 - The Weight of Political Accountability on Regulatory Decisions

In their empirical analysis, Gasmi, Noumba Um and Recuero Virto (2009) explore the relationship between regulatory performance, proxied by telecommunications outcomes, and political accountability, captured by variables on corruption, bureaucracy, law and order, expropriation, currency risk, and checks and balances. The authors find a relatively weak effect of political accountability on the performance of regulation in developed countries, but a clearly strong effect in the case of developing countries where the greater the political accountability, the better the regulatory performance. These quantitative results suggest that in developed countries political accountability is already well established and practiced through the electoral process. The findings suggest that the focus in those countries should be on the governance structures of the regulatory institutions themselves. In developing countries, political accountability is at an early stage of development and hence this calls for additional means and resources from development partners to promote good governance which will in turn enhance the quality of regulation. Indeed, building regulatory institutions in developing countries should be part of a broader strategy of "good governance" and not only be considered, as it has been in the past years, as a sectoral matter. Consequently, international donors, including the World Bank, the Department for International Development, and others have been strong advocates for good governance since many years

Source: Gasmi, F., Noumba Um, P. and L. Recuero Virto (2009), "Political Accountability and Regulatory Performance in Infrastructure Industries: An Empirical Analysis," World Bank Economic Review 2591.

Box 10 - When Regulation Fails

In Senegal, a second cellular license was issued in the 199Os to Sentel, a subsidiary of the US company Millicom International. However, when a new government took over in 2000, the price paid by Sentel was considered too low and the license was unilaterally withdrawn without any renegotiation. The creation of the regulatory agency had been deliberately delayed and the "Direction de la Réglementation" that was acting as a regulator had no effective power. In Benin, the government also decided to retrospectively increase licence fees. In Cameroon, Research ICT Africa has found evidence that the granting of frequencies and licences is not transparent. In Namibia, the failure to pass the reform legislation through Parliament for more than seven years has left the country without a regulator. In Côte d'Ivoire, even though the regulatory agency is run by well-trained officials, political interference is widely present. In South Africa, political interference is present in licensing and regulatory processes and the Ministry of Communications has a veto on the regulator. This mechanism of control has been recently removed by the Electronic Communications Act.

Source: Gasmi, F. and L. Recuero Virto (2005), "Telecommunications Technologies Deployment in Developing Countries: Role of Markets and Institutions," Communications & Strategies, No. 58, and Esselaar, S., Gillwald, A. and C. Stork (2007), "Towards an Africa e-Index: Telecommunications Sector Performance in 16 African Countries", Research ICT Africa, www.researchICTafrica.net.

Where the muscle is needed

Research ICT Africa undertook a survey of industry leaders, regulators and civil society in 14 Sub-Saharan countries in 2006 which highlights the perceived inefficiency of the regulatory environment.

There is a high correlation between the Telecommunications Regulatory Environment (TRE) scores in Figure 7 and the extent of market reforms and performance. In countries where the TRE scores are higher, regulation encourages investment. Countries that are seen to be more inefficient, Rwanda, Namibia, Ethiopia and Kenya, have been slow to launch market reforms. Fixed-line traditional operators were still state-owned in Namibia and Ethiopia in 2007. In all four countries, the performance of the fixed-line operator is disappointing, with a penetration rate of less than 2 per cent of the population. In Ethiopia the mobile market remained under monopoly in 2008 and less than 2 per cent of the population had a cellphone. In Rwanda where a second mobile phone licence was granted only in late 2008, the penetration rate is only 8.3 per cent. In Kenya and Namibia, where the cellular penetration rates in 2008 were 38 per cent and 62 per cent respectively, the negative perceptions were associated

with the strong interference of the fixed-line operator in Kenya and with stagnant reforms in Namibia.

In contrast, the most efficient countries in terms of regulatory environment, Nigeria and Côte d'Ivoire, have partially privatized fixed-line operators with penetration rates of about 10 per cent in 2007 and have a large number of competitors in the mobile phone segment, 7 and 4, respectively, both with penetration rates of around 40 per cent in 2008. The case of Nigeria is quite exceptional since together with these mobile phone operators, two national carriers, 22 telephony operators, 52 VSAT operators and 36 internet service providers are present.

Fixing the fixed-line operators

Governments have been good at adopting the 'converged licensing regime' in a bid to rescue traditional fixed-line operators who have lost telephone and other communications traffic to mobile rivals. Under the old system a new licence had to be issued each time a new service or technology was developed. The new regime gives more flexibility. Under the technologically neutral licences, the operator chooses the technology to provide. Mobile operators can choose between GSM

97

Figure 7 - Telecommunications Regulation Environment in 2007

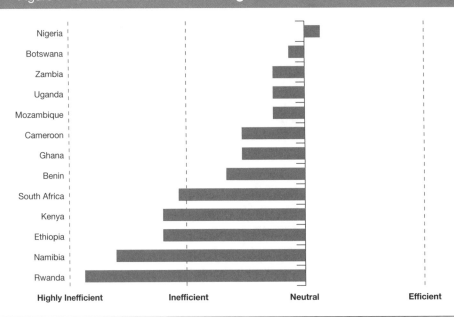

Source: Esselaar, S., Gillwald, A. and C. Stork (2007), "Towards an Africa e-Index: Telecommunications Sector Performance in 16 African Countries," Research ICT Africa, www.researchICTafrica.net.

StatLink ⬛ᴵ⬛ http://dx.doi.org/10.1787/568357251507

98

or CDMA wireless technologies. Under a service neutral licence, operators can select services that are in greater demand or are most cost effective. This new licence helps traditional fixed-line operators since they can get out of high-cost fixed-line connections and use wireless technologies instead. Fixed-line operators in Africa are increasingly turning to CDMA wireless technology for the final 'last mile' connection with customers. Fixed-line operators are pursuing mobile technology more aggressively to attack the now dominant position of mobile phone operators.

This neutral technology attitude by regulators is also helping the spread of universal service schemes in rural areas. Fixed-lines are not the best choice for low density, low income areas. In Uganda, the fixed-line operator, UTL, a technology neutral licensee, MTN and a mobile operator, Celtel, all bid for a competitive subsidy tender for universal service provision in rural areas. 'Neutral' technology and services are gaining ground across Africa, including in Botswana, Egypt, Mali, Mauritius, Morocco, Nigeria, Tanzania, Uganda and South Africa. Africa has a high share in the relatively small number of countries using converged licences. But Australia, the

European Union, Japan, Malaysia, Pakistan and Singapore also use them.

Fixed-line operators also need regulatory help on call termination charges between fixed and mobile operators. The initially high 'termination charges' made from fixed-line operators to mobile networks were financing cellphone operators' investments and are still present even though mobile phone networks are now more widespread than fixed-line networks. In addition, call termination costs in mobile networks are decreasing as traffic increases so these tariffs need to be reformed to prevent the abuse of dominance of mobile markets that are becoming mature (see Box 11).

Taxing the upwardly mobile

With large informal sectors which in some countries reach more than 70 per cent of the population, African governments often rely on a narrow tax base, frequently businesses that are major exporters. Mobile companies get their revenues from an increasingly large mass of the population, giving fiscal authorities the opportunity to broaden their tax base. One study of 15 countries

Box 11 - Capacity Building for Interconnection Disputes between Fixed and Mobile Operators

The liberalisation of telecommunications markets in Sub-Saharan Africa led to increased competition on the provision and pricing of communication services. But, due to the lack of appropriate regulatory tools, newly established regulators are poorly equipped to arbitrate increasing interconnection disputes between competing operators.

The World Bank has built a cost model, prepared to provide Sub-Saharan Africa regulators and operators with a sound regulatory tool allowing the determination of accurate interconnection costs, thus facilitating the settlement of lengthy and costly interconnection disputes between fixed and mobile operators.(*) Based on bottom-up Forward Looking – Long Run Incremental Costs (FL-LRIC) cost modelling, this tool has been used to set interconnection call termination prices between 2002-2007 in 6 African countries and has been used by 18 African regulatory agencies for skill upgrading.

(*) Gille, L., Noumba Um, P., C. Rudelle and L. Simon (2002), "A Model for Calculating Interconnection Costs in Telecommunications," The World Bank, Eds.

Source: Laurent Gille, Professor, Télécom ParisTech and Paul Noumba Um, Lead Economist, Economic Support Unit, Middle East and North Africa Region, World Bank Group.

99

Figure 8 - Mobile Operators' Contribution to Government Tax Revenues

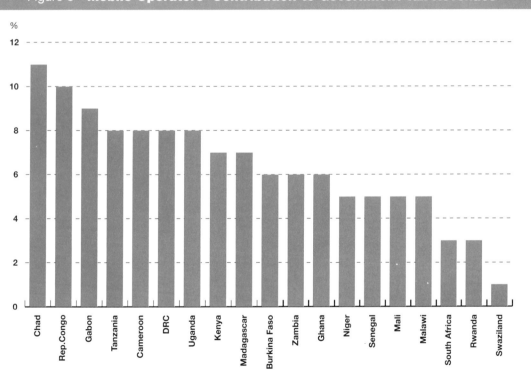

Source: GSM World, 2006, "Taxation and Growth of Mobile Services in Sub-Saharan Africa."

StatLink ⎯ http://dx.doi.org/10.1787/568380815516

(Figure 8) showed that mobile operators provided more than 8 per cent of government tax revenues in 7 of them.

Taxes represent on average 29.4 per cent of operators' revenue, but are as high as 53 per cent in Zambia, 45 per cent in Madagascar and 43 per cent in Tanzania and Gabon, and as low as 16 per cent in Democratic Republic of Congo. The GSMA association estimated that mobile operators in Africa in 2006 had contributed over USD 5 billion in taxes with about 77 per cent generated by operators in Nigeria and South Africa.

An analysis of the 15 Sub-Saharan countries surveyed in 2006 shows that the average tax on handsets is 31.1 per cent of their price, way above the average tax on network equipment (21.2 per cent), on connection and subscription (15.3 per cent) and on airtime

(18.3 per cent). Handsets are often treated as luxury goods in tax classifications. There are hidden differences however. Uganda, Tanzania and Kenya apply the highest taxes on usage, more than 25 per cent of the prices charged by operators, while they are at the lower end for levies on handsets, with taxes below 20 per cent.

In some countries, taxes on handsets can be avoided because the second hand market is huge. However, airtime taxes cannot be bypassed and because mobile services expenditures represent a large percentage of average income in Africa, the sensitivity of demand to price is larger than in OECD countries. One concern is that the high price of mobile phone usage (including taxes) is slowing their penetration rates among informal small and medium enterprises (SMEs) (see Box 12).

Box 12 - Mobile Phone Prices Penalise Informal SMEs in Africa

According to a Link Centre survey, SMEs respondents in 17 countries in Sub-Saharan Africa state that mobile phones are either important or very important for their business. While the percentage of respondents supporting this argument is around 95 per cent across formal, semi-formal and informal businesses, the importance attributed to other ICT items such as fixed-lines, fax, computers and internet connection decreases significantly with the degree of informality. Interestingly, the main reason highlighted by informal SMEs (50.8 per cent of respondents) for not possessing ICT is the high price of mobile telephony. This percentage drops to 31.5 and 22.9 in semi-formal and formal businesses. Thus, any decreases in mobile phone prices would help informal businesses the most.

Source: Gillwald, A. and C. Stork (2008), "Towards Evidence-Based ICT Policy and Regulation: ICT Access and Usage in Africa," Vol. I, Policy Paper Two, Research ICT Africa, www.researchICTafrica.net.

Business Environment and Financing

Mobile Operators charge high tariffs

Subscribers in resource-scarce North African and Sub-Saharan countries generate the lowest Average Revenue Per User (ARPU), closely followed by Latin America and Caribbean customers (Figure 9). In contrast, subscribers in rich resource Sub-Saharan countries generate a large ARPU, around USD 13, more than in Latin America, the Caribbean and the Asia-Pacific region in 2008. ARPU is not determined solely

by income levels since the average GDP per capita in Latin America, the Caribbean and the Asia-Pacific was around 4 times larger than in resource rich countries in Africa in 2007. Since minutes of use are fairly similar between these three regions, it is likely that ARPU is more due to higher tariffs. According to the ITU, in resource rich countries in Africa prices per 3 minute communications for peak hours are 0.9 USD, compared to USD 0.7 in Latin America and the Caribbean and USD 0.6 in Asia and Pacific. Another interesting feature of Figure 9 is the high number for minutes of use per user in North Africa, more than twice that of other regions.

Figure 9 - Revenue and Usage per Mobile Phone User

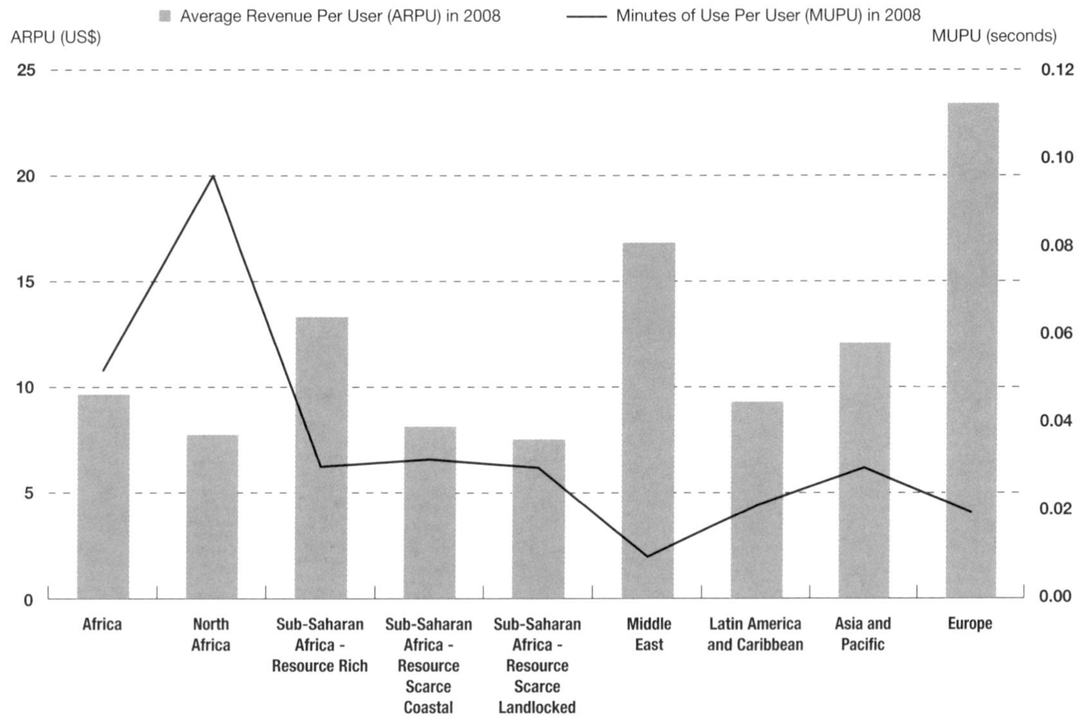

Average Revenue Per User (ARPU) in 2008 ——— Minutes of Use Per User (MUPU) in 2008

ARPU (US$) — categories: Africa, North Africa, Sub-Saharan Africa - Resource Rich, Sub-Saharan Africa - Resource Scarce Coastal, Sub-Saharan Africa - Resource Scarce Landlocked, Middle East, Latin America and Caribbean, Asia and Pacific, Europe. MUPU (seconds)

Source: Wireless Intelligence (www.wirelessintelligence.com).

StatLink http://dx.doi.org/10.1787/568387827637

101

Even though the sample of countries is not large, there is evidence (Figure 10) that capital and operating expenditures in Africa are below those in Latin America, the Caribbean and Asia. At the same time, mobile operators in Africa perform well in terms of liquidity, with larger earnings than other regions. Returns on investment are attractive for investors in African networks even if there is increasing competition (see figure 11).

The Rise of the Pan-African Mobile Operator

Mobile networks have quickly spread in recent years into once unserved areas. This has been helped by Orange, Vodacom, Zain, MTN, Moov, and Tigo all becoming players in several countries. MTN is South African, Zain and Moov belong to Middle East investors and Orange, Vodafone and Tigo (Millicom) are European-based. Zain and Tigo are present in East, Central and West Africa, Orange is present in East and

West Africa, Moov is mainly in West Africa and Vodafone in southern Africa. Their strategies concentrate on lowering prices to increase market share at a time when investment growth in network expansion is slowing due to the financial crisis. A key element of the African-style communications revolution has been reducing roaming charges — applying local charges to a network user even if the individual is located abroad. Regional integration will benefit as these strategies scale-up across operators and eventually erode price differences between countries.

These six operators accounted for 52 per cent of total subscriptions for mobile phones in Africa in 2008 (Figure 12). The average growth rate in Africa has been 41 per cent, but two entrants, Orange (68 per cent) and Tigo (82 per cent) were much better as were two established operators, Zain (52 per cent) and MTN (60 per cent). Vodafone and Zain have lower growth rates but are in more mature markets.

Figure 10 - Mobile Operators' Profits and Expenditures

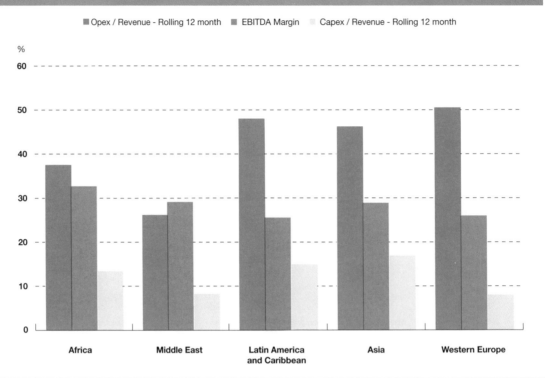

■ Opex / Revenue - Rolling 12 month   ■ EBITDA Margin   Capex / Revenue - Rolling 12 month

Source: Wireless Intelligence (www.wirelessintelligence.com). Data for 2008.

StatLink ⟨⟩ http://dx.doi.org/10.1787/568403347067

Even though competition is increasing among operators, the low penetration rates suggest considerable scope for strong growth. Orange is turning its attention to Africa after its abortive USD 40 billion bid for the Nordic operator, TeliaSonera. Orange invested in Kenya and Nigeria in 2008 where it is providing a package of mobile, fixed-line and internet services under the converged licensing regime. Orange also expects to cover 30 cities in Niger. It has a strategy of targeting markets with the potential to generate strong revenue growth with a bigger consumer base. In 2008, Orange mobile subscribers and revenue grew by 42.5 and 17 per cent respectively in Africa, compared to 28 per cent and 8.3 per cent for the Orange group worldwide. Tigo is expected to see substantially lower growth in 2009 because of the economic crisis. In 2008, it saw lower revenue growth in Senegal, Chad and Ghana.

In 2008, Zain invested in expanding network capacity and upgrading transmission capability, particularly in Ghana, Sudan, Malawi, Zambia and Nigeria. Most of its growth comes from Nigeria which accounts for 43 per cent of its subscriptions in Africa. Zain could build on its knowledge of third generation networks which it has deployed in Bahrain and Kuwait. Vodafone is also turning to Africa. In 2008, the group purchased 70 per cent of Ghana Telecom for USD 90 million. Vodafone is largely concentrated in South Africa which accounted for about 50 per cent of its consumer base in 2008. Vodafone South Africa is the largest mobile operator in Africa in terms of subscriptions per country. Both Zain and Vodafone are seeking to expand their consumer base by reducing prices. MTN has the largest number of subscribers in Africa and it seeks to consolidate this position by providing an attractive three-service package like Orange. In 2008, MTN acquired Arobase Telecom, the second fixed line operator, and an internet service provider, Afnet, in Côte d'Ivoire. MTN's largest mobile subscriber bases are in Nigeria and South Africa.

Figure 11 - Degree of Competition (Herfindahl Index) in Mobile Markets in Africa

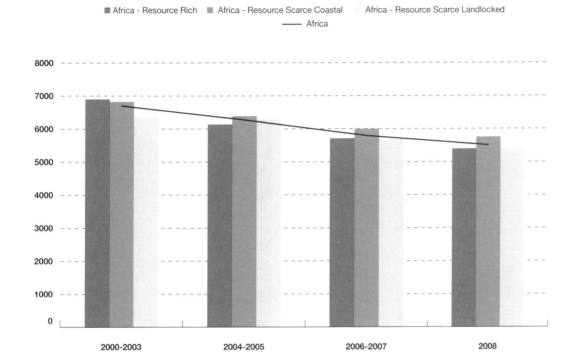

■ Africa - Resource Rich ■ Africa - Resource Scarce Coastal □ Africa - Resource Scarce Landlocked
—— Africa

Source: Gutierrez, L. H., S. Lee and L. Recuero Virto (2009), "Market Concentration and Performance in Mobile Markets in Africa and Latin America," OECD Development Centre (mimeo).

StatLink ⬛️🖳 http://dx.doi.org/10.1787/568414640007

Operators that have larger subscriptions bases in Africa, such as Vodacom, Zain and MTN, are those that have higher average market shares in the countries where they operate (Figures 12 and 13). The three operators each have more than 11 per cent of total subscriptions in Africa. Vodacom and MTN each have an average market share of more than 50 per cent of subscriptions in countries where they operate. Zain is close behind with 46 per cent of market share per country. At the other end, Moov and Tigo both have a lower number of subscriptions, below 3 per cent, as well as lower average market share per country, around 20 per cent. Orange has a small share of subscriptions in Africa but a large market share per country. There is also a close relationship between an operator's average market share and the number of countries targeted. Operators present in a larger number of countries, tend to have larger subscription share in each market and larger economies of scale. The only exception is

Vodafone which operates in a relatively small number of countries.

Zain is seeking larger potential markets (454 million people in 2007) by providing services in countries that have a lower per capita median GDP (USD 282 in 2007). Orange and MTN are concentrating on slightly smaller potential markets, with a per capita GDP median of about USD 450.

Vodafone has access to a larger potential market than Orange even if it is present in only six countries as compared to the French group's 14. All the countries where Vodafone is present, except Lesotho, have large populations. Vodafone is focusing on countries with a relatively high median per capita GDP (USD 452 in 2007) although this is not reflected in the average revenue per user in their networks which is USD 7.5 in 2008 as compared to Zain's USD 11.2 and MTN's USD 12.7.

Figure 12 - Penetration of Major Mobile Operators in Africa

■ Conexions Per Operator in 2008 (% Total Conexions in Africa in 2008)
—— Annual Growth Rate Per Operator in 2008

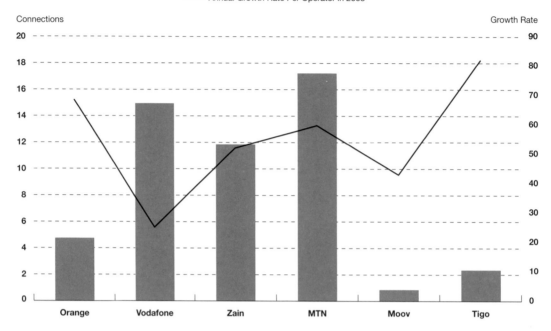

Source: Gutierrez, L. H., S. Lee and L. Recuero Virto (2009), "Market Concentration and Performance in Mobile Markets in Africa and Latin America," OECD Development Centre (mimeo).

StatLink ⫘ http://dx.doi.org/10.1787/568421528705

Vodafone is pursuing an aggressive pricing policy to reach lower income households since 90 per cent of its consumer base use prepaid services. As Zain and MTN are in tight competition in Sudan, Uganda, Congo, Nigeria and Zambia prices are likely to fall in these markets. Zain is already offering innovative price schemes

(see Innovative Business Models) in an effort to increase market share after reporting losses in two quarters of 2008. At the other extreme, Moov and Tigo, which are present in six and seven countries, respectively, have focused on middle size countries in terms of population and with median per capita GDP of about USD 270.

Table 1 - Market Positioning of Major Operators in Africa

Operator	Population (millions)[a]	GDP per Capita (median)[a] - USD	GDP per Capita (mean)[a] - USD	Presence in Resource scarce Coastal Countries: Presence in African Countries[b]
Orange	184	431	1 535	6 out of 14
Vodafone	249	452	1 146	4 out of 6
Zain	454	282	629	3 out of 15
MTN	355	500	813	4 out of 12
Moov	70	260	887	3 out of 7
Tigo	119	283	293	3 out of 6

Note: GDP per capita in 2000 usa. a. 2007 data, b. 2008 data.
Source: Gutierrez, L. H., S. Lee and L. Recuero Virto (2009), "Market Concentration and Performance in Mobile Markets in Africa and Latin America," OECD Development Centre (mimeo).

StatLink ⫘ http://dx.doi.org/10.1787/574554774088

Figure 13 - Market Concentration of Major Operators in Africa

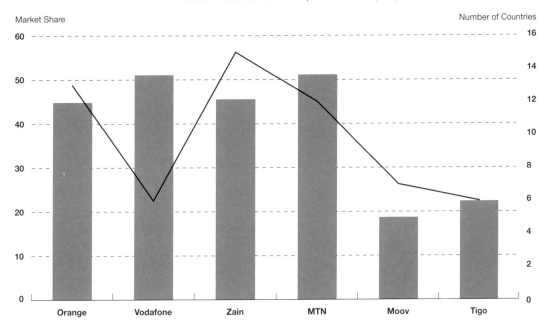

■ Average Market Share Per Country (2008)
— Number of Countries where the Operator is Present (2008)

Source: Gutierrez, L.H., S. Lee and L. Recuero Virto (2009), "Market Concentration and Performance in Mobile Markets in Africa and Latin America," OECD Development Centre (mimeo).

StatLink http://dx.doi.org/10.1787/568436163413

The domination of mobiles hits fixed line operators

Over the past decade telephone traffic has switched dramatically from fixed-line phones to mobiles. Mobiles account for 64 per cent of total telephone revenues and Africa is the only region in the world where mobiles outstrip fixed lines. Small fixed-line networks are suffering as a result in terms of their cost structure. Mobile network per minute costs are fast decreasing while those of fixed-line rivals are increasing as their traffic goes down (Figure 14).

Mobile phone networks are constituted by transmission towers which make up to 70 per cent of total capital costs. Each transmission tower has seven transceivers. While the number of transceivers increases linearly with the traffic, Figure 15 shows how total network investment per transceiver decreases very fast with the traffic increases.

Because of the increasing volumes, mobile phone charges could fall if the lower variable costs were passed on to consumers. The current per minute cost of a mobile call is still four times higher than fixed-line calls (Figure 16). In Africa, a fall in the price of mobile calls would probably lead to a significant increase in traffic and further cut costs, while fixed line costs are likely to keep rising. But taking into account that OECD countries, which benefit from substantial economies of scale with high mobile penetration rates, have prices comparable to those in Africa, it is not clear that mobile prices in Africa will fall as networks build up.

Price and choice in national networks

In 2007, there were 508 000 km of terrestrial backbone infrastructure in Sub-Saharan Africa. Of this, only 32 per cent was owned by fixed-line operators, while 68 per cent was owned by mobile operators.

Figure 14 - Variable Network Costs for 21 African operators

■ Mobile Networks ■ Fixed-Line Networks

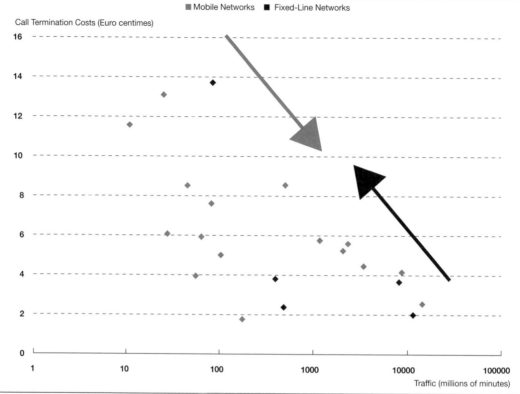

Call Termination Costs (Euro centimes)

Traffic (millions of minutes)

Source: Field work based on Gille, L., Noumba Um, P., C. Rudelle and L. Simon (2002), "A Model for Calculating Interconnection Costs in Telecommunications," The World Bank Eds.

StatLink ᴍᴸᴸᴸ http://dx.doi.org/10.1787/568451462288

Figure 15 - Mobile Network Costs for 14 African Operators

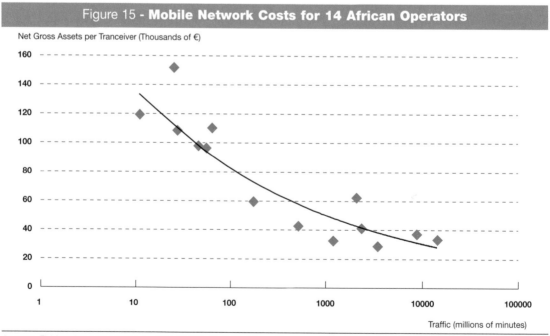

Net Gross Assets per Tranceiver (Thousands of €)

Traffic (millions of minutes)

Source: Field work based on Gille, L., Noumba Um, P., C. Rudelle and L. Simon (2002), "A Model for Calculating Interconnection Costs in Telecommunications," The World Bank Eds.

StatLink ᴍᴸᴸᴸ http://dx.doi.org/10.1787/568474415748

Figure 16 - Comparison between Fixed-Line (local) and Mobile per Minute Prices

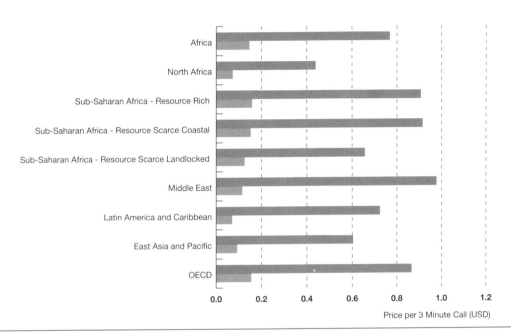

Data for 2006, in constant 2000 USD. Mobile prices for prepaid, on-net.
Source: International Telecommunication Union World Telecommunication/ICT Indicators 2008.

StatLink ⌨ http://dx.doi.org/10.1787/568475607336

Almost all the satellite-based backbone infrastructure is also operated by mobile operators. In the past, fixed-line operators did not meet the demands of mobile operators for high-capacity transmission so the mobile operators launched their own terrestrial backbone networks to connect their transmission towers to the rest of their own network. Ninety-nine per cent of the backbone network length run by mobile operators in Sub-Saharan Africa is microwave technology which can be easily upgraded, only 1 per cent is fibre optic. On average, transmission accounts for less than 10 per cent of the total mobile costs.

Fixed-line operators use fibre optic technology for 40 per cent of their backbone networks. Only the costs of transmission equipment depend on the traffic and these are less than 10 per cent of the total. Between 60 per cent and 80 per cent of the cost of the fibre optic network is fixed and related to the cost of laying the cables. Since the fibre optic choice only becomes optimal when the traffic volume rises above 2 000 Mbps and

it becomes cheaper than microwave technology, fixed-line operators must invest ahead of demand and so need long-term financing. Mobile networks only invest in new capacity when projected revenues are large enough to quickly pay back the investment.

Most fixed-line networks in Africa were designed only for voice services and now need major upgrading to carry data. Fixed-line operators' staff also need to be trained for the shift from analogue to digital technology. Some small operators such as Kasapa in Ghana are outsourcing this task. Neotel, the second fixed-line operator in South Africa, is a rare operator with a 100 per cent digital network. Compared to analogue, a digital network is 30 to 50 per cent less expensive in terms of investment and 30 per cent less expensive in terms of operating costs. Traditional fixed-line operators are therefore penalised, compared to mobile firms and newcomers in the fixed-line segment, unless regulators let them raise private capital and increase customer prices to cover their operating and capital costs.

Box 13 - Rwanda: Regional ICT Hub

Rwanda government plans to lay 2 300 km of fibre optic cable between February and September 2009 to deploy a national backbone network connecting 35 nodes across the country and 350 sites. Rwanda currently accesses internet through satellite connections at USD 3 000 Mbps/month. The price is expected to drop to USD 25 Mbps/month once the national grid is connected with the future submarine fibre optic cables on the east coast. A 135 km network has already been deployed in Kigali at a cost of USD 5 million. Private sector operators are also contributing to ICT development. The development of Kigali ICT Park, which comprises three components, namely: Established ICT companies, Incubated companies (ICT startups) and a Multi-disciplinary Centre of Excellence in ICT (MCE-ICT), is one such example. Rwanda is expecting to position itself as a regional ICT hub.

Source: Rwanda's 2009 *African Economic Outlook* country note and author.

With fixed-line operators experiencing financing difficulties in Africa, high retail tariffs for backbone networks are still common, a result of cross subsidisation between local and long distance and international communications. While tariffs are changing, this has mainly been through an increase in local tariffs for voice (see Box 14). Indeed, local voice tariffs in Africa are close to those applied in OECD countries. Long distance voice calls and internet services (which should have fallen) remain expensive. There is also a wide difference in price between members of the same consortium, such as the SAT-3 submarine cable off western Africa, where retail prices can vary between USD 1 316 charged by Senegalese incumbent Sonatel to the USD 11 000 by Telkom South Africa. With international backbones soon offering wholesale prices of about USD 500 for bringing traffic from the other side of the world, it will become increasingly difficult for African fixed-line operators to justify high retail prices for low distance national links. Even if international backbone capacity is accessible at low wholesale prices, African consumers will only benefit if fixed-line operators pass on these lower tariffs or use their profits to expand capacity and improve service.

Box 14 - The Impact of the Privatisation of Traditional Fixed-Line Operators

In theory, whether the privatisation of fixed-line telecommunication operator leads to improvements in network expansion or quality depends on the institutional and political context in which it is applied. Governments have often perceived full privatization as a trade-off between benefiting from one shot licence fees while abandoning the future stream of revenues generated by the operator[1]. In any case, privatisation typically leads to higher local tariffs to fully cover costs including a rate of return on investment. Recently, Gasmi, Noumba Um and Recuero Virto (2009) reported on the main findings of an analysis of 1985-1999 data across different world regions classified by geography and wealth[2]. The developed countries included in the sample had all partially or totally privatized their historical state-owned operator during the period considered. As to the developing countries, 15 from Latin America and 13 from Africa had privatized during the period. Hence, 60 per cent of the Latin American countries in the sample had privatised their operators;

1. Wallsten, S., 2004, "Telecommunications Privatization in Developing Countries: The Real Effects of Exclusivity Periods" *Journal of Regulatory Economics*, 26(3).

2. Gasmi, F., P. Noumba Um and L. Recuero Virto (2009), "Privatisation of Fixed-Line Incumbents: Regional Differences" OECD Development Centre (mimeo).

this figure comes down to 30 per cent for the African countries. African countries were therefore at their early stages of privatisation during the period under study.

The difference in the results between the developed and the developing countries mainly reflect the extent to which there was excess supply in developed countries and hence no perceptible effect on network expansion in the former. The existence of unmet demand in developing countries, instead did lead to network expansion and greater labour productivity. The network expansion in developing countries followed increases in local tariffs. Indeed, the population in developing countries is willing to pay a price for communications that is often reported to be higher than state-owned subsidised prices. However, privatisation of the fixed-line operator in developed countries lead to decreases in the prices of fixed-line services due to increased competition in well supplied markets.

Once the developing countries sample is disaggregated interesting regional differences were found. Latin American and African resource scarce coastal countries show very similar results to those of the overall developing countries sample, with increases in both output and prices. In contrast, in African resource scarce landlocked countries, privatisation was associated with increases in tariffs which did not translate into network expansion. In these countries, privatisation was also associated with lower labour efficiency. In African resource rich countries, privatisation has no impact on any performance measure.

The extent to which these results can be explained by institutional quality is subject to further research. For the time being, according to the ICRG indices, while Latin American and African resource scarce coastal countries in the sample have very similar institutional endowments, African resource scarce landlocked and resource rich countries both lag behind.

Source: Farid Gasmi, Professor, Toulouse School of Economics and author.

High retail prices often result from countries allowing national transmission monopolies. An operator with a transmission monopoly in Sub-Saharan Africa can get 65 per cent of its revenue from international traffic. In Zambia the liberalisation of international traffic transmission is being continuously delayed. Some countries seem to prefer a monopoly over international facilities even at the expense of letting in new entrants to develop domestic markets.

To maintain benefits from international traffic, some delegations at International Telecommunication Union (ITU) meetings have argued for a premium on international traffic exchange[3]. An ITU-T recommendation was passed at the World Telecommunication Standardisation Assembly (WTSA) in October 2008 to analyse whether such a premium should be paid for traffic passing between operators in developed and developing countries. The so-called 'network externality premium' is only feasible in markets where there is a transmission monopoly and no incentive to expand network access. The increase in net outpayments and incoming international traffic to Africa from developed countries suggests that the premium is not needed (see Box 15).

There is a big difference in interconnection rates from fixed to mobile networks in Africa. In 2006, Kenya, Benin and South Africa's rates were almost 200 per cent higher than in Rwanda, Senegal and Uganda. These charges make fixed line subscribers increasingly attracted by mobile phone networks which bypass these charges.

---

3. OECD, 2009, "Network Externality Premiums and International Telecommunications Traffic Exchange," DSTI/ICCP/CISP(2008)4.

Box 15 - **Boost in International Net Outpayments and Incoming Traffic to Africa**

With international traffic exchange based on termination charges under a liberalised environment, many operators generate greater termination revenues than they did in the past when this exchange was based on accounting rates between countries' monopoly telephone companies. Net outpayments from operators, based in the United States, to African counterparts, for example, are frequently greater today than they were under the accounting rate system. In total, operators in African countries received payments of around USD100 million greater in 2006, than they did in 1996, and more than USD200 million greater than 1994. In fact, the total net outpayments from the United States to Africa were the highest ever recorded in 2006, the latest year for which data are available (see Figure 17).

Figure 17 - Net Outpayments from the United States to Africa

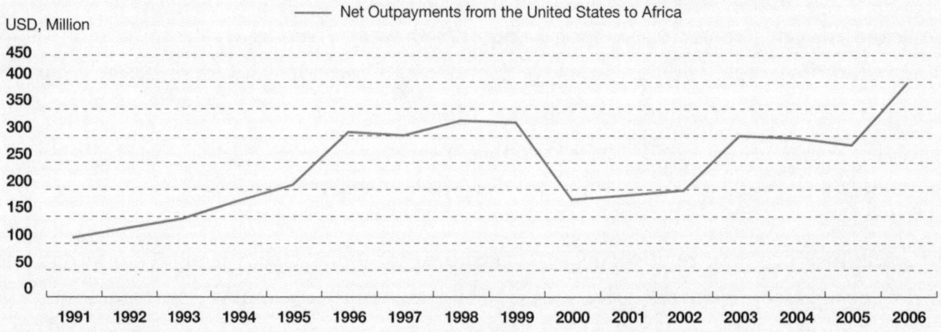

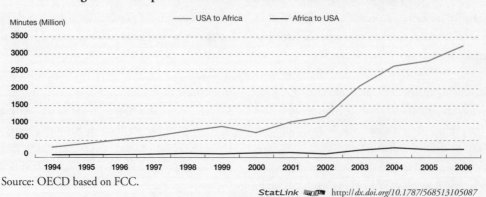

Source: OECD based on FCC.

StatLink http://dx.doi.org/10.1787/568485764447

One reason for this increase, in aggregate revenue at the national level, is that although interconnection between networks has become more cost-oriented, the volume of international traffic has increased enormously over recent years. Between 2000 and 2006 outgoing traffic from the United States to Africa increased by 344 per cent (see Figure 18). Traffic in the opposite direction increased 80 per cent. The primary reason for this increase is that accounting rates kept the prices for international telephony artificially high to the point of being prohibitive for many users to make calls. It is also the case that network expansion, as a result of liberalisation, has created many more calling opportunities. As such the increase in traffic volume is the result of lower prices for international calls and network expansion.

Figure 18 - Telephone Traffic between the United States and Africa

Source: OECD based on FCC.

StatLink http://dx.doi.org/10.1787/568513105087

Source: Sam Paltridge, Principal Administrator, Directorate for Science, Technology and Industry, OECD.

Figure 19 - Interconnection Rates from Fixed-Line to Mobile Networks

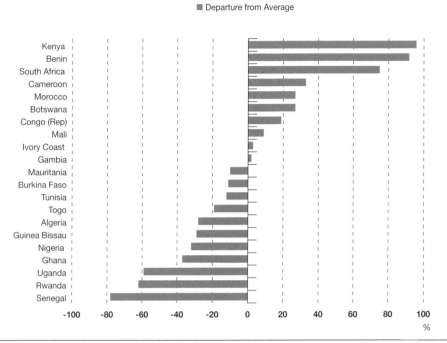

■ Departure from Average

Source: Esselaar, S., Gillwald, A. and C. Stork (2007), "Towards an Africa e-Index: Telecommunications Sector Performance in 16 African Countries," Research ICT Africa, www.researchICTafrica.net.

StatLink http://dx.doi.org/10.1787/568518126306

Faced with ever tougher competition from mobile operators, many fixed-line networks plan to offer broadband services to add value and attract consumers. Although fixed-line networks have a comparative advantage over wireless in terms of broadband capacity, there are doubts whether fixed-line operators will find a large enough market in Africa.

Business models for low incomes

Operators are having to come up with new ideas to keep services affordable for a region dominated by low income households. According to surveys in 16 countries in Sub-Saharan Africa in 2006 and 2007 done by Research ICT Africa, people who do not have mobile phones will only be brought into the market through offers of cheap calls[4]. People who did not have a mobile phone or SIM card in Côte d'Ivoire, Ghana, Nigeria and Uganda were only ready to pay

between USD 5 and USD 10 a month and in Ethiopia below USD 2.

The same study indicated that people in seven countries did not want to spend more than USD 10 for a handset. Only two countries, Côte d'Ivoire and Namibia, signalled a willingness to spend up to USD 30 for a cellphone. The average cost in the countries is between USD 16 and USD 27.

Low cost handsets can be easily obtained on the second hand market. But the survey indicates that a small reduction in the cost of equipment and services could bring increased uptake and a significant growth in revenue for operators. Charges for call time in peak hours are also coming under pressure in places like South Africa where Virgin Mobile has recently begun offering the same flat rates to consumers for peak and off-peak hours for data and SMS. In Kenya, Zain has

4. Gillwald, A. and C. Stork (2007), "Towards an African e-Index: ICT access and usage across 16 African countries," LINK Centre, Witwatersrand University.

Box 16 - Evidence on Mobile Phone Price Elasticity's: The Cost of Alternatives

Using a Vodacom cross-sectional data set on 6 936 individuals collected in May 2005 in South Africa, Gasmi, Invaldi and Recuero Virto (2008) develop a structural demand-and-supply structural model based on the multinomial specification that investigates voice and SMS prepaid communications. Their findings reveal high price elasticity's in the range of -2 to -6, typically higher than those found in developed countries. All consumers attach the largest valuation to peak hours (or working hours) but since these hours are highly priced, demand for peak hours is significantly more elastic than for off-peak hours (or leisure time). Indeed, both for urban and rural consumers and for voice and SMS, price elasticities for off-peak hours are on average -1, while for peak hours, this number is on average -3. At the time of the survey Vodacom's prepaid prices for peak voice and SMS communications more than doubled those applied during off-peak hours.

At first sight, price cuts on prepaid services could be rewarding both for consumers and for the firm (peak hours). For rural areas networks, close to full capacity, it would be necessary to verify that the increase in revenues would be sufficient to cover incremental investments on base stations. In addition, this research suggests that reducing the gap between urban and rural economies, calls for investment in networks in rural areas since the usage in these regions appears to support economic activity with high value and relative low elasticity attached to working hours. This can be explained through the cost of alternatives in rural areas. A Vodafone study on cellular users in Tanzania and South Africa illustrates this idea, where 50 per cent to 70 per cent of respondents claimed that their cellular phones led to large savings in travel time and cost.

Source: Gasmi, F. and Ivaldi, M. and Recuero Virto, L., 2008, "An Empirical Analysis of Cellular Demand in South Africa," IDEI Working Papers 531, Institut d'Économie Industrielle (IDEI), Toulouse.

also begun offering the same flat rates for both peak and off-peak hours.

The reluctance to pay for mobile equipment and services can be understood from figures from 17 countries on the average monthly mobile expenditures of subscribers as a percentage of monthly disposable income (Figure 20). For the top 25 per cent income earners in Zambia and Rwanda, the percentage exceeds 40 per cent. In another seven countries, the percentage was between 30 and 40 per cent. Turning to the bottom 75 per cent earners, the percentages are larger – in six countries it was between 60 and 80 per cent. This explains why market penetration rates remain low — only a small fraction of households can afford these services – and why pre-paid phone deals are preferred.

Banana Cellular introduced prepaid mobile phone services in the United States in 1993. By 2008, 71 per cent of mobile subscribers throughout the world were using this kind of service, in Africa it was 96 per cent. This 'pay as you go' service has also been adopted by electricity and water utilities, notably in South Africa. After new meters have been installed in a home, credit can be purchased by phone or internet. The consumer is given a code which can be used on a meter.

Other ideas to tempt lower income households in Africa include micropayment accounts — consumers can use SMS to put a few cents on their accounts — microfinance funding for handsets and subscriptions and phone sharing (see Box 17).

SMS messages that were intended by their inventor to enable communications between operators' staff were soon to alert people to a voice mail message with the first commercial service launched in Sweden in 1993. To adapt to the lower incomes in Africa, a mobile instant messaging service, MXit, is set to expand across the continent with the cost of sending an SMS falling below a fraction of one cent (ZAR) (see Box 18).

Figure 20 - **Monthly Mobile Expenditure as Percentage of Income Quartiles**

■ Monthly Mobile Expenditure (US$) / Monthly Disposable Income (US$) Bottom 75% in Terms of Disposable Income
■ Monthly Mobile Expenditure (US$) / Monthly Disposable Income (US$) Top 25% in Terms of Disposable Income

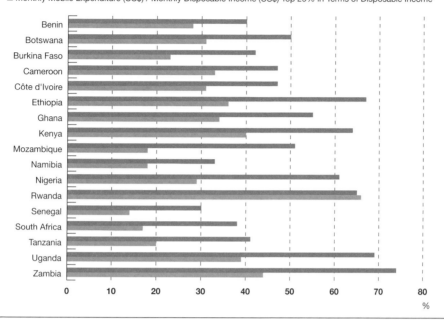

Source: Gillwald, A. and C. Stork (2008), "Towards Evidence-Based ICT Policy and Regulation: ICT Access and Usage in Africa," Vol. I, Policy Paper Two, Research ICT Africa, www.researchICTafrica.net.

StatLink ⬛⬛ http://dx.doi.org/10.1787/568542055713

Box 17 - **New Business Models to Reach Low Income Deciles**

Nokia Siemens Networks is developing new business models for African consumers (see Figure 21). Beyond the well known postpaid and prepaid options, the following solutions are incorporated:

• With microprepayment consumers can load electronically (by SMS) some cents onto their accounts. In the past operators have used vouchers (e.g. USD 10)[5]. However, in emerging markets, even this is a large sum to spend. Reducing the value of the voucher was difficult for operators, as the small value and distribution costs of the voucher were above the potential revenue. Nokia Siemens Networks was a pioneer in developing SMS-based solutions by which any amount could be uploaded to a prepaid account. Micropayment is also a very common way of recharging in Africa.

• Microfinance is funding support to enable hard-up consumers to purchase a handset and subscription. The loan is paid back in installments. The most famous case can be found in Bangladesh, where GrameenPhone launched the "Village Phones" programme. It has since been used in Uganda and Rwanda. In Rwanda, Village Phone aims to create over 3 000 new small businesses within the next three years. Five thousand new businesses have been created in Uganda since 2003. The Grameen Foundation and Nokia are looking into replicating the model in other countries.

5. The mobile operator Orange for example, is offering prepaid cards for USD 10 cents at much lower tariffs than in France where the lowest price is EUR 10.

A microfinance loan of approximately USD 200 allows the Village Phone operator to purchase a mobile phone kit. The kit comprises a Nokia handset, a SIM card preloaded with prepaid airtime, an external antenna set (including a booster antenna, a coupler, and a cable), and marketing materials. The loan is usually for up to nine months, at an interest rate of not more than 4 per cent. Village Phone operators are typically able to repay their loan within six months, from their revenues.

• Phone sharing is widely used in the low income segment. A phone is shared within a family or among friends, whoever uses the phone and has some small change available pays to upload the prepaid account.

Figure 21 – The Global Income Pyramid

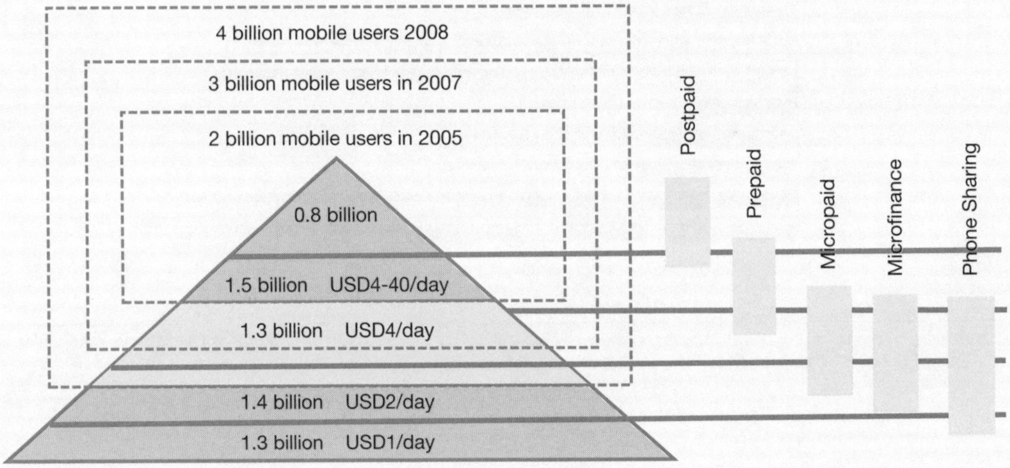

4 billion mobile users 2008
3 billion mobile users in 2007
2 billion mobile users in 2005

0.8 billion
1.5 billion   USD4-40/day
1.3 billion   USD4/day
1.4 billion   USD2/day
1.3 billion   USD1/day

Postpaid   Prepaid   Micropaid   Microfinance   Phone Sharing

Source: Frank Oehler, Head of Business Development, New Growth Markets, Nokia Siemens Networks.

StatLink http://dx.doi.org/10.1787/568545403552

Box 18 - Below one cent price for a message (SMS)

MXit which was originally an acronym for "message exchange" is a free instant messaging software application developed in South Africa that runs on internet enabled (GPRS/3G) mobile phones. MXit allows the user to send and receive text and multimedia messages to and from phones and PCs connected to the Internet. These messages are sent and received via the Internet, rather than with standard SMS technology. MXit does not charge for sending and receiving messages but some mobile operators do charge for GPRS/3G data although this is much cheaper than traditional SMS messages, a fraction of 1 cent (ZAR) per message compared to the normal SMS rates of approximately 75 cents (ZAR). For the price of one SMS, MXIt users can send several thousand messages.

MXit has now more than 11 million registered subscribers, of whom 9 million are located in South Africa. There are more than 1 million subscribers in more than 150 countries. On a typical day, MXit receives about 25 000 new subscribers and more than 250 million messages have been transmitted over its network. Its servers, located in Mauritius, Cape Town and Frankfurt, receive 25Gigabytes of data and transmit 145 Gigabytes of data per day.

Source: Herman Heunis, founder and CEO, MXit.

With such small amounts of money spent on phone calls, Africa has become a leader in advanced mobile advertising. Vodacom in South Africa has launched one service aimed at the high-end market, "Vodafone Live!", and two services for low income consumers, "Ad-Me" and "Please Call Me Back". The "Vodafone Live!" site has about 20 million page impressions per month and has about 1.5 million customers per month, making it the largest digital advertising property in South Africa.

In addition to running banner ads, Vodacom offers branded content. In its "Ad-Me" service, a subscriber signs up, provides limited amounts of personal information and then receives targeted advertising messages. In return for receiving advertisements, discount vouchers, free competitions, special offers and give-aways are offered. The most successful service has been "Please Call Me Back" with 20 million messages a day in a country of 48 million people (see Box 19).

Box 19 - Ad-Funded Mobile Service Fulfilling Consumer Needs

In South Africa, when people had low call credit they would phone parents or friends, let the phone ring twice and then get a return call. This was a way of keeping in touch but consumed network time without spending. In response, Vodacom, set up the ad funded targeted at pre-paid subscribers, "Please Call Me Back". The message is sponsored by advertising and users set up an SMS which is free to send and the receiver gets an advert of up to 115 characters with the message. This allows the recipient to call back for free. Vodacom avoids the cost of missed calls and created an opportunity for advertising revenue.

Source: Vodacom.

The roaming phone war

Roaming allows customers to use their mobile phones while outside their home network. This is made possible through agreements between the customer's phone service provider and at least one network provider in the country visited. Now several operators in Africa are providing free roaming services.

Celtel, which was founded by the Sudanese Mo Ibrahim, launched the world's first borderless network across East Africa in September 2006 (see Box 20). Under this initiative, customers can make and receive calls and send SMS messages at local rates, they can also use recharge cards bought in any of those countries. Prices are still not the same in each country. It still costs twice as much to call a Celtel customer in Tanzania

Box 20 - Regional Integration: World's First Borderless Network

In September 2006 after Celtel was acquired by Zain of Kuwait it launched "One Network", the world's first borderless network in East Africa (Uganda, Kenya and Tanzania). Celtel expanded this in November 2007 to a further nine African countries. Democratic Republic of Congo, Republic of Congo, Gabon, Burkina Faso, Chad, Malawi, Niger and Nigeria became connected offering over 400 million people in 12 countries the opportunity to communicate freely across geographical borders without roaming call surcharges.

On 14 April 2008, Zain extended the service to Bahrain, Iraq, Jordan and Sudan where more than 14 million Zain customers now have the same benefits. Zain has linked the Middle East to the 12 African One Network countries. The service is now available to more that 63 million Zain Group customers in 17 countries spread across Africa and the Middle East. Another three Middle East and three African countries were recently added.

Source: Mamadou Kolade, Director, Regulatory Affairs, Zain.

or to send an SMS from Tanzania compared to Uganda. But new initiatives are coming. Zain has launched a strategy in Kenya with the same price for local peak and off-peak calls and for local communications to subscribers of all networks. The 'Vuka' tariff undercuts the competition by 68 per cent for a local call to another network. Zain is applying a preferential rate for international calls to Zain subscribers in East Africa, and a slightly less advantageous rate for non Zain subscribers in East Africa.

Zain's model is being copied by competitors. In East Africa, Vodacom Tanzania, MTN Uganda and Safaricom Kenya established reciprocal free roaming agreements in 2007. But as of 2008, Vodacom prepaid

consumers had only restricted access to roaming. MTN Rwanda recently joined this roaming agreement, which now covers 15 million subscribers on four networks. MTN is scaling up the offer by providing a free-roaming service, 'MTN One World', in all 21 countries where it is present in Africa and the Middle East. It has already started in Cameroon, Ghana, Nigeria and Benin.

With these free-roaming agreements, Africa is showing technological and business innovation. It is also an example of how telecommunications operators and regulatory authorities can work together to develop cost-effective solutions. Regulation concerns have prevented similar arrangements in the European Union, when for example Vodafone and Mannesman sought

Box 21 - Solar Panel Energy: Distribution through Microfranchising

The use of kerosene for lighting in developing countries causes serious health, environmental, educational and income problems for poor communities. SolarAid, a new and fast-growing non-profit organisation, estimates that there are 200 million kerosene lamps in Africa, with each one generating approximately a tonne of CO_2 over 10 years. It wants to replace all of them with solar lamps by 2020, either through its own operations or in partnership with others.

Sunny Money is SolarAid's new micro-franchise brand that applies the proven marketing and operational concepts of traditional franchising to small businesses in the developing world, and allows the rapid creation of distribution networks in rural and urban areas.

Sunny Money is recruiting a large network of micro-franchisees from poor communities in East Africa to sell solar lamps and replace kerosene. It works with local communities to recruit and train micro-franchisees, with strict training and sales targets. Sunny Money supports them with new product development, manufacturing, marketing and branding.

Results are surpassing expectations, promising huge potential for scale-up. Micro-franchisees show a high success rate and customer feedback is overwhelmingly positive. The plan is to scale this up across Africa and then into OECD markets too.

As well as microsolar entrepreneurship, SolarAid installs larger solar systems at schools, health clinics and community centres, carries out educational work on solar power and climate change in schools in the UK and East Africa, and is building the capacity of the East African solar industry through the construction of a Solar Academy in Lusaka, Zambia. It is also starting a pilot project in South America with indigenous communities.

Source: Nicolas Sireau, Executive Director, Solar Aid (www.solar-aid.org).

a merger in 2000. It was approved on the condition that the merging parties provide roaming tariffs to affiliated and unaffiliated mobile operators. As a result, the new entity had no incentive to offer pan-European services with low or zero roaming charges. The fact that African operators are present in a large number of countries and that regulatory intervention is limited has enabled the expansion of these pan-African networks tariffs.

Renewable Energy Phones

Solar panels are increasingly being used in Africa to power telecommunication networks. Orange has used this to extend affordable coverage to remote areas. Traditional fuels had to be brought by trucks, often over huge distances. Fossil fuels are expensive and unreliable, since there can be blackouts when supplies run out. Orange has substituted traditional power by solar panels at 200 radio stations in Africa where there is no electricity grid. Energy costs account for up to 25 per cent of total costs. Solar radio stations have two generators, one permanent and the other on backup. Solar base stations do not need air-conditioning and consume little. Batteries to stock solar energy can last up to four days. These radio stations are currently producing excess energy eleven months of the year and it is given to local communities to recharge mobile phones. About 1 000 solar radio stations are planned for 2009 in Africa in line with Orange's target to have 25 per cent of its energy based on solar technology by 2015 and to attain 20 per cent reduction in its CO_2 emissions by 2020.

Pro-Development Innovative Applications

E- Banking for Africa

In the absence of collateral to secure loans from banks, extended families in Africa create their own 'family pot" of money. There are also a revolving credit schemes called "susu" in Ghana, "esusus" in Yoruba, "tontines" or "chilembe" in Cameroon and "stokvel" in South Africa. In a typical scheme, each member of a group of perhaps 10 people agree to contribute USD 100 to a fund. When the fund reaches a threshold, say USD 1 000, it is lent to one member. As soon as the money is repaid it can be lent to another member. This funding, which requires a lot of trust, is often the primary source of capital in the informal sector and generally works well because of peer pressure. According to an Research ICT Africa survey in 2007/2008, around 30 per cent of respondents in 17 Sub-Saharan countries, borrow from family and friends[6]. The bill of exchange, which is a Western Union type of service, is also largely used in Africa to make remote payments from one individual to another.

Digital technology is helping traditional banking and payment practices in Africa. The Sente service is an informal practice in Uganda to send money from one individual to another using mobile technology. A person who wishes to send money buys a mobile top-up voucher from a local seller. This person charges the mobile of a local village middleman who passes an agreed amount of cash to someone else living in a different area. The middleman retains a commission on his phone in the form of pre-paid minutes that he sells to other villagers, becoming also a small-scale service provider. The M-Pesa service in Kenya formalises the Sente service by allowing its customers to transfer money using their Safaricom mobile phones. M-Pesa users do not need a bank account – only about 26 per cent of the population had a bank account in 2007, according to a household survey[7]. M-Pesa has attracted 5 million customers, about 13 per cent of the population in less than two years.

The M-Pesa model is being copied in different forms across Africa. The technologies and business models used vary considerably. SMS, voice or Interactive Voice

117

---

6. Gillwald, A. and C. Stork (2007), "Towards and African e-Index: ICT Access and Usage across 16 African countries," LINK Centre, Witwatersrand University.

7. Gillwald, A. and C. Stork (2008), "Towards Evidence-based ICT Policy and Regulation: ICT Access and Usage in Africa," *Vol. I, Policy Paper Two, Research ICT Africa*, www.researchICTafrica.net.

Box 22 - M-Pesa leads Mobile-Payments in Kenya

M-Pesa was launched in March 2007 in Kenya, where it has reached 5 million customers. Money is transferred from one individual to another by SMS with any mobile phone that has a SIM-enabled card. Individuals can register at any agent kiosk by showing an identity card and pay no registration fees. Individuals buy airtime that is transferred to the mobile phone account of the recipient who can cash out at another agent kiosk. Most transactions are below KSH 2 000.

Figure 22 - Transactions with M-Pesa in Kenya

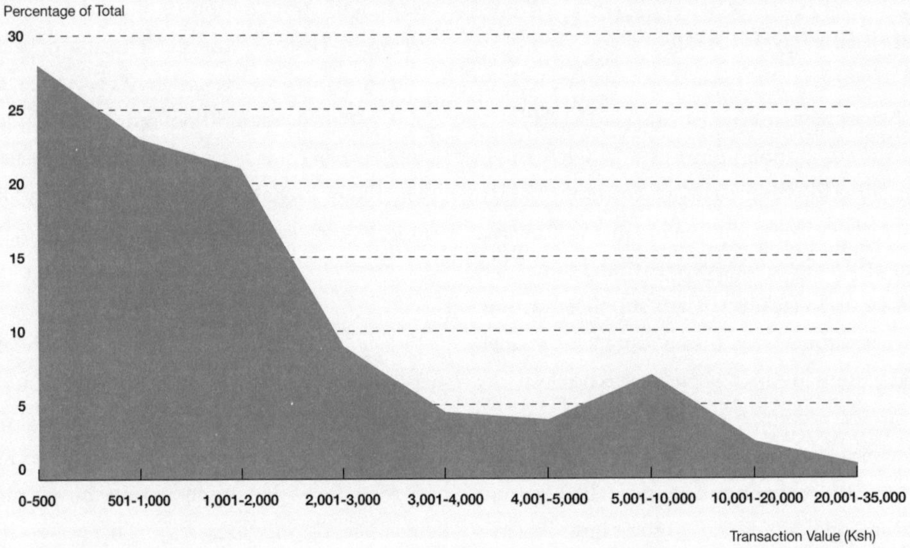

Percentage of Total

Transaction Value (Ksh)

Source: Vodafone.

StatLink http://dx.doi.org/10.1787/568575565355

M-Pesa has been successful because it relies on traditional practices and structures and modernises these features. It is indeed a model based on indigenous payment practices, extended mobile phone networks and a large distribution network. The distribution network is based on agents who were already present in markets. Agents receive basic training from M-Pesa. Only three months after the launch of M-Pesa, the service had 400 agents, compared to 450 bank branches and 600 ATMs in Kenya. By 2009 M-Pesa had 3 400 agents. It is simple and quick, taking less than 30 seconds to carry out a transfer.

Another important aspect of M-Pesa is its adaptability to local specificities. It recently started in Afghanistan, instead of using the Kenyan SIM toolkit menu on the mobile, the provider is delivering a user interface model based on voice recognition that is adapted to the low literacy levels in the country. In Kenya, M-Pesa plans eventually to include bill payments and international remittances.

Source: Vodafone Status Reports in December 2008 and author.

Response (IVR), Unstructured Supplementary Services Data (USSD) and SIM toolkits can be used on standard mobile phones typically present on a large scale in Africa. SMS, voice and USSD are used in South Africa by Wizzit, First National Bank (FNB) and Amalgamated Banks of South Africa (ABSA). These are open systems independent of the mobile network operator. SIM toolkits are used by M-Pesa in Kenya and MTN Banking in South Africa. These use proprietary systems where only members can transfer funds.

Box 23 - WIZZIT: First Entity to Offer Mobile-Banking to the Unbanked

WIZZIT targets 13 to 16 million people who do not have bank accounts or do not use accounts they have. WIZZIT is the first entity to offer a mobile phone based bank account.

- The WIZZIT is a fully functional bank account against which you can set up debit orders and have your salary deposited electronically from any bank.
- Through the use of secure technology, clients can conduct financial transactions, remit money, pay accounts, buy airtime, and get their balance all through their mobile phone 24 hours a day.
- Account opening takes about two minutes and only requires a copy of an identity document.
- Accounts have affordable transaction fees, no monthly fees and no minimum balance.
- The technology works on any cell phone and across all networks.
- Payments can be made to any bank account or be received from any account.
- An alternative to the high costs, security and inconvenience of accessing and storing cash.
- A way to avoid long queues, travel costs, time and inconvenience.

WIZZIT has, through relationships with the South African Post Office - 2800 outlets- and ABSA -800 outlets-. (WIZZIT is a recently launched Division of The South African Bank of Athens Limited.)

Source: Brian Richardson, Founding Director, Wizzit.

More advanced technologies such as Wireless Application Protocol (WAP) and HTTPS are being used by NedBank, FNB and ABSA in South Africa. These are only accessible to those who have enabled handsets. Payments are also being facilitated by Near Sound Data Transfers (NSDT) software developed by Tag Attitude which is compatible with standard mobile phones. NSDT is being tested in Zambia, South Africa, the Republic of Congo, and Democratic Republic of Congo and is about to be launched in Ghana, Nigeria and Mali.

The African business models provide new channels for payment and banking. When the services have the support of banks, they comply with banking regulations. Wizzit in South Africa belongs to the Bank of Athens and can be used by any mobile phone operator (see Box 23). A joint venture MTN Banking in South Africa between the mobile phone operator MTN and Standard Bank is another example.

There is a regulatory gap with banking services provided by mobile phone operators. While mobile phone operators are accountable to telecommunications authorities, the scope of intervention of financial

regulation is often undefined. Central banks responsible for monetary and fiscal policy in Africa have not started looking at e-payments, e-banking and other services. There is presently no mention of electronic transactions and e-currency in regulatory frameworks. M-Pesa in Kenya belongs to the telecommunications operator Safaricom and is not supported by any bank. M-Pesa was only able to start after lengthy discussions with local authorities. M-Pesa argued that it was transferring money, not taking deposits and so remains out of the scope of financial regulation.

However, the difference between a payment and a deposit is merely defined by the time the money remains in the system. Frontiers between telecommunications and financial services are easily blurred. And as African banks rely heavily on revenues from transaction fees, M-Pesa represents a strong competitor and has made a strong impact in its two years of operation. However, when the company announced in December 2008 that it would expand into initiating and receiving international remittances from the UK through an arrangement with Western Union, Kenya's Ministry of Finance announced plans to audit M-Pesa arguing there was a risk to customers. It appears that much of the pressure for the audit originated from the 48 commercial banks in Kenya. Last year Kenya received approximately USD 1.6 billion in international remittances which is around 5 per cent of GDP. At an estimated amount of USD 283 billion in 2008 according to the World Bank, global remittances attract much interest. Inward remittances are larger than ODA flows (excluding debt) in countries such as Botswana, Ghana and Kenya, six times larger in Nigeria and three times in South Africa in 2007[8]. Orange, Zain and MTN are already exploring the possibility of launching this service.

Mobile-payments and banking are quick and easy to use. This could enable rapid take up by unbanked population. According to the 2007/2008 Research ICT Africa survey the main reason people do not have a bank account is because they do not have enough regular income. Zero transaction costs were highlighted by many respondents as a reason for sending air-time instead of cash. M-Pesa for example, is particularly attractive for small transactions. In order to send KSH 1 000, Western Union would charge a fee of KSH 500 while M-Pesa would ask 30 KES if the money is sent to M-Pesa users and 75 KES if it is sent to non users[9]. The technology could eventually be used to collect the transaction history of customers, enabling them to obtain a favourable credit rating.

Recent entrants planning to expand or begin providing similar services are CelPay in Democratic Republic of Congo and Zambia, Orascom in Algeria, Tunisia, Egypt and Zimbabwe, Monitise in Uganda, Burundi, Democratic Republic of Congo, Ethiopia, Kenya, Rwanda, Tanzania and Zambia, Globacom in Nigeria, Zain in Kenya, Tanzania and Uganda, Orange in Mali, Côte d'Ivoire, Kenya and Egypt and the Cooperative Bank of Kenya in Kenya. With only 19.8 per cent of individuals keeping their money in a bank account in a sample of 17 African countries, and more than 30 per cent worried about being robbed or losing the cash, the potential for developing mobile-banking seems high.

Sunny future for E-Agriculture

Market information is difficult to obtain in Africa and costly because of the poor state of telecommunications and transport. Market Information Systems (MIS) have long been established to collect data on prices and sometimes quantities of widely traded agricultural products. This is sent to farmers, traders, government officials and consumers through message boards, radio and print media.

ICT-based systems have started to emerge in Africa, providing a fast and relatively affordable flow of information on agriculture and fisheries. There are two major initiatives in East Africa. In Kenya, SMS Sokini provides agricultural information through SMS text messages for a fee. The project is run by a partnership between the Kenyan Agricultural Commodities Exchange (KACE) and mobile operator Safaricom. Information kiosks are located near where agricultural commodity buyers and sellers meet, providing low cost access to farmers. KACE workers collect the information from the kiosks and send it to farmers, buyers and exporters on text messages. In 2005, in Uganda, the Women of Uganda Network (WOUGNET) started to send SMS texts with market prices to 400 rural farmers with financial support from the Technical Centre for Agricultural and Rural Cooperation ACP-EU (CTA). Workers collect information from markets and data is posted on the Busoga Rural Open Source Development Initiative (BROSDI) website. Other workers translate the information to Luo, a local language, and send it to farmers by SMS. Farmers can request more information by replying to the SMS. WOUGNET is providing free mobile phones and free access to this service.

---

8. Comninos, A., S. Esselaar, A. Ndiwalana and C. Stork (2009), "Mobile Payment Systems: Unlocking Africa's Development Potential," *Towards Evidence Based ICT Policy and Regulation in Africa, Volume 1, Policy paper 4, ISSN: 20730845.*

9. Comninos, A., S. Esselaar, A. Ndiwalana and C. Stork (2009), "Mobile Payment Systems: Unlocking Africa's Development Potential," *Towards Evidence Based ICT Policy and Regulation in Africa, Volume 1, Policy paper 4, ISSN: 20730845.*

Box 24 - Manobi: African Innovation for Smallholder Farming

Since 2002, Manobi a company based in Senegal, brings farmers services to fill their market linkage gaps:

- In Niayes, a farmer checks market prices in real time on his/her mobile phone to negotiate with the wholesaler and obtain the best prices.
- In Tambacounda, Senegal, groups of Sterculia gum growers use their mobile phone to inform their contract buyers about their inventory.
- In Sikasso, Mali, mango growers record information on every step of the process to trace their products for export markets in compliance with Global Gap requirements.

These examples show how Manobi uses mobile phone technology to help small scale farmers play a more active role in the product value chain. An innovative business model developed by Manobi supports the delivery of the services while creating a sustainable ecosystem for the farmers and all the value chain operators.

This model is going to be extended in West and Central Africa in partnership with international organisations and private foundations which have joined Manobi aiming to reach 650 000 farmers by 2011. Mobile operators and suppliers also support the project which makes rural communities much more attractive by transforming the mobile phone into a business tool.

Source: Daniel Annerose, CEO, Manobi.

121

In West Africa, two initiatives are expanding. Xam Marsé ("Know your market" in Wolof) in Senegal established by the Manobi Development Foundation provides commodity prices information for farmers (see Box 24). This was launched on 2002 after two year of research. It allows farmers in their fields to access market prices which are collected by specialists. For a small fee farmers can receive market information for selected crops, mainly vegetables. Farmers can access information on their crops and the prices in markets where they normally sell as well as in other distant markets. Xam Marsé makes use of all currently available communication channels on mobile phones — SMS text messages, Multimedia Messaging Service (MMS) that includes images, video and audio and the Wireless Application Protocol (WAP) that enables access to internet on a mobile phone.

Esoko Networks (known previously as TradeNet) was started in 2004 by the Ghanian software company BusyLab. Esoko has a website where more than 800 000 prices from hundreds of markets are quoted, with a focus on Sub-Saharan Africa. Because only a small percentage of users are active on the internet, Esoko has relied on an SMS platform. Users can sign up to receive weekly SMS alerts on commodities for a fee and the cost of the SMS. Users can also upload offers to buy and sell products via mobile phone and make precise price requests on commodities in a country receiving the information by SMS.

The SMS messages enable farmers to access accurate information at an affordable price, typically 1/7th of the cost of a call and up to an estimated 1/10th of the travel cost in some cases. The information has increased the bargaining power of farmers, who in the past had little alternative but to sell their goods to the wholesalers located nearest to them.

There are several obstacles to the wider use of e-agriculture technology however. Even though 39.1 per cent of the African population owned a mobile phone in 2008, many unprofitable rural areas are not covered by mobile services. E-agriculture cannot anyway answer all of farmers' problems such as poor transport.

Box 25 - Esoko: Large Scale Market for Agricultural Products in West Africa

Far from consumer zones in northern Ghana, where infrastructure is notoriously lacking and production is seasonal, Kujo Asumah is a smallholder farmer cultivating groundnuts, soya and maize. Like many farmers on a small wage, knowing the price of his crop in numerous markets is essential to his livelihood. Recently, his producer co-operative registered him for Esoko's price alerts for all major markets in Ghana. When he was offered GHS 320 for his product in Tamale, he knew he could get much more 700 km away. With the information received on his mobile phone, he decided to ship the groundnuts to Accra and sold the crop for a higher price, doubling the income earned.

Agriculture in developing countries is one of the final frontiers to benefit from the technology revolution of the last two decades, and Esoko's web and mobile based market information system (MIS) is on the forefront. Esoko seeks to improve incomes and build healthier, more efficient markets by disseminating market information via mobile. Built by Ghanaian software company BusyLab, Esoko began in 2004 as a platform used to collect and distribute price information using SMS and email. Since then, various partners have used the software and helped Esoko evolve and respond to the realities and opportunities in the field. Currently in ten countries, projects range from establishing a regional MIS covering three value chains for USAID's Agribusiness and Trade Promotion (ATP) project in four West African countries to helping a Ghanaian animal feed company better manage its local supply chain for maize.

With Esoko's suite of tools, farmers and traders can receive targeted, scheduled text messages on prices for different commodities, offers, or weather. Scout, a new feature to be released later in 2009, includes an automated polling system to track and monitor crop activities among suppliers or inventory among distributors; responses are sent by SMS and displayed on GIS maps. Esoko's platform also helps businesses and associations market their services by creating websites and publishing SMS messages to thousands of users profiled on the system. Partner organisations can license Esoko — as a small business; a large association or project; or a franchise rolling out a country-wide program — and also benefit from Esoko's training and support services to assist with the design and implementation of a successful and sustainable market information system.

Source: Sarah Bartlett and Laura Drewett, Esoko Communication Director and Partner Director.

The information systems are difficult to sustain. In Ghana, TradeNet has had to hire and train agents to collect information, which anyway can be easily pirated. Manobi subsidises the collection of market data. Esoko has been subsidising SMS alerts for individuals, but most people prepay for their text messages, so it is now only subsidising SMS alerts for individuals in Ghana. The challenge is to provide information that farmers feel they have to pay for. Farmers and traders are not using radio-based MIS in Sub-Saharan Africa because the information does not meet their needs so the providers will have to tailor their services more to the needs of users.

Capacity building, even literacy programmes for farmers, is also important for the internet and SMS usage. But e-farming is continuing to evolve and not just in Africa. In Cambodia, the Canada Agricultural Market Information Project (CAMIP) is developing an SMS system that enables farmers to access commodity price information. The difference with respect to existing initiatives in Africa is that in this case farmers are trained through Farmer Marketing Schools (FMS) not only to use the system but also to improve their operations by focusing on packaging, bargaining, post harvest quality and peer networking.

Box 26 - Bringing People and Markets Together: The Impact of ICT on Grain Markets in Niger

The majority of the population in Niger are rural subsistence farmers. Grains (primarily millet) are dietary staples, accounting for over 75 per cent of rural households' caloric consumption. These are transported from farmers to consumers through an extensive system of markets that run the length of the country, which is roughly three times the size of California.

As grain markets occur only once per week, traders and farmers have historically travelled long distances to markets to obtain market information. This not only requires the cost of travel, but also the opportunity costs of traders' time. Between 2001 and 2006, however, cell phone service was phased in throughout the country, providing an alternative and cheaper search technology to grain traders, farmers and consumers.

Aker (2008) shows that the introduction of cell phone towers in Niger reduced differences in grain prices across markets by 20 per cent and the intra-annual variation of grain prices by 12 per cent. Cell phones had a greater impact on price dispersion for markets that are farther away, and for those that are linked by poor-quality roads. This effect also intensified over time: the reduction in inter-market price dispersion increased as a higher percentage of markets have cell phone coverage, suggesting that ICT is more useful as a greater percentage of people have coverage.

The reduction in price differences seems to be linked to a reduction in search costs: Since cell phones reduced traders' search costs by 50 per cent, they were able to change their marketing behaviour. Grain traders operating in cell phone markets searched over a greater number of markets, had more market contacts and sold in more markets as compared to their non-cell phone counterparts. This suggests that traders in cell phone markets were better able to respond to surpluses and shortages, thereby allocating grains more efficiently across markets and dampening the price differences.

Cell phones have not only helped traders in Niger. Between 2001-2006, cell phones were associated with a 3.5 per cent reduction in average consumer grain prices, as well as an increase in traders' profits. Holding all else equal, this would have enabled rural households to purchase an additional 5-10 days' worth of grain per year. In 2005, the year that Niger experienced a severe food crisis, cell phone markets in food crisis regions had relatively lower consumer grain prices. This suggests that the presence of cell phone towers could have averted a worse food crisis. Since a majority of rural households in Niger are net consumers, lower consumer prices suggest that people were better off. In sum, the experience in Niger provides powerful evidence of the potential impacts of information – and in particular ICT – on agricultural markets and producers', traders' and consumers' welfare.

Source: Jenny C. Aker, Visiting Fellow (Centre for Global Development) and Tufts University.

E-Education's steep learning curve

The adoption of ICT technologies in education is moving from small projects to national government programmes. With the exception of South Africa and Mauritius, ICT educational policies have only been developed in the last five years. By 2007, 39 countries had ICT education policies in place or under implementation. While in North Africa and countries such as Mauritius, Ghana and Botswana, ICT education programmes have made significant progress, in the rest of Africa the lack of accessibility to a mainstream

123

Box 27 - Mistowa: Capacity Building for e-Agriculture

The USAID Market Information Systems and Trader's Organizations in West Africa (MISTOWA) partnered with a private company, BusyLab, by helping to establish over 100 "Agribusiness Information Points" (ABIPs) in 13 countries throughout West Africa. The ABIP managers were trained in the use of Tradenet and the collection of data to feed into the system, and in turn trained producers and traders to use the system. While the MISTOWA project has ended, TradeNet (now rebranded "Esoko") continues in widespread use.

Source: Judith E. Payne, e-Business Advisor and AFR ICT Coordinator, US Agency for International Development.

network and the shortage of trained staff are acute and threaten the implementation.

National ICT educational policies in 53 countries surveyed by the World Bank in 2007, highlighted that beyond the need for connectivity and skills, technology training for teachers, development of digital content and increasing access to ICT tools are key factors to be reinforced[10]. There are important regional initiatives on teacher training. The Teacher Training Initiative for Sub-Saharan Africa (TTISSA) is a 2006-2015 programme co-ordinated by UNESCO that aims to increase the quantity and quality of teachers in 46 Sub-Saharan countries. Concentrating on mathematics and science, the African Virtual University teacher ICT education project has since 2006 involved 10 countries in partnership with the AfDB and NEPAD. The NEPAD e-schools initiative will focus on ICT training under its Teacher Professional Development and Training framework (see Box 28). Schoolnet Africa and World Links are also involved in ICT teacher development in 41 African countries. South Africa plans to introduce an Advanced Certificate for Education on ICT Integration that will be compulsory for school principals.

Among interesting initiatives, the Virtual University for Small States of the Commonwealth (VUSSC) was set up to create post-secondary skills courses. Botswana, Comoros, Gambia, Lesotho, Namibia, Seychelles, Sierra Leone and Swaziland are taking part. The courses were created with WikiEducator which enables materials to be adapted to local demands. Staff from universities are being trained to develop course content. The African Academy of Languages has been supported by the African Union to promote the use of African languages in internet, with education as a special axis. Intel is developing the skools.com project to provide e-learning. Edubuntu, Learnthings and Mindset Network organisations are also promoting local digital content in Africa.

Second hand and refurbished computers are widely used. Computer Aid International collects old computers from UK companies which are data-wiped, refurbished and tested. Non profit organisations can apply for refurbished computers and are charged a 39 pound sterling (GBP) handling fee plus shipping. More than 80 000 computers have been distributed in Eritrea, Kenya, Tanzania, Uganda and Zambia. The UK based charity Computers for African Schools (CFAS) has similarly distributed 13 000 donated computers mostly in Zambia, Zimbabwe, Malawi and Zanzibar. Digital Links, another UK-based entity, has distributed 50 000 refurbished computers. The US-based World Computer Exchange has sent more than 42 shipments of second-hand computers to 25 countries. The NGO SchoolNet Africa has distributed second-hand computers in Cameroon, Mali, Mozambique, Namibia, Nigeria, Senegal, Swaziland, Zambia and Zimbabwe. Importantly, SchoolNet Namibia, Mozambique, Nigeria and Uganda, Computers for Schools Kenya and World

10. Farell, G. and S. Isaacs (2007), "Survey of ICT and Education in Africa: A Summary Report, Based on 53 Country Surveys," Washington, DC: infodev/World Bank.

Box 28 - E-Schools NEPAD's Initiative: Africa's Schools Connect to the 21st Century

First announced in 2003 at the Africa Summit of the World Economic Forum in Durban, the NEPAD e-Schools Project focuses on providing end-to-end ICT solutions that will transform schools across Africa into NEPAD e-Schools and connect them to the Internet. The solution also includes the provision of content and learning material and the establishment of health points at schools. In each country, the programme aims to assist African governments to transform 50 per cent of their secondary schools into NEPAD e-Schools by 2015 and all primary and secondary schools within a further ten years of this date. In total more than 600 000 schools across the continent will enjoy the benefits of ICT and connectivity to the Internet upon completion of the project.

Five consortia consisting of private sector companies and non-governmental organisations led by AMD, HP, Oracle, Microsoft, and Cisco Systems sponsored the demonstration project, which aims to implement six NEPAD e-Schools in each of the 16 participating countries during a 12 month period. The Demo aims to accrue a body of knowledge about implementing ICT in schools across the African continent in based on real life experiences, in order to inform the massive rollout of the NEPAD e-Schools Initiative. Participating countries are Algeria, Burkina Faso, Cameroon, Egypt, Gabon, Ghana, Kenya, Lesotho, Mali, Mauritius, Mozambique, Nigeria, Rwanda, Senegal, South Africa and Uganda. Ten countries have already launched NEPAD e-Schools in their countries, equipment has been installed, teachers have been trained and pupils have been exposed to the wonders of new technology in more than 80 community schools in Africa.

Source: Dr. Katherine W. Getao, NEPAD e-Schools: Project Manager.

125

Links Zimbabwe are creating computer refurbishment centres that support the installation and maintenance of projects. The shipment of refurbished and second hand computers to Africa is nevertheless raising increasing environmental concerns since a high rate of imported devises are out of use and are improperly disposed of.

There are three large initiatives on new low-cost computers. The One Laptop per Child non-for-profit project distributes a low-power computer for USD 188. 31 000 devises are already present in Ethiopia, Ghana and Rwanda. It targets poor children and uses free and open source software, but the results have been disappointing. Education ministries in India and China saw the teaching materials as a challenge to their authority and cultural systems. Unlike Linux, the project did not develop innovative ways to attract independent developers to build up open source software. In addition, the companies financing the project, Google, AMD, Qanta, Marvell and Red Hat

are suffering from the crisis and 50 per cent of One Laptop per Child workers will be fired in 2009. The project aims at creating now an educational hub in Sub-Saharan Africa. ClassMate PC is another initiative where low cost USD 230 - USD 300 computers are being sold to Africa with greater success (see Box 29). The Indian Institute of Technology and the Indian Institute of Science were developing a USD 10 laptop, claiming that the One Laptop per Child USD 100 was still unaffordable for the population, but by 2008 the price was already at USD 100.

Almost all African countries are making use of open source and proprietary software. Despite a lack of qualified personnel, some initiatives such as the Free and Open Source Software Foundation for Africa (FOSSFA), Bokjang Bokjef in Senegal and LinuxChix Africa are still promoting the use of open source in Africa. The NGO SchoolNet has been a pioneer in promoting open source software through its OpenLab model in Namibia, soon to be copied in Mozambique.

Box 29 - ClassMate Project: South – North Innovation

The Intel-powered classmate PC is Intel's low cost personal computer developed for children in developing countries. The model launched in 2006 and a new convertible design (an addition to the Intel-powered classmate PC family, joining the successful clamshell design), has been designed to promote inventiveness, interactiveness and conviviality at schools through the results of more than two year period ethnographic studies. Initially designed in Mexico and Egypt and implemented in Nigeria (first pilot), the computer is quickly expanding to Europe and US. The price and functionalities of this computer (light, hard, water-resistant keyboard, with touchscreen, virtual keyboard, electronic blackboard, 180° screen rotation, built-in microphone, speakers and wireless) have indeed attracted consumers in OECD countries. In Portugal, the government has put in place a programme "Magalhães Initiative" to provide PCs to all elementary school children via the local computer manufacturer and telecom service providers. Same locally build schemes have been developed through Axioo and Zyrex (Indonesia), HCL Infosystems Mileap-X (India), CMS Computers (UK), and MPC, M&A technology and Computer Technology Link (US). Intel-powered classmate PC allows open source and proprietary software and OS.

Source: Isabelle Flory, Institutional Relations, INTEL.

Catching up on e-Government

E-governance is intended to improve government services but it has not yet got a big foothold in Africa. The United Nations has developed an e-government indicator that marks governments on their online presence, telecommunications infrastructure and human capital. The survey shows that Africa is lagging behind other regions with less than two thirds of the average scores obtained by the Americas, Asia and Oceania and with less than half of the score obtained by Europe. There is a large gap between North Africa and Sub-Saharan Africa resource poor landlocked countries as can be seen in Figure 23.

Some attempts are being made to advance government through the web however. In Cape Verde, all government services are being integrated through a one-stop-shop which can be accessed physically, by mobile phone or internet. One of the major challenges, as acknowledged by the Operational Centre for the Information Society in Cape Verde, was to eliminate bureaucratic barriers to create a single front office. It required a lot of political will to create a portal that service-oriented rather than directly referring to the various government branches. The key element to

support the transfer of powers and competences in this reduction of intermediation was strong political will.

A wide range of services are available, including electronic payments through mobile phones and the internet through a system developed with the Interbanking Society for Payment Systems, in which all commercial banks in the country are shareholders. All forms are available in electronic format. Birth, marriage and other certificates can be requested online and through mobile phones in a system that many OECD countries cannot match for the degree to which paperwork is cut out. All state systems are integrated through a unified information system. Individuals can now create a firm in 60 minutes, where in the past it took 63 days by visiting several offices and filling in many forms. A unified document for car registration is also accessible online.

The government says it no longer uses paper format for any internal activity within or between ministries. Information is exchanged online through a unified system that integrates all activities, including registration, health and education, notarial, electoral and municipal services. The principle is to record information once and then consult it as necessary through the information

Figure 23 - UN E-Readiness Indicator 2008

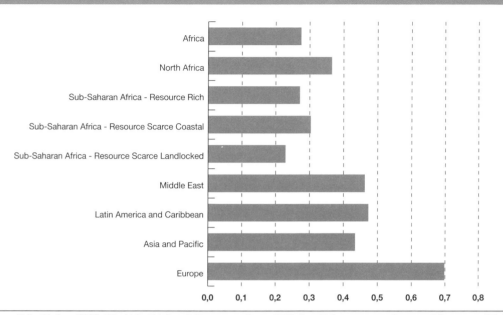

Source: United Nations (2008), "The United Nations E-Government Survey 2008: From E-Government to Connected Governance," United Nations Press.

StatLink 🖳📊 http://dx.doi.org/10.1787/568585134470

127

system. A database has been created with biometric information that is used by passport, security and criminal justice services. A new biometric identification card is being issued to citizens. E-government has also changed budget management (see Box 30).

The third Annual African E-Government forum held in Rwanda in March 2009 highlighted the growing interest in e-government services. In Nigeria, the government aims to use telephones and computers to automate government paper services. In the region around the capital, Abuja, authorities are starting to build a website so citizens can access information and send messages to the government. In Burkina Faso, the government is computerising accounting services so officials can check how much money has been collected and how much government departments need each day. In Rwanda and Ghana, the World Bank is supporting e-government applications to improve efficiency and transparency. South Africa is developing a paper-free tax declaration and payment programme (see Box 31) and Ethiopia in revenue management (see Box 32).

Despite the initial success of e-government services, the performance depends a lot on a country's institutional capacity and will to adapt to new ways, the transparency of processes seen as threatening jobs and cultural resistance to broad change in many societies. A lack of power, low literacy rates, the high cost of telecommunications and the shortage of broadband networks can also hamper e-government. In Cape Verde, the government has sought to maximise the use of mobile phones for e-government services since the penetration rate for mobile subscribers is 40 per cent, compared to 11.5 per cent for computer usage, 6 per cent for the internet and 0.35 per cent for broadband. In addition, the government is creating special centres for service delivery. Private telecentres can also provide certain services. The wide range of services available electronically is likely to create business opportunities helping people who lack access and/or skills.

E-reforms are needed for e-trade

E-government applications should also transform customs clearance, an area in crucial need of attention

Box 30 - Cape Verde's Financial Management System: Recent Developments

The aim of Cape Verde Government is to transform the archipelago into a "modern, competitive country, with social cohesion and justice, and environmental quality"(*). Consequently, the development of Information and Communication Technologies to establish an Information and Knowledge Society was defined as a strategic option and Electronic Government, in particular, was identified as a key pillar. Two main strategic orientations were defined for the E-Government platform:

i) Improve the performance and the efficiency of the Public Administration and;
ii) Re-engineer, streamline and automate processes to improve quality and reduce public service delivery time.

The financial management system also known as "SIGOF" integrates tax revenue, the federal government budget, the Controller's Office, and the Treasury. The system is being enhanced to incorporate monitoring and evaluation, increase security, and integrate with a Geographical Information System.

The Budget Office has reaped most gains in efficiency. The process of auditing and approving budgets for each State Department, which used to take one to three months, has now been shortened to just four days. The government is now also able to provide financial information more quickly and efficiently to foreign aid donors.

This transformational process has increased transparency, increasing the openness of government processes and procedures while reducing intermediaries and public service delivery time. Furthermore, it has enhanced tax collection, and reduced opportunities for fraud and corruption.

(*) Message by H.E., The Prime Minister of Cape Verde, Dr.Jose Maria Neves, Information Society Strategic Program, pg 15.

Source: Jorge Lopes, General Manager, Operational Centre for the Information Society, Cape Verde.

in Africa. The EU and United States are about to move to completely paperless trade and all exports from the EU will have to comply with paperless legislation by July 2009. EU importers will go paperless by January 2011, which could increase non-tariff trade barriers for African products, underscoring the need for African countries to accelerate the conversion to e-trade.

E-trade is present across the entire exporter-importer chain, from the time a product is bought and shipped, until it has been paid for and received. But there are also different customs procedures and regulations to comply with. A transaction typically involves 27 to 30 different parties, 40 documents for export, 90 per cent

of which are currently done on paper. In addition, each transaction requires 200 data elements, 30 of which are repeated 30 times at least, and the re-writing of 60 to 70 per cent of the data at least once. As a result, 10 per cent of the value of all goods shipped worldwide in 2008 was spent on administration, an estimated USD 550 billion. To reduce these costs there are several initiatives promoting e-trade such as the United Nations Electronic Documents (UNeDocs), the European Fiscalis Program on Customs 2013, the US Customs and Border Protection and Canada's and Australia's Paperless Trade Adoption. These promote the development of a single window where data is available in any way that a regulator wishes to view it.

Box 31 - South Africa: Paperless Tax Procedures

In early 2007, the South African Revenue Service (SARS) embarked on an ambitious programme to maximize tax payer compliance through the use of ICT. The greatest improvements have been obtained so far in the individual income tax return process where a complex, paper-based, labour intensive process was simplified and automated through an electronic format.

The 2008/2009 Employers Tax season has been a huge success with the receipt of more than 250 000 submissions representing 15.5 million employee tax certificates, up from 11.7 million in 2007. More than 90 per cent of submissions were received electronically using a new electronic channel, branded e@syFile. Employees no longer needed to complete blank tax returns. For the first time no blank tax forms were dispatched to tax payers, which saved SARS considerable printing and postal charges. The SARS electronic internet platform (e-Filing) is growing rapidly with more than 2 million tax payers registered by 2009. This e-Filing system has shown the greatest gains. The number of returns submitted electronically by the deadline has increased from 580 852 in 2007 to 1 376 702 in 2008, an increase of 137 per cent.

One of the key challenges faced in 2008 was the accuracy of personal information on employee tax certificates, which affected the ability of SARS to match certificates and tax payers. Some tax payers requesting returns electronically also faced uncertainty of which fields to fill in, indicating that further enhancements and education were still required. The next wave of modernisation will focus on other forms of income tax, such as Corporate Income Tax, and modernizing customs.

Under the auspices of the India-Brazil-South Africa (IBSA) Dialogue Forum, the three heads of Revenue Administration have agreed to share information on tax and customs matters, especially abusive tax avoidance and on common positions for trade facilitation, which is soon to go paperless in a large number of economies.

Table 2 – Comparative Statistics for Tax Season 2007 and 2008

Measure	As at deadline 2007	As at deadline 2008	Per cent change
Income Tax returns received	2 930 641	3 020 910	+3.08
Income Tax returns submitted manually	1 922 528	410 548	-78.65
Income Tax returns submitted electronically via branch	655 180	944 082	+44.10
Income Tax returns submitted via e-Filing	580 852	1 376 702	+137.01
Income Tax returns assessed	1 658 112	2 492 683	+50.33
Per cent of Income Tax returns assessed within 24 hours	10.1 per cent	76.1 per cent	+532.87

Source: International Relations Office, South African Revenue Service (SARS).

StatLink http://dx.doi.org/10.1787/574554881606

Paperless trade in Africa could decrease the time and costs of commercial exchanges. While South Asia is the worst performer in terms of the number of documents for export/import activities, Sub-Saharan Africa leads in terms of the time and cost of exports and imports: on average 75.8 days and USD 4 157 per container,

according to the World Bank Doing Business 2009 report. These costs are twice as high as for OECD countries, Latin American and North African countries. In North Africa, import and export transactions on average require 35.25 days and cost USD 1 881 per container. These burdens on Sub-Saharan trade,

129

Box 32 - Fully Automated Services in Revenue Management in Addis Ababa

The Integrated Revenue Management System project in Ethiopia has fully automated services to over 300 000 customers of the Revenue Agency of the Addis Ababa City Administration, including new taxpayer registration, assessment of different tax types based on the relevant regulations, payment and collection, and clearance certificate generation. It has enabled the Tax Authority to collect more revenue as the system has facilities for tracking unsettled liabilities which in turn helps to track unsettled liabilities for further legal enforcement. The project has been fully operational since the 2003/2004-budget year.

Source: UNECA (www.aarevenue.net).

highlight the potential benefits of developing cross-frontier collaborative innovation (see Box 33). The extent to which SMEs can benefit from e-trade is not clear however. According to a recent survey undertaken by UNECA, small and medium companies in Kenya, Egypt, South Africa, Ghana, Senegal and Ethiopia have very varied levels of e-readiness and so their ability to integrate e-trade activities is compromised.

Another related issue is that of the health requirements of importing countries to prevent the spread of diseases. International food safety and food hygiene regulations now require all food be traceable from source. Radio frequency identification (RFID) tracking systems are being used in Africa to comply with these regulations. In Botswana there is one of the world's largest RFID livestock tracking, monitoring and management systems, involving every cow in the country, 3 million in 2008. This Livestock Identification Trace-back System (LITS) has a database on the production, processing and sale of meat. Although this project was set up to comply with EU regulations, it also allows livestock operators to optimise feeding regimes and to meet reporting requirements to health authorities. In Namibia, authorities are increasing the use of RFID to every cow in the country. In Kenya, a pilot RFID programme is being developed for cows (see Box 33). In South Africa, sheep and ostrich farmers use RFID systems.

The traceability of agricultural products is a new requirement in international trade and there is a global shortage of experienced agricultural supply chain traceability analysts. In addition, new standards such as the Global Partnership for Good Agricultural Practice (GlobalGap) and the Hazard Analysis Critical Control Point System (HACCP), are still evolving which makes it difficult to develop a computerised application. Traceability also has to accommodate the needs of different government departments and private companies, increasing the cost for businesses. Experience in Kenya shows that the cost of certification and meeting other requirements lead to smallholders dropping out. Community sites operated in Kenya and Senegal show that costs for external certification can be reduced significantly. A successful example of community group certification is the Fresh Food Trace web platform of the fruit-and-vegetable export company FRUILEMA GIE in Mali set up with Manobi and IICD on February 2008. This helps mango exporters in Mali to enhance the traceability of their products and to maintain GlobalGap certification standards. Farmers can use mobile phones to provide updates on their activities, information that is integrated in a system that can be accessed by buyers.

ICT could be cleaner

While ICTs account for 2.5 per cent of total greenhouse gas emissions, according to the International Telecommunication Union, their potential to reduce their own emissions and those who account for the other 97.5 per cent is large[12]. The impact on Africa is not yet clear however. New generation devises usually

---

12. International Telecommunication Union (2008), "ICTs and Climate Change: ITU Background Paper".

130

Box 33 - ICT to Overstep North-South Trade Barriers

Information and Communication Technology (ICT) enables people and organisations to work better across distances, to co-ordinate more closely and to bring together multiples sources of information on a common platform. These advantages are increasingly relevant in international trade to facilitate complex import and export procedures.

Over the past 10 years, developing countries have also become more engaged in international trade. Africa traded USD424 billion in 2007 – an increase of 16 per cent from 2006 – providing a significant source of income and economic growth to the continent. Microsoft believes that encouraging greater access to technology in the developing world provides an opportunity to facilitate trade, emulate best practices and overcome North/South barriers.

For example, in Senegal, the local ICT company Gainde2000 developed ORBUS, a paperless electronic single window solution based on Microsoft technology to facilitate preclearance formalities by linking multiple Government agencies, banks and importers and exporters. By putting in place the best available infrastructure from the outset, Senegal has been able to provide a full end-to-end secure paperless customs platform that enables the country to trade more effectively with the rest of the world. The solution is also being implemented in Kenya.

Another Microsoft partner, TradeFacilitate, developed an electronic platform that updates existing customs systems, including ASYCUDA (Automated SYstem for CUstoms DAta system implemented by the UNCTAD in the 1970s), to the latest technology standards for paperless trade – leapfrogging gradual improvements in infrastructure. This platform has specifically targeted small and medium enterprises (SMEs) in developing countries throughout Africa, Latin America and South East Asia so that they can benefit from the latest technology and meet paperless trade requirements from the US and EU. An African and APEC program will be rolled out in 2009 with the EU CP3 Group on Import/Export Electronic Trade for SMEs, with an initial pilot project launched in April 2008 for Ethiopian exporters. It is estimated by CP3 that the time elapsed between the initial transmission of data by an exporter and the receipt of permission to export will become minutes rather than the current paper-based 30 days through the use of the TradeFacilitate platform. CP3 warns that Ethiopian exports of USD923 million could be in jeopardy by 2011 and that 400 Ethiopian exporters are expected to benefit from access to the solution by 1 July 2009. Other countries currently in discussion to use the platform are Taiwan, Vietnam and Thailand.

As technology skills develop globally, innovative applications are increasingly being created locally to address the specific needs of developing countries thus benefiting them directly and enabling the North to learn from the South. In Kenya, Microsoft partner Virtual City Ltd. built a unique radio frequency identification (RFID) tracking solution to help Kenya's cattle farmers keep track of data on the medical history and whereabouts of each cow destined for the export market. By inserting a low-cost tracking device in cows' stomachs and digitizing the relevant data, cattle farmers in Kenya now meet EU food traceability regulations, thus reopening a market that had been closed in the past. The system can also easily be adapted for use in other countries.

As global trading systems change, large trading partners (US and EU) are increasingly imposing more stringent requirements on imports. Technology will help developing countries meet these requirements, ensuring continued market access and the ability to remain competitive in the long-run

Source: Frank McCosker, Managing Director, Global Strategic Accounts, Microsoft.

consume more energy for operating and cooling (for example third generation mobile phones) though environment-friendly innovations are increasingly being developed so that temperature requirements and adaptative power needs are less demanding. ICTs could have most impact in Africa by reducing the need for travel, which accounts for 14 per cent of the total worldwide greenhouse gas emissions. There will also be

a key role in supporting early-warning, climate change mitigation and relief systems in Africa. According to the Intergovernmental Panel on Climate Change (IPCC), temperatures are could increase by an average of 1.4 to 5.8°C worldwide by 2100 in the absence of policies to stabilise and eventually reduce emissions, which will increase Sub-Saharan Africa's desertification. Countries most at risk due to climate change are Malawi, Ethiopia,

Box 34 - Technological Innovation for Climate Change Patterns in the Sahel Region

The Sahel region of West Africa experiences marked variability in rainfall associated with changes in atmospheric circulation and in tropical sea surface temperature patterns in the Pacific, Indian and Atlantic Basins. In particular, the decreasing rainfall in the Sahel region is among the largest effects of climate change worldwide. Since the 1990s, a variety of government and non-government organisations in The Sahel have worked with community-based structures to develop early warning systems (CEWS) for data on rainfall and food security. The major constraints for the sustainability of these traditional systems was the cost collecting and disseminating the information through monthly or bi-monthly meetings at local, regional and national levels. ICT-based CEWS are being increasingly implemented to assemble, analyze, and disseminate information that can mitigate the impact of crisis periods of drought. Taking into account that, according to the UN Emergency Relief, every USD 1 spent on preventing disasters saves between USD 4 and USD 7 in humanitarian emergency after a disaster, the use of ICTs on early warning systems is crucial

The Famine Early Warning Systems Network (FEWS NET) USAID-funded activity collaborates with international (for example, NASA), regional and national partners to provide timely and rigorous early warning and vulnerability information on emerging and evolving food security issues. With this system, professionals in US and Africa monitor various information including remotely sensed and ground-based metereological and crop data, as indicators of potential threats to food security. This is fundamental taking into account that according to the Human Development Report 2007/2008, Sub-Saharan Africa has the lowest density of meteorological stations in the world.

On another project between UNEP and Google, up to 120 environmental hotspots have been identified currently in the "UNEP Altas of our Changing Environment" publications. With images such as the forest fires in Sub-Saharan Africa and the decline of the Lake Chad, this application helps the environmental community to keep pace with recent changes. The TIGER Initiative is another project launched by the European Space Agency to focus on water resource management in Africa with the use of space technology. Their current projects in the Sahel include the tele-detection of humid areas, the evaluation and management of water resources, methods of groundwater development to remedy the inadequate natural recharge systems of the aquifers in the Chad Basin in North Eastern Nigeria, and the development of integrated resource management policies in the Gash basin of the Sudan, Eritrea and Ethiopia which can serve as reference basin.

Radar Technologies France/USGS/UNESCO Watex, has identified an aquifer potential in Central Darfur over an area of 135 000 km². Such identification was made possible using new radar remote sensing technologies. The study has revealed vast stretches of land in central Darfur hosting enough ground water reserves to sustain 33 million people year round with 15 litres of water per day. These aquifers are renewable and easily accessible within a depth ranging from subsurface to 50 meters in unconsolidated sediments easy to drill. In an area which hosts 2.5 million people in Internally Displaced Persons (IDP) champs, this is a major achievement to ensure water supply.

In another initiative, Canada's International Development Research Centre (IDRC) has sponsored the Cyber Shepherd Initiative to enable Sahelian pastoralists to access accurate information on the status of grazing lands in order to help them co-ordinate their movements. Project members are working closely with communities to identify innovative ways in which ICTs can be used to harness traditional knowledge on natural resource management. In another project, the Food Insecurity and Vulnerability Information and Mapping Systems (FIVIMS) in collaboration with the Food and Agricultural Organisation (FAO) are working on building in Niger a more integrated food insecurity and vulnerability information system at national and sub-national levels to provide timely information to the policy-makers and members of civil society.

Source: International Telecommunication Union (ITU).

Zimbabwe, Mozambique, Niger, Mauritania, Eritrea, Sudan, Chad and Kenya (drought), Mozambique and Benin (floods) and Egypt, Tunisia, Mauritania and Senegal which have low lying coasts (see Box 34).

Information and communications technology can however have a negative environmental impact through e-waste, the biggest and fastest growing segment of manufacturing waste with between 20 million and 50 million tonnes generated worldwide each year, according to the UN Environment Programme. E-waste has been increasing in Africa since 2006, following dumps in China, India and Pakistan. Nigeria is becoming one of the fastest growing computer dumping grounds. At the port of Lagos trade in used computers is flourishing with 500 40-foot containers per month, 75 per cent of which are not repairable or resalable, according to the Basel Action Network (BAN), an environmental non government organisation. In addition, despite the growth of its ICT industries, Nigeria does not have the infrastructure for electronics recycling. So in shipyards, unprotected workers, many of them children, dismantle computers and televisions to find the copper, iron and other metals that can be sold. Workers earn about USD 2 a day this way. The remaining plastic, cables and casings are burned or dumped. Agbobloshie dump site in Accra, Ghana, is another bad example. According to research by the environmental journalist Mike Anane, only 10 per

cent of imported computers are put into use, while the 90 per cent remain dumped at the site.

The Nigeria's University of Ibadan has found evidence of excess heavy metals in the soil, plants and vegetables near dumps. In Ghana, Green Peace found toxic metals 100 times above regular levels. The organisation also found chemicals such as phthalates which interfere with sexual reproduction and chlorinated dioxins that promote cancer. Even though the Basel Convention, a United Nations treaty, has banned the transfer of hazardous waste from developed to less developed countries since 1992, it has proven difficult to enforce. A 1995 Basel Ban Amendment prohibits the export of hazardous waste even for recycling.

In Ghana, European computer imports are often labelled "refurbished" or "usable second-hand goods", even if they prove to be of no use. According to the Nigerian Environmental Ministry, most of the 500 tonnes of electronic equipment imported each day is accompanied by unclear documentation. Since measures set by Nigerian authorities to halt imports of old computers, telephones and other material are not sufficient, the government is setting up a national committee. In South Africa, though levels or e-waste are not recorded, the Information Technology Association has partnered with the Swiss government to develop an e-waste model. African countries need

133

to strengthen their own regulatory regimes to protect human health and the environment and donors are willing to help.

According to the US National Safety Council, in the United States alone there are more than 300 million obsolete computers, so policies that restrict hazardous materials in computers and stronger controls on re-exporting have to be pushed. Manufacturers must have recycling programmes that cover the entire lifecycle of their products. The European Union recently adopted a directive to restrict the use of certain hazardous substances in electrical and electronic equipment sold in the EU. There are a lot of programmes aimed at promoting the use of refurbished computers in Africa, which raises many questions especially when low cost new computers are becoming more available.

Human Capacity Building in ICT and Innovation Skills

Efforts to improve educational levels are crucial and are already being carried out by companies and organisations to fill critical skilled shortages in Africa. Several expanding ICT companies are unable to find adequately trained personnel. Microsoft's South African Innovation Centres and the International Youth Foundation promote the Student2Business job enablement programme that aims to place 10 000 graduates in jobs by 2010. IBM is setting up an Innovation Centre in Johannesburg to help companies develop ICT skills and workers meet business challenges. The centre will give access to 38 innovation centres and 60 R&D laboratories that IBM has worldwide. MTN is investing in skills development to deal with South Africa's human resources shortage. CISCO is also investing in skills development with the Global Talent Acceleration Program in South Africa.

The AfDB is investing in information and technology skills at two regional Centres of Excellence in ICT in Tunisia and Rwanda and in a High Tech Centre in ICT in Mali. These centres train senior level

managers, entrepreneurs, government and private sector employees, and university students pursuing advanced ICT studies. The International Telecommunication Union (ITU) is promoting a scholarship for ICT studies, a Youth Education Scheme (YES), and an internship to develop ICT professional skills, the Youth Incentive Scheme (YIS). Applications for YES can be 12 times higher than for scholarships. Only Alcatel-Lucent and Thales Communications are participating on YIS by offering training, but taking into account the large number of ICT companies in Africa, more should be involved[13]. The ITU is also promoting a project aiming to raise ICT awareness in indigenous communities. The UN Conference on Trade and Development (UNCTAD) is providing custom training for engineers and technicians from least developed African countries under its Connect Africa project. Lesotho is the first pilot project and gets 220 computers and open source software. UNCTAD is also working on courses that concentrate on biotechnology and ICTs. Nine courses were held between 2006 and 2008 in China, Egypt, India, South Africa, Tanzania and Tunisia. There are three times more applications than there are places. (See Box 35)

To help the staff of regulatory agency personnel, the World Bank and InfoDev are working with the ITU on an ICT in Regulation Toolkit. The World Bank Institute has since 2001 worked with the Centre d'Études de Politiques pour le Développement (CEPOD) in Senegal, to create the first francophone platform for training on infrastructure regulation. Between 2001 and 2005, CEPOD organised 21 seminars and has trained 736 students from 22 countries. The World Bank Institute has also supported a research centre on infrastructure regulation, the Centre de Recherche Micro-économiques du Développement (CREMIDE) in Côte d'Ivoire. The centre has trained a large number of economists who were later hired by operators and regulators. There is a masters in Telecommunications Regulation organised by the World Bank, Télécom ParisTech and regulatory authorities in France, Burkina Faso and Senegal, that seeks to upgrade skills in regulatory agencies, ministries, and operators in francophone Africa.

---

13. For further information see URL: http://www.itu.int/ITU-D/youth/YouthIncentiveScheme/index.html.

Box 35 - The Pan-African E-Network: South-South Capacity Building

The Pan-African E-Network African Union initiative estimated at INR5429 million envisages setting up a network connecting Indian institutions with the 53 African countries, through satellite and fibre optic links (http://www.panafricanenetwork.com/). The network is designed to have 169 VSAT terminals, with 3 VSAT terminals in each country to provide e-education, e-health and Heads of State connectivity with a satellite hub in Senegal.

The e-education services will be provided from 7 reputed universities in India and 5 leading universities in Africa. The e-health services for specialist healthcare services in Africa will be provided through 12 hospitals in India and 5 in Africa. The project is conceived as a mechanism triggering e-education and e-health services that should be sustainable in Africa. African countries should be able to carry on with their own services after 5 years.

The pilot project in Ethiopia has been successful. 40 students in Addis Ababa and Haramaya universities are taking the MBA course from IGNOU at New Delhi through tele-education. The Black Lion and the Nekempte hospitals are receiving online medical consultation from medical specialists of CARE Hospital in Hyderabad in India. It is expected to scale up quickly. By 2009, 32 African countries have signed agreements with Telecommunications Consultants India Limited to implement the Pan-African E-Network. ICT has been estimated to be the main growth area in India-Africa trade relations.

Source: Telecommunications Consultants India Limited (TCIL).

135

Incubating African business

Africa is mainly an importer of information and communications technology. The NEPAD initiative has sought to promoting technical change and innovation by building skills in local software R&D. The project will be implemented through the African Virtual Open Initiatives and Resources (AVOIR) programme that currently works in Kenya, Mozambique, Senegal, South Africa, Tanzania and Uganda. To support and promoting access to scientific knowledge for African scientists, decision makers, students and researchers, UNECA has launched the "Access to Scientific Knowledge in Africa (ASKIA)" initiative seeking to provide ways for African scientists to tap into global scientific knowledge and develop indigenous knowledge that supports economic and industrial growth.

Microsoft has opened the Innovation Laboratory in Cairo with cutting edge technology. To promote business and social values in local cultures, efforts are made to measure, analyse and enhance Web searches in Arabic and to digitalise books in Arabic by using images instead of the optical character recognition used for the Latin alphabet and others. The laboratory is trying to make it easier to browse and search multimedia content through platforms with limited connectivity such as mobile phones. Microsoft's 3 innovation centres in South Africa promote software innovation and help open source solution builders test software on Microsoft to ensure compatibility. Other Innovation Centres are going to be launched in Morocco, Nigeria, Uganda and Rwanda.

Compared to other regions of the world, new business incubation is in its infancy in Africa and the opportunities for innovation and entrepreneurial networking are not as developed as in Eastern Europe, Central Asia and Latin America. There are still some interesting initiatives. The World Bank is developing InfoDev's Business Incubator Initiative in Africa to work on more than 26 ideas, with a special focus on micro and small and

Box 36 - Business Process Outsourcing in Ghana: The Bangalore of West Africa?

Ghana Cyber City is a technology cluster on a 36 acre technology park being built in Accra. It is setting the stage for work between SMEs to encourage outsourcing to come to Africa. According to Gartner, Business Process Outsourcing (BPO) was a USD 128.8 billion market in 2005 and is forecasted at USD 191.3 billion market by 2010 with the offshore ICT industry growing at 21 per cent. Ghana's BPO could create 37 000 jobs with revenues of USD 750 million over 5 years.

According to the AT Kearney's Global Services Location Index, Ghana scored better than India and China in financial attractiveness in 2007 and had a similar business environment. The volume of talent pool is however half that of China and India. The government is seeking stronger training. Ghana is competitive in low-skill, low-margin areas such as transcription services, account activation, surveys and basic consumer care. Major Indian players are moving towards higher-value work such as transaction processing and analysis of consumer behaviour.

Source: Author.

medium sized companies. This financial and technical assistance aims to help entrepreneurs to leverage ICT on a global level. Knowledge sharing is a key element promoted across Africa through the pan-African network on business incubation (ANI) launched in 2006. Seeking to work with Asia, Eastern Europe and Central Asia, Latin America and the Caribbean and Middle East, infoDev has its Incubator Support Centre (iDISC). This is a virtual platform seeking the technology to help entrepreneurs and new business creation in developing countries.

Several InfoDev incubators are being developed in North Africa. The Elgazala Park of Communications Technologies is the first of 24 incubators in Tunisia, the Casablanca Technology Park, Al Akhawayn University Incubator and Morocco Incubation and Spin-off Network are being developed in Morocco and the Biotechnology and Engineering Technology in Libya. In Sub-Saharan Africa, BusyInternet in Ghana was created in 2001 and has already seen 11 ICT companies set up. In Nigeria, InfoDev's first privately owned and managed incubator, Nextzon Business Incubator, has brought on 15 companies. In Uganda, the Industrial Research Industry offers training to rural companies that turn raw products into semi-finished or processed commodities. Other examples can be

found in Angola, Kenya, Mozambique, Rwanda, Senegal and South Africa.

Measuring Africa's technology progress

There is no doubt that Africa is making strides in technological and scientific development and innovation. But indicators are crucial to formulate policies. The ITU, OECD, UNCTAD, UNESCO Institute for Statistics, the UN Regional Commissions, the World Bank and EUROSTAT all took part in the development of indicators for ICT for Development in 2004. It was an important attempt to compare experience across several countries, but does not fully account for the continent's innovation. NEPAD is going to develop a pan-African Science, Technology and Innovation Indicator (STII) and an African Science, Technology and Innovation Observatory that will prepare an African Innovation Outlook. These are expected to be developed with the OECD, Eurostat and UNESCO. The African Ministerial Council on Science and Technology recently confirmed the decision of the first inter-government meeting on STII in Maputo in 2007 to adopt the Frascati and Oslo manuals for collecting statistics on Africa. There is widespread agreement between the OECD, EU and Africa on the definition of innovation in Africa.

136

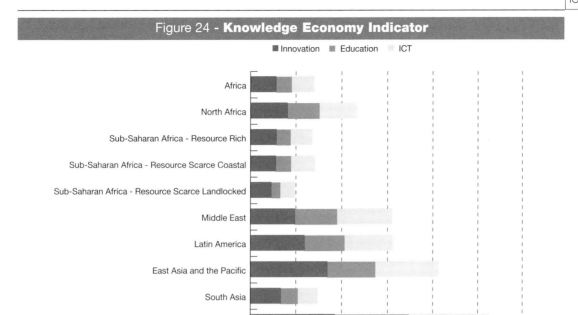

Figure 24 - **Knowledge Economy Indicator**

■ Innovation ■ Education ☐ ICT

Source: World Bank Knowledge Assessment Methodology (www.worldbank.org/kam).

StatLink ⊞⬛ *http://dx.doi.org/10.1787/568604734845*

137

The World Bank uses a knowledge economy indicator (KEI) composed of ICT, education and innovation parameters that can be seen in Figure 24. Fifteen countries are missing but the data still gives good preliminary evidence[14]. Africa's knowledge information indicator lags behind the Middle East, Latin America, East Asia, the Pacific and Western Europe. Sub-Saharan countries, especially resource scarce landlocked countries, are the worst African performers and they are closely followed on the world scale by South Asia. The score of North African countries is between Sub-Saharan and Middle East and Latin American nations. While the educational sub-index is smaller in all developing regions than in Western Europe, this component is particularly low in Sub-Saharan Africa. This indicator might not be the best way of measuring innovation, but it indicates the scarcity of education in Sub-Saharan Africa to build innovation-based economies.

---

14. There are no innovation surveys in Africa with the exception of South Africa. This indicator includes inputs to innovation such as patents granted by USPTO per 1 000 people on average for 2002-2006 and scientific and technical journal articles per 1 000 People in 2005. The indicator also includes total royalty payments and receipts in USD per population in 2006.

Part Three

Statistical Annex

List of Tables

143

Methodology

When used, the oil exporting countries group refers to Algeria, Angola, Cameroon, Chad, Congo Dem.Rep, Congo Rep., Cote d'Ivoire, Egypt, Equatorial Guinea, Gabon, Libya, Nigeria, Sudan

Tables 1 to 6.

Where indicated, the figures are reported on a fiscal-year basis. Figures for Egypt, Ethiopia, Kenya, Lesotho, Liberia, Malawi, Mauritius, Tanzania, and Uganda are from July to June in the reference year. For South Africa, Namibia and Botswana, fiscal year 2007 is from April 2007 to March 2008.

Table 7. Exports, 2007

The table is based on exports disaggregated at 6 digit level (following the Harmonised System, rev.1)

Table 8. Diversification and Competitiveness

The diversification indicator measures the extent to which exports are diversified. It is constructed as the inverse of a Herfindahl index, using disaggregated exports at 4 digits (following the Harmonised System, rev.1). A higher index indicates more export diversification. The competitiveness indicator has two aspects: the sectoral effect and the global competitivity effect. In order to compute both competitiveness indicators, we decompose the growth of exports into three components: the growth rate of total international trade over the reference period (2003-2007) (not reported); the contribution to a country's export growth of the dynamics of the sectoral markets where the country sells its products, assuming that its sectoral market shares are constant (a weighted average of the differences between the sectoral export growth rates –measured at the world level – and total international trade growth, the weights being the shares of the corresponding products in the country's total exports); the competitiveness effect, or the balance (export growth minus world growth and sector effect), measuring the contribution of changes in sectoral market shares to a country's export growth.

Table 10. Foreign Direct Investment, 2002-07

The UNCTAD Inward Potential Index is based on 12 economic and structural variables measured by their respective scores on a range of 0-1 (raw data are available on: www.unctad.org/wir). It is the unweighted average of scores of: GDP per capita, the rate of growth of GDP, the share of exports in GDP, telecom infrastructure (the average number of telephone lines per 1 000 inhabitants, and number of mobile phones per 1 000 inhabitants), commercial energy use per capita, share of R&D expenditures in gross national income, share of tertiary students in the population, country risk, exports of natural resources as a percentage of the world total, imports of parts and components of electronics and automobiles as a percentage of the world total, and inward FDI stock as a percentage of the world total (Source: UNCTAD, *World Investment Report* 2008).

Table 11. Aid Flows, 2002-07

The DAC countries are: Australia, Austria, Belgium, Canada, Denmark, Finland, France, Germany, Greece, Ireland, Italy, Japan, Luxembourg, the Netherlands, New Zealand, Norway, Portugal, Spain, Sweden, Switzerland, United Kingdom, United States and the Commission of the European Communities.

Table 13. Demographic Indicators

Infant mortality rate: under one-year-old child deaths per live birth per year.

Total fertility rate: average number of children per woman.

Mortality under age 5: probability that a newborn infant would die before the age of 5.

Table 14. Poverty and Income Distribution Indicators

National poverty line: absolute poverty line corresponding to the value of consumption necessary

144

to satisfy minimum subsistence needs. International poverty line: absolute poverty line corresponding to a level of income or consumption of $1 or $2 a day.

Gini index: index measuring the intensity of inequality in income or consumption expenditure distribution. Perfect equality leads to a Gini index of zero and maximum inequality to a Gini index of 100. Share of consumption: share of total consumption for a decile of the population ranked by level of consumption.

Table 15. Access to Services

The Sanitation coverage is the percentage of the population with access to improved sanitation technologies (connection to a public sewer, connection to septic system, pour-flush latrine, simple pit latrine or ventilated improved pit latrine). The water supply coverage is the percentage of the population with access to improved water supply (household connection, public standpipe, borehole, protected dug well and protected spring or rainwater collection).

Table 16. Basic Health Indicators

Life expectancy at birth is the average number of years a newborn infant would live under the hypothesis that, during its life, the conditions of mortality remain the same as observed at its birth. Life expectancy at birth with AIDS is the estimated average number of years a newborn infant would live under the hypothesis that, during its life, the conditions of mortality remain the same as observed at its birth in particular the characteristics of AIDS epidemic. Life expectancy at birth without AIDS is the estimated number of years a newborn infant would live under the hypothesis of absence of AIDS during its life. Under nourishment prevalence is the proportion of the population that is suffering insufficient food intake to meet dietary energy requirements continuously. Food availability is the available nutritious food for human consumption expressed in kilo-calories per person per day (note

that the recommended daily caloric intake for an active healthy life is 2 100 calories). Public share of total health expenditure is calculated by defining public health expenditure as current and capital outlays of government, compulsory social security schemes, extra-budgetary funds dedicated to health services delivery or financing and grants and loans provided by international agencies, other national authorities and commercial banks. Private share of total health expenditure is calculated by defining private expenditure as private insurance schemes and prepaid medical care plans, services delivered or financed by enterprises, outlays by non-governmental organisations and non-profit institutions serving mainly households, out-of-pocket payments, and other privately funded schemes not elsewhere classified, including investment outlays.

Table 17. Major Diseases

Healthy life expectancy at birth is the average equivalent number of years in full health a newborn infant would live under the hypothesis that, during its life, the conditions of mortality and ill-health remain the same as observed at its birth.

People living with HIV/AIDS is estimated whether or not they have developed symptoms of AIDS.

HIV/AIDS adult prevalence is the estimate of the adult population (15-49) living with HIV/AIDS. Malaria notified cases are cases of malaria reported from the different local case detection and reporting systems. These figures should be considered with caution because of the diversity of sources and probable underestimation. The Measles incidence is the number of new cases of measles reported during the reference year.

MCV: Measles Containing Vaccine.

DTP3: Third dose of Diphtheria and Tetanus toxoids and Pertussis vaccine.

145

Table 19. School Enrolment

Gross enrolment ratio: population enrolled in a specific level of education, regardless of age, expressed as a percentage of the official school-age pupils enrolled in that level. Net enrolment ratio: official school-age population enrolled in a specific level of education expressed as a percentage of the total population enrolled in that level.

Table 20. Employment and Remittances

Participation rate: measure of the proportion of a country's working-age population that engages actively in the labour market, either by working or looking for work. It provides an indication of the relative size of the supply of labour available to engage in the production of goods and services.

Total unemployment: proportion of the labour force that does not have a job and is actively looking for work.

Inactivity rate: percentage of the population that is neither working nor seeking work (that is, not in the labour force).

Table 21. Corruption Perception Index, 2002-08

The Corruption Perception Index (CPI) is a composite indicator based on surveys of business people and assessments of country analysts. A background paper presenting the methodology and validity of the CPI is available on the Transparency International website:
http://www.transparency.org/policy_research/surveys_indices/cpi/2008/methodology

Table 22 to 24. Political Indicators

The political indicators were built on information taken from the weekly newspaper *Marchés Tropicaux et Méditerranéens* according to a methodology first proposed by Dessus, Lafay and Morrisson[1]. Since 2008, the source used to calculate the indicators has changed, now being Agence France Presse. This introduces a break in the series and comparison of 2008 indicator with past values must be done with caution. The qualitative information is either computed as 0-1 variables with 0 being the non-occurrence of the event and 1 its occurrence or as 4-value indicators (with 0: non-occurrence, 1: occurrence but weak intensity, 2: medium intensity and 3: strong intensity). From these indicators, three main political indexes are constructed: an index of conflicts, a measure of the softening of the political regime and one of its hardening. The annual aggregation method has been improved in 2008, and applied to all the series. The average value across quarters is now taken and computed according to the following formula:

$$PI_i = (I_i - \min i)/(\max i - \min i)$$

Where PI_i is the political indicator for country i, I is the average indicator across quarters, $\min i$ is the minimum quarterly value for country i, and $\max i$ is the maximum quarterly value for country i.

In 2008/09 AEO report, the names of political troubles and hardening of the regime indicator were changed to Civil Tensions and State Pressure over Civil Liberties.

Table 22. Civil Tensions

• **Strikes**
0 = non-occurrence,
1 = 1 strike or number of strikers lower than 1 000 (inclusive),
2 = 2 strikes or number of strikers between 1 000 and 5 000 (inclusive),
3 = 3 strikes or number of strikers higher than 5 000.

• **Unrest and violence (number of dead and injured)**

---

1. Dessus. S., D. Lafay and C. Morrisson (1994), "A Politico-economic Model for Stabilisation in Africa", *Journal of African Economies*.

Dead

0 = none,

1 = between 1 and 10 (non inclusive),

2 = between 10 and 100 (non inclusive),

3 = higher than 100.

Injured

0 = none,

1 = between 1 and 50 (non inclusive) or if the number of dead is between 1 and 10,

2 = between 50 and 500 (non inclusive) or if the number of dead is between 10 and 100,

3 = higher than 500 or if the number of dead exceeds 100.

• **Demonstrations**

0 = non-occurrence,

1 = 1 demonstration or number of strikers lower than 5 000 (non inclusive),

2 = 2 demonstrations or number of strikers between 5 000 and 10 000 (non inclusive),

3 = 3 demonstrations or number of strikers higher than 10 000.

• **Coup d'état and attempted coups d'état**

Table 23. Softening of the Regime

• **Lifting of state of emergency**

• **Releases of political prisoners**

• **Measures in favour of human rights**

• **Improvement of political governance (fight against corruption…)**

• **Relinquishment of political persecution, rehabilitation, return from exile**

• **Political opening (measures in favour of democracy)**

1 = Discussion with the opposition,

2 = Entry of the opposition to power,

3 = Opening of a regime to elections.

• **Lifting of bans on strikes or demonstration**

• **Lifting of bans on press or public debates**

Table 24. State Pressure over Civil Liberties

• **State of emergency**

• **Arrests, incarcerations**

0 = non-occurrence,

1 = between 1 and 10 (non inclusive),

2 = between 10 and 100 (non inclusive),

3 = higher than 100.

• **Additional resources for the police, propaganda or censorship**

• **Toughening of the political environment (expulsions, dismissals, curfew, and dissolution of political parties)**

• **Violence perpetuated by the police (number of dead and injured)**

Dead

0 = none,

1 = between 1 and 10 (non inclusive),

2 = between 10 and 100 (non inclusive),

3 = higher or equal to 100.

Injured

0 = none,

1 = between 1 and 50 (non inclusive),

2 = between 50 and 500 (non inclusive),

3 = higher or equal to 500.

• **Prosecutions, executions**

• **Bans on strikes and demonstrations**

• **Bans on press or public debates**

• **Closing of schools**

• **Obligatory demonstrations**

A principal component analysis was undertaken in order to determine a relevant weight for each qualitative variable within the synthetic indexes.

147

Weights in "Civil Tensions"

	Weights
Strike	0.286
Dead	0.950
Injured	0.958
Demonstration	0.543
Coups d'état and attempts	0.059

Weights in "Softening of the Regime"

	Weights
Lifting of state of emergency	0.282
Release of political prisoners	0.709
Measures in favour of human rights	0.373
Improvement of political governance	0.089
Relinquishment of political persecution	0.502
Political opening	0.373
Lifting of bans on strikes	0.323
Lifting of bans on public debates	0.522

Weights in "State Pressure over Civil Liberties"

	Weights
State of emergency	0.631
Violence perpetuated by the police: Dead	0.261
Injured	0.423
Arrests	0.402
Additional resources for the police	0.603
Toughening of the political environment	0.253
Prosecutions, executions	0.583
Bans on strikes	0.383
Bans on demonstrations	0.292
Closing of schools	0.092

Tables

Table 1 - Basic Indicators, 2008

	Population (thousands)	Land area (thousands of km²)	Population Density (pop/km²)	GDP (PPP valuation, USD million)	GDP per Capita (PPP valuation, USD)	Annual real GDP growth (average over 2000-2008)
Algeria	34 373	2 382	14	208 113	6 054	3,8
Angola	18 021	1 247	14	134 722	7 699	12,4
Benin	8 662	111	82	12 521	1 345	4,3
Botswana	1 921	567	3	24 673	12 948	5,1
Burkina Faso	15 234	274	54	18 478	1 215	5,2
Burundi	8 074	26	331	2 997	338	2,4
Cameroon	19 088	465	40	44 167	2 334	3,7
Cape Verde	499	4	132	1 971	3 634	6,4
Central Afr. Rep.	4 339	623	7	3 866	874	1,9
Chad	10 914	1 259	9	11 697	1 055	8,4
Comoros	661	2	336	785	913	1,9
Congo	3 615	342	11	16 071	4 177	4,4
Congo, Dem. Rep.	64 257	2 267	28	21 264	329	3,6
Côte d'Ivoire	20 591	318	61	34 863	1 777	0,0
Djibouti	849	23	36	1 980	2 336	3,4
Egypt *	81 527	995	76	454 460	5 914	5,0
Equatorial Guinea	659	28	18	17 462	33 600	20,3
Eritrea	4 927	101	48	3 743	748	0,3
Ethiopia*	80 713	1 000	79	68 307	802	6,8
Gabon	1 448	258	5	23 454	17 371	2,1
Gambia	1 660	10	171	1 587	905	5,1
Ghana	23 351	228	103	29 965	1 251	5,4
Guinea	9 833	246	38	10 691	1 117	3,0
Guinea Bissau	1 575	28	60	905	519	1,4
Kenya	38 765	569	66	81 832	2 123	3,9
Lesotho	2 049	30	66	2 862	1 417	4,0
Liberia	3 793	96	39	1 948	494	3,7

Table 1 - Basic Indicators, 2008 (cont.)

	Population (thousands)	Land area (thousands of km²)	Population Density (pop/km²)	GDP (PPP valuation, USD million)	GDP per Capita (PPP valuation, USD)	Annual real GDP growth (average over 2000-2008)
Libya	6 294	1 760	3	73 923	11 765	5,1
Madagascar	19 111	582	34	16 951	839	4,0
Malawi	14 846	94	148	8 602	602	3,8
Mali	12 706	1 220	10	14 649	1 152	4,6
Mauritania	3 215	1 031	3	6 488	2 025	4,4
Mauritius	1 280	2	622	16 069	12 637	3,6
Morocco	31 606	446	69	139 852	4 425	4,8
Mozambique	22 383	786	27	27 563	1 264	7,5
Namibia	2 130	823	3	12 869	6 122	4,8
Niger	14 704	1 267	11	9 795	665	4,4
Nigeria	151 212	911	162	315 823	2 085	8,4
Rwanda	9 721	25	395	8 837	883	6,8
São Tomé and Principe	160	1	165	257	1 605	5,7
Senegal	12 211	193	64	21 048	1 659	4,2
Seychelles	84	0,5	185	1 817	20 881	3,0
Sierra Leone	5 560	72	82	5 194	870	10,3
Somalia	8 926	627	14	...	...	...
South Africa	49 668	1 214	39	461 767	9 456	4,1
Sudan	41 348	2 376	16	87 020	2 206	7,6
Swaziland	1 168	17	67	5 397	4 700	2,5
Tanzania	42 484	886	46	48 229	1 163	6,8
Togo	6 459	54	121	4 884	722	1,3
Tunisia	10 169	155	66	91 264	8 742	4,9
Uganda	31 657	197	157	43 739	1 371	7,0
Zambia	12 620	743	16	17 374	1 429	5,0
Zimbabwe	12 463	387	35	...	...	-5,5
Africa	987 092	29 367	85	2 675 993	2 777	5,3

Note: * Fiscal year July (n-1)/June (n)
Sources: United Nations, Department of Economic and Social Affairs, Population Division, World Population Prospects, The 2008 Revision. Special extract. For GDP data, authors' estimates, IMF *World Economic Outlook* (October 2008), World Bank *World Development Indicators* (March 2009).

Table 2 - Real GDP Growth Rates, 2000-2010

	2000	2001	2002	2003	2004	2005	2006	2007	2008 (e)	2009 (p)	2010 (p)
Algeria	2.2	2.1	4.7	6.9	5.2	5.1	2.0	3.0	3.3	0.2	3.7
Angola	3.0	3.1	14.5	3.3	11.2	20.6	18.6	21.0	15.8	-7.2	9.3
Benin	4.9	6.2	4.4	3.9	3.1	2.9	3.8	4.6	5.0	5.3	5.6
Botswana	5.9	3.6	8.8	6.3	6.0	1.6	5.1	4.4	3.9	2.6	2.9
Burkina Faso	1.9	7.1	4.7	8.0	4.6	7.1	5.5	3.6	4.2	6.0	4.2
Burundi	-0.9	2.1	4.5	-1.2	4.4	0.9	5.5	3.6	3.2	2.9	3.0
Cameroon	4.2	4.5	4.0	4.0	3.7	2.3	3.2	3.4	4.1	3.1	3.4
Cape Verde	7.3	6.1	5.3	4.7	4.4	5.8	10.8	6.9	6.1	3.6	4.6
Central Afr. Rep.	1.3	2.7	0.3	-4.6	3.5	3.0	4.3	4.2	2.6	3.2	5.0
Chad	-0.5	11.5	8.5	14.3	33.7	7.9	0.2	0.1	0.2	-0.7	2.7
Comoros	1.4	3.3	4.1	2.5	-0.2	4.2	1.2	0.5	0.5	1.7	2.5
Congo	7.6	3.8	4.6	0.8	3.5	7.8	6.2	-1.6	7.0	7.7	5.2
Congo Dem. Rep.	-6.9	-2.1	3.5	5.8	6.6	7.9	5.6	6.3	5.7	-0.6	2.7
Côte d'Ivoire	-3.7	0.0	-1.4	-1.6	1.8	1.2	-0.3	1.8	2.3	3.8	4.1
Djibouti	0.5	2.0	2.6	3.2	3.0	3.2	4.8	5.3	5.9	6.5	6.8
Egypt *	5.4	3.5	3.2	3.2	4.1	4.5	6.8	7.1	7.2	4.3	4.0
Equatorial Guinea	13.1	67.8	20.4	14.4	32.7	8.8	5.3	10.3	9.9	3.7	2.9
Eritrea	-12.4	8.8	3.0	-2.7	1.5	2.6	-1.0	1.3	1.2	2.0	6.0
Ethiopia*	5.9	7.7	1.2	-3.5	12.3	8.7	5.4	11.5	11.6	6.5	7.0
Gabon	-1.9	2.1	-0.3	2.5	1.4	3.0	1.2	5.6	5.5	4.0	4.6
Gambia	5.5	5.8	-3.2	6.9	7.0	5.1	6.5	6.3	5.7	5.0	5.0
Ghana	3.7	4.2	4.5	5.2	5.6	5.9	6.4	6.3	6.4	5.8	6.1
Guinea	2.5	3.7	5.2	1.2	2.3	3.0	2.5	1.8	4.7	3.8	4.4
Guinea Bissau	7.5	0.2	-7.1	-0.6	2.2	3.2	1.8	2.5	3.2	3.1	3.3
Kenya	0.5	4.5	0.5	2.9	5.1	5.8	6.4	7.0	2.6	5.0	4.3
Lesotho	4.5	3.0	1.6	3.9	4.6	0.7	8.1	5.1	4.2	3.8	5.3
Liberia	25.7	2.9	3.7	-31.3	2.6	5.3	7.8	9.5	7.3	10.8	11.2

Table 2 - Real GDP Growth Rates, 2000-2010 (cont.)

	2000	2001	2002	2003	2004	2005	2006	2007	2008 (e)	2009 (p)	2010 (p)
Libya	3.7	-4.3	-1.3	13.0	4.4	10.3	6.7	6.8	6.5	3.4	3.7
Madagascar	4.5	6.0	-12.4	9.8	5.3	4.6	5.0	6.2	7.0	4.8	7.6
Malawi	0.8	-4.1	1.9	4.2	5.0	2.3	8.2	7.9	8.4	6.5	5.4
Mali	-3.1	11.2	4.4	7.7	2.8	6.1	5.3	3.2	3.6	4.2	5.1
Mauritania	1.9	2.9	1.1	5.6	5.2	5.4	11.4	1.0	5.2	3.4	4.5
Mauritius	2.6	2.6	1.9	4.3	5.8	1.2	3.9	5.4	4.8	3.0	3.3
Morocco	1.8	7.6	3.3	6.1	4.8	3.0	7.8	2.7	5.7	5.4	5.4
Mozambique	1.5	12.3	9.2	6.5	7.9	8.4	8.7	7.0	6.2	4.0	5.2
Namibia	3.5	1.2	4.8	4.2	12.3	2.5	7.1	4.1	3.4	2.7	3.1
Niger	-2.6	7.4	5.3	7.7	-0.8	7.2	4.8	5.7	4.8	1.8	5.7
Nigeria	5.3	8.2	21.2	9.6	6.6	6.5	6.0	6.2	6.1	4.0	4.4
Rwanda	8.1	6.7	9.4	0.9	5.3	7.2	7.3	7.9	8.5	6.6	5.7
São Tomé and Principe	0.4	3.1	11.6	5.4	6.6	5.7	6.7	6.0	5.8	6.0	6.0
Senegal	3.2	4.6	0.7	6.7	5.9	5.6	2.3	4.8	3.7	3.5	3.6
Seychelles	4.2	-2.3	1.2	-5.9	7.5	8.3	7.3	5.5	1.5	-0.4	2.9
Sierra Leone	3.8	18.2	27.4	9.5	7.4	7.3	7.4	6.4	5.4	6.3	5.5
Somalia	..	..	..	..	..	..	..	..	..	..	..
South Africa	4.2	2.7	3.7	3.1	4.9	5.0	5.3	5.1	3.1	1.1	3.5
Sudan	8.4	6.2	5.4	7.1	5.1	6.3	11.3	10.2	8.4	5.0	5.2
Swaziland	2.0	1.0	1.8	3.9	2.5	2.2	2.9	3.5	2.6	2.5	2.0
Tanzania	4.9	6.0	7.2	6.9	7.8	7.4	6.7	7.1	6.8	6.1	6.7
Togo	-1.0	-1.3	-1.3	4.8	2.5	1.2	3.9	1.9	0.8	3.9	4.1
Tunisia	4.7	4.9	1.7	5.6	6.0	4.0	5.5	6.3	5.1	4.1	4.2
Uganda	2.3	8.8	7.1	6.2	5.8	10.0	7.0	8.6	7.0	5.6	6.1
Zambia	3.6	4.9	3.3	5.1	5.4	5.2	6.2	6.1	5.5	2.8	4.1
Zimbabwe	-7.3	-2.7	-4.4	-10.4	-3.6	-4.0	-5.4	-6.1	..	..	..
Africa	3.7	4.2	5.4	5.0	5.6	5.7	6.0	6.1	5.7	2.8	4.5

Note: * Fiscal year July (n-1)/June (n)
Sources: Authors' estimates and forecasts, various domestic authorities; IMF *World Economic Outlook* (October 2008).

153

154

Table 3 - Demand Composition and Growth Rate, 2007-2010

	2007						2008(e)						2009(p)						2010(p)					
	Final Consumption		Gross Capital Formation		External Sector		Total Final Con-sump-tion	Gross Capital Forma-tion - Total	Exports	Imports			Total Final Con-sump-tion	Gross Capital Forma-tion - Total	Exports	Imports			Total Final Con-sump-tion	Gross Capital Forma-tion - Total	Exports	Imports		
	Private	Public	Private	Public	Exports	Imports																		
	Percentage of GDP						Real Percentage Growth						Real Percentage Growth						Real Percentage Growth					
Algeria	31.3	11.9	23.9	11.1	46.9	25.0	4.2	5.5	1.8	6.0			4.9	8.0	-6.0	11.4			4.8	6.3	1.0	5.9		
Angola	32.6	21.2	2.2	11.6	71.3	39.0	17.7	48.2	10.2	18.4			7.1	-34.1	-4.4	0.5			7.3	6.0	5.8	3.4		
Benin	75.8	12.3	12.6	8.1	19.5	28.3	4.1	12.8	4.8	7.5			6.7	11.6	-2.6	6.7			6.9	13.0	-0.1	9.9		
Botswana	40.3	20.2	19.4	7.5	49.5	36.9	3.9	11.9	1.3	6.0			4.2	6.1	-1.0	2.9			4.7	8.3	-0.2	5.9		
Burkina Faso	76.2	22.9	9.5	5.7	10.5	24.8	3.7	10.1	4.8	6.2			3.4	4.5	5.9	-2.4			3.7	8.0	4.9	4.9		
Burundi	85.1	30.7	2.3	9.3	6.8	34.2	2.7	6.2	0.6	1.9			0.9	6.6	3.7	-3.2			2.1	10.0	0.5	2.0		
Cameroon	71.3	10.1	14.5	2.2	24.2	22.4	2.6	6.9	6.6	3.2			3.1	4.7	1.7	3.0			2.9	4.7	4.0	3.2		
Cape Verde	75.7	18.5	40.5	4.9	17.7	57.2	4.3	14.6	14.9	12.1			4.5	8.2	-16.7	2.4			2.5	9.3	10.1	6.5		
Central Afr. Rep.	91.3	6.2	6.1	3.8	14.8	22.3	4.9	16.7	-11.9	6.9			3.7	18.1	-8.9	4.0			4.3	13.4	1.7	4.7		
Chad	28.2	23.4	12.0	4.0	54.7	22.4	-2.1	-35.7	1.3	-31.8			0.4	1.0	-1.5	1.0			4.8	5.2	3.7	14.7		
Congo	52.5	18.6	15.6	10.6	80.3	77.6	-1.2	5.8	9.0	1.7			0.4	5.9	6.8	0.6			0.9	5.2	4.7	1.3		
Congo Dem. Rep.	76.0	9.4	15.9	2.3	46.0	49.5	0.9	11.9	18.6	6.4			0.7	-9.0	-6.9	-5.8			0.1	5.5	5.9	0.9		
Côte d'Ivoire	75.2	8.7	6.1	2.7	47.7	40.5	1.7	14.7	1.5	3.3			2.7	12.9	2.0	2.4			3.8	15.0	3.8	6.4		
Djibouti	50.1	27.3	42.3	11.5	62.2	93.4	3.6	17.5	6.1	10.9			5.1	10.1	5.5	7.0			4.4	6.9	6.3	4.6		
Egypt *	72.4	11.3	12.9	7.9	30.2	34.8	5.3	15.5	29.0	26.0			4.4	10.4	4.3	8.6			5.1	9.4	1.9	9.0		
Equatorial Guinea	6.9	2.7	11.3	19.9	95.8	36.5	1.7	7.1	6.3	3.0			4.7	5.0	0.2	0.2			3.0	5.6	1.6	2.7		
Ethiopia*	84.0	10.5	9.3	15.7	12.8	32.2	13.9	7.0	17.2	23.1			7.5	3.9	3.9	6.3			7.7	7.2	8.6	9.4		
Gabon	32.1	12.2	17.4	6.2	65.0	32.9	7.4	4.5	3.2	4.0			6.7	1.4	1.7	2.6			7.4	3.2	2.3	4.2		
Gambia	80.2	10.7	13.1	11.9	53.8	69.7	17.5	10.3	-6.1	22.4			-0.6	9.5	4.4	-4.7			3.5	7.2	3.0	1.4		
Ghana	74.4	18.4	19.5	14.2	39.8	66.3	3.2	4.5	5.8	1.6			6.5	5.1	3.2	4.8			4.2	5.0	6.9	3.8		
Guinea	78.7	6.7	17.2	2.7	27.5	32.8	0.8	13.7	5.6	2.4			4.9	-8.6	3.2	-7.6			2.5	7.6	5.7	2.3		
Kenya	74.8	17.2	15.5	4.6	26.6	38.8	4.2	10.5	-2.0	5.3			4.8	8.0	1.2	3.5			5.8	9.0	1.6	7.2		
Lesotho	99.0	33.8	20.6	3.7	55.6	112.8	2.2	4.3	2.3	1.2			2.6	4.2	0.9	0.9			1.1	5.2	6.5	1.4		
Liberia	70.3	30.1	57.3	12.5	50.4	120.6	6.2	7.1	5.9	6.1			6.0	7.2	1.4	2.8			5.5	13.5	8.8	8.2		

Table 3 - Demand Composition and Growth Rate, 2007-2010 (cont.)

	2007						2008(e)					2009(p)					2010(p)				
	Final Consumption		Gross Capital Formation		External Sector		Total Final Consumption	Gross Capital Formation - Total	Exports	Imports		Total Final Consumption	Gross Capital Formation - Total	Exports	Imports		Total Final Consumption	Gross Capital Formation - Total	Exports	Imports	
	Private	Public	Private	Public	Exports	Imports															
	Percentage of GDP						Real Percentage Growth					Real Percentage Growth					Real Percentage Growth				
Libya	26.0	11.8	6.8	19.3	65.6	29.5	10.3	14.8	-0.8	26.3		8.5	5.5	-4.6	17.2		3.9	9.6	2.4	11.2	
Madagascar	78.0	11.7	19.7	6.7	28.6	44.6	13.4	50.2	-2.9	47.1		11.2	-17.8	0.8	-4.4		7.2	-2.3	19.6	5.6	
Malawi	86.1	12.2	10.2	14.1	23.0	45.7	7.3	18.8	19.0	16.3		7.4	7.8	-4.2	4.6		5.1	4.0	2.6	2.7	
Mali	75.0	10.9	13.6	8.8	26.4	34.7	3.6	5.8	2.3	4.0		3.3	3.4	3.2	0.9		5.7	6.3	4.0	6.8	
Mauritania	73.7	21.7	16.4	6.0	54.5	72.2	11.9	15.4	1.1	14.3		3.6	4.1	0.5	2.5		1.7	5.3	4.9	1.5	
Mauritius	70.4	13.1	21.4	5.5	58.8	69.2	4.1	3.0	4.4	3.1		2.9	0.9	-0.2	-0.5		2.5	3.4	2.7	1.8	
Morocco	58.4	18.2	29.7	2.8	35.8	44.9	7.0	5.8	4.0	6.8		6.8	7.2	4.3	8.6		4.4	7.4	8.6	7.8	
Mozambique	78.1	11.8	6.3	11.7	37.6	45.5	4.5	27.3	2.6	10.5		4.1	13.5	1.4	8.3		4.6	7.8	3.7	4.9	
Namibia	61.8	19.2	14.0	6.9	47.9	49.7	6.6	13.0	-2.2	6.7		6.4	8.4	-3.5	5.2		3.7	9.8	2.5	6.4	
Niger	71.9	17.2	17.9	7.3	19.0	33.4	7.1	4.6	1.4	8.6		2.8	4.2	-11.1	0.6		5.6	4.3	14.5	7.5	
Nigeria	46.7	18.8	16.0	8.0	40.3	29.7	11.6	16.3	-2.1	12.8		3.9	7.3	2.4	4.5		4.5	7.3	2.8	5.1	
Rwanda	86.3	10.9	12.4	8.8	10.0	28.3	9.6	13.3	2.3	14.0		9.4	1.9	1.4	12.0		6.4	6.6	5.8	9.0	
Senegal	77.3	13.7	20.6	6.5	23.0	41.2	3.2	7.0	1.2	3.5		3.4	3.0	0.9	1.4		3.2	6.0	1.4	3.1	
Seychelles	59.3	35.1	26.8	5.6	96.6	123.4	-4.6	-3.0	4.2	-4.1		-6.6	-4.5	-3.6	-11.0		3.2	1.6	1.0	0.9	
Sierra Leone	83.4	10.5	10.0	3.5	20.9	28.3	7.9	5.0	-2.6	10.4		8.2	12.1	8.2	15.5		6.1	14.3	1.1	8.3	
South Africa	61.4	19.7	15.8	6.2	31.5	34.6	1.7	7.1	1.7	1.1		0.4	1.9	-0.6	-1.3		3.2	8.4	2.0	4.9	
Sudan	61.6	15.6	17.0	9.6	20.1	23.9	3.4	14.0	22.6	8.3		4.2	6.6	5.1	4.7		3.6	9.2	6.5	6.4	
Swaziland	73.5	14.9	6.1	6.8	79.9	81.2	-1.8	11.0	2.6	-0.4		0.3	0.9	-0.8	-3.2		2.6	7.3	2.7	4.3	
Tanzania	67.9	19.3	21.8	7.8	24.2	41.1	7.6	19.7	2.6	16.9		7.1	4.4	0.9	4.0		7.8	10.0	3.4	10.7	
Togo	99.6	10.1	8.9	2.0	42.0	62.6	1.5	21.0	1.5	6.2		1.2	16.4	3.0	1.5		3.1	13.5	5.6	6.0	
Tunisia	62.0	14.7	19.6	6.0	55.8	58.1	5.1	9.3	3.0	5.1		5.4	8.9	5.8	10.2		3.4	5.8	5.5	4.7	
Uganda	80.4	11.9	17.5	5.1	16.1	31.1	7.7	16.5	2.5	13.3		5.3	3.0	1.9	0.7		7.0	10.0	2.4	9.6	
Zambia	53.7	18.9	16.7	5.6	39.6	34.3	6.5	11.5	7.6	12.2		2.4	-1.3	-4.4	-5.2		3.7	5.0	4.1	4.0	

Note: * Fiscal year July (n-1)/June (n).
Sources: Authors' estimates and projections, Various domestic authorities and IMF *World Economic Outlook* (October 2008).

155

156

Table 4 - Public Finances, 2007-2010 (percentage of GDP)

	2007			2008(e)			2009(p)			2010(p)		
	Total revenue and grants	Total expenditure and net lending	Overall balance	Total revenue and grants	Total expenditure and net lending	Overall balance	Total revenue and grants	Total expenditure and net lending	Overall balance	Total revenue and grants	Total expenditure and net lending	Overall balance
Algeria	39.3	34.5	4.8	39.1	32.3	6.8	28.9	40.3	-11.5	29.1	40.1	-10.9
Angola	45.1	34.0	11.2	47.2	36.4	10.8	36.8	45.5	-8.7	36.2	43.1	-6.9
Benin	24.0	22.2	1.9	22.2	22.7	-0.5	21.3	22.3	-1.0	21.7	22.3	-0.7
Botswana**	40.7	34.2	6.5	37.5	37.7	-0.3	31.0	31.5	-0.5	32.3	31.9	0.4
Burkina Faso	20.1	25.8	-5.7	19.9	26.3	-6.4	18.5	25.5	-6.9	18.4	25.7	-7.3
Burundi	35.9	38.8	-3.0	31.1	40.0	-8.9	69.3	36.9	32.4	30.1	39.8	-9.8
Cameroon	19.9	15.6	4.4	21.7	15.7	5.9	18.8	16.0	2.8	18.7	16.0	2.7
Cape Verde	28.5	29.3	-0.8	28.3	29.5	-1.2	28.2	31.8	-3.7	26.8	30.5	-3.7
Central Afr. Rep.	14.3	12.7	1.5	13.8	13.3	0.5	13.2	13.7	-0.5	13.3	13.8	-0.5
Chad	25.8	19.0	6.8	27.2	14.5	12.7	22.5	17.2	5.3	23.3	17.3	6.1
Comoros	20.3	22.3	-2.0	23.6	21.6	2.0	18.5	21.1	-2.6	19.1	21.2	-2.1
Congo	43.1	32.0	11.1	48.9	24.0	24.9	39.2	29.3	9.9	40.4	26.8	13.6
Congo Dem. Rep.	17.5	17.8	-0.3	15.5	21.3	-5.8	14.2	23.2	-9.0	13.1	20.9	-7.9
Côte d'Ivoire	20.0	20.7	-0.8	20.3	20.6	-0.2	18.8	20.1	-1.3	19.7	21.3	-1.6
Djibouti	35.4	38.0	-2.6	36.0	38.5	-2.4	36.1	38.0	-1.9	36.5	38.4	-2.0
Egypt *	24.2	29.8	-5.6	24.7	31.5	-6.8	25.0	32.1	-7.1	24.9	31.6	-6.7
Equatorial Guinea	41.4	23.2	18.2	41.6	18.5	23.0	38.3	30.6	7.8	38.0	29.8	8.2
Eritrea	25.3	35.3	-10.0	25.5	33.8	-8.3	25.6	33.7	-8.1	27.9	35.0	-7.1
Ethiopia*	17.7	21.4	-3.7	17.2	20.3	-3.1	18.0	19.8	-1.8	16.8	18.1	-1.3
Gabon	29.9	21.3	8.6	30.6	17.7	12.9	28.6	21.9	6.7	28.6	20.3	8.4
Gambia	22.9	22.7	0.2	23.9	24.9	-1.1	22.4	24.8	-2.4	22.9	26.7	-3.8
Ghana	28.6	37.0	-8.4	28.0	38.0	-10.0	25.9	35.1	-9.2	26.0	35.2	-9.1
Guinea	15.7	15.2	0.5	17.4	16.4	1.0	14.7	15.0	-0.3	14.1	16.4	-2.3
Guinea Bissau	31.6	41.9	-10.3	41.9	40.8	1.1	25.0	37.6	-12.6	25.0	37.5	-12.5
Kenya*	22.6	23.7	-1.1	25.4	31.5	-6.1	22.3	25.2	-3.0	21.3	24.4	-3.0
Lesotho*	60.4	48.3	12.2	84.9	74.1	10.8	70.1	54.9	15.2	72.0	55.4	16.6
Liberia*	29.3	24.3	5.0	23.4	22.3	1.1	27.5	25.9	1.6	26.6	24.0	2.6

Table 4 - Public Finances, 2007-2010 (percentage of GDP) (cont.)

	2007			2008(e)			2009(p)			2010(p)		
	Total revenue and grants	Total expenditure and net lending	Overall balance	Total revenue and grants	Total expenditure and net lending	Overall balance	Total revenue and grants	Total expenditure and net lending	Overall balance	Total revenue and grants	Total expenditure and net lending	Overall balance
Libya	61.4	35.2	26.2	66.8	32.3	34.5	47.4	46.4	0.9	48.9	46.3	2.6
Madagascar	15.2	17.8	-2.6	17.5	22.0	-4.5	15.7	18.9	-3.2	15.1	18.9	-3.9
Malawi*	31.7	33.0	-1.3	30.1	32.8	-2.7	31.3	34.3	-2.9	32.1	34.2	-2.2
Mali	21.7	25.1	-3.4	20.8	26.1	-5.4	19.7	23.6	-3.9	20.1	24.4	-4.3
Mauritania	26.5	29.2	-2.7	27.4	31.2	-3.7	26.2	30.9	-4.7	25.2	30.6	-5.4
Mauritius*	19.2	23.5	-4.3	21.5	24.8	-3.4	20.1	23.4	-3.2	20.5	22.6	-2.1
Morocco	25.0	24.8	0.2	24.2	23.4	0.8	23.9	23.5	0.4	24.1	23.5	0.6
Mozambique	25.3	28.2	-2.9	28.7	33.1	-4.4	30.3	35.5	-5.2	28.8	34.1	-5.2
Namibia**	28.9	28.0	0.9	27.3	30.9	-3.6	27.8	31.2	-3.4	31.4	30.3	1.1
Niger	25.1	22.3	2.8	27.2	22.2	5.1	26.1	22.9	3.2	25.6	22.6	3.0
Nigeria	28.3	27.8	0.4	27.3	26.4	0.9	19.0	30.1	-11.1	18.8	30.5	-11.7
Rwanda	25.2	26.9	-1.7	26.9	27.2	-0.3	24.7	24.7	-0.1	23.7	24.8	-1.1
São Tomé and Principe	160.2	40.0	120.2	74.3	32.7	41.6	26.2	31.0	-4.8	26.5	30.2	-3.7
Senegal	23.4	27.2	-3.8	23.5	28.0	-4.5	22.2	26.5	-4.3	22.1	26.8	-4.7
Seychelles	36.0	40.8	-4.7	36.9	36.8	0.1	35.6	39.1	-3.5	35.2	38.6	-3.4
Sierra Leone	42.8	17.6	25.2	16.8	16.8	0.0	15.3	16.0	-0.7	14.0	15.6	-1.5
Somalia	...	...	...	...	...	...	...	...	...	...	...	...
South Africa**	27.1	26.3	0.9	26.4	27.4	-1.0	26.1	29.8	-3.7	27.3	30.1	-2.9
Sudan	20.7	26.1	-5.4	25.1	24.5	0.5	17.8	28.4	-10.6	17.8	28.7	-10.9
Swaziland	43.0	32.5	10.5	40.5	33.9	6.5	42.9	33.0	9.8	39.9	30.9	9.0
Tanzania*	19.0	23.0	-4.0	23.2	23.3	0.0	21.2	23.3	-2.1	20.5	22.0	-1.5
Togo	18.7	19.4	-0.7	19.8	20.1	-0.3	20.4	20.1	0.4	20.9	19.9	1.0
Tunisia	23.9	26.8	-2.8	23.8	26.9	-3.0	23.5	26.7	-3.2	23.2	26.6	-3.3
Uganda*	18.0	19.9	-1.9	18.3	20.5	-2.2	16.7	19.0	-2.4	15.5	18.1	-2.6
Zambia	21.2	24.1	-3.0	23.1	25.2	-2.1	25.5	27.9	-2.3	24.3	27.3	-3.0
Zimbabwe	97.4	97.8	-0.4	...	...	...	...	...	...	...	...	...
Africa	30.2	28.2	1.9	31.0	28.2	2.8	25.7	31.1	-5.4	25.8	30.8	-5.0

Note: * Fiscal year July (n-1)/June (n) ** Fiscal Year April (n)/March (n+1).
Sources: Authors' estimates and projections, various domestic authorities and IMF *World Economic Outlook* (October 2008).

157

Table 5 - Monetary Indicators

	Inflation (%)				Exchange Rate (LCU / USD)				Broad Money (LCU billion) 2008			Reserves, excluding gold (USD million) 2008	
	2007	2008(e)	2009(p)	2010(p)	2006	2007	2008	Level	% of GDP	Growth 2007/08	Stock at year-end	Eq. Months of imports
Algeria	3.5	4.3	3.3	3.1	72.6	69.3	64.4	7 697.6	65.0	25.0	136 599.0	59.2
Angola	11.8	13.2	9.8	9.4	80.4	76.8	72.7	1 286.1	18.4	25.1	19 786.5	9.9
Benin	1.3	8.1	6.3	4.5	522.6	479.2	452.8	916.7	30.6	8.4	1 365.6	12.2
Botswana	7.1	12.6	9.2	6.3	5.8	6.1	6.8	39.4	44.4	22.2	10 197.2	30.0
Burkina Faso	-0.2	9.3	5.4	3.5	522.6	479.2	452.8	893.0	25.2	9.8	980.6	6.2
Burundi	8.3	24.5	13.1	3.7	1 028.7	1 081.9	1 184.4	390.7	28.6	18.4	211.1	10.4
Cameroon	1.5	5.7	5.4	5.0	522.6	479.2	452.8	2 219.5	20.6	9.2	3 104.0	7.0
Cape Verde	4.3	6.7	3.8	2.1	87.9	80.6	76.1	107.8	81.7	14.0	...	3.2
Central Afr. Rep.	0.9	9.2	5.6	2.9	522.6	479.2	452.8	111.0	12.5	-6.3	127.8	3.6
Chad	-9.0	8.1	3.2	2.1	522.6	479.2	452.8	462.1	11.9	16.2	1 241.8	16.7
Comoros	4.5	5.9	3.8	3.0	0.0	0.0	0.0	34.5	19.2	6.9	112.0	7.8
Congo	2.6	5.4	3.2	3.4	522.6	479.2	452.8	795.6	14.0	11.4	3 394.8	9.1
Congo, Dem. Rep.	16.7	26.2	25.2	21.7	468.3	516.0	560.0	889.5	12.6	38.7	213.2	0.5
Côte d'Ivoire	1.9	6.4	5.4	2.9	522.6	479.2	452.8	3 062.9	29.9	8.0	2 289.2	3.1
Djibouti	5.0	11.9	7.6	6.5	177.7	177.7	177.7	134.0	77.5	13.5	171.0	3.1
Egypt	11.2	11.7	13.0	7.3	5.7	5.6	5.4	...	...	...	32 907.2	7.4
Equatorial Guinea	2.8	5.5	4.7	4.2	522.6	479.2	452.8	622.3	7.2	38.3	4 632.5	15.8
Eritrea	9.3	11.0	10.5	9.7	15.4	15.4	15.4	27.0	118.7	7.7	...	...
Ethiopia	17.8	25.0	15.1	10.0	8.7	8.8	9.2	68.9	29.5	21.2	...	...
Gabon	5.0	5.4	3.2	3.2	522.6	479.2	452.8	1 139.5	16.6	8.8	1 696.2	6.7
Gambia	5.4	6.4	5.6	6.2	28.1	24.9	20.6	9.3	51.8	12.2	142.1	6.7
Ghana	10.7	14.1	8.1	7.3	9 169.5	9 355.0	10 524.3	75 264.1	42.9	30.5	...	...
Guinea	22.9	19.3	11.0	11.2	3 644.3	4 485.0	4 639.3	4 216.1	20.3	24.1	...	...
Guinea Bissau	4.6	9.6	6.2	2.7	522.6	479.2	452.8	83.6	44.4	20.7	148.1	6.9
Kenya	9.8	25.8	9.1	6.8	72.1	67.3	67.6	933.1	44.1	20.0	3 264.0	2.8
Lesotho	8.0	10.7	9.8	7.0	6.8	7.0	8.3	4.4	34.3	12.9	...	...
Liberia	11.4	17.5	7.9	7.7	1.0	1.0	1.0	15.6	1684.1	30.3	148.6	1.7

Table 5 - Monetary Indicators (cont.)

	Inflation (%)				Exchange Rate (LCU / USD)				Broad Money (LCU billion) 2008			Reserves, excluding gold (USD million) 2008	
	2007	2008(e)	2009(p)	2010(p)	2006	2007	2008	Level	% of GDP	Growth 2007/08	Stock at year-end	Eq. Months of imports
Libya	6.7	11.2	7.1	7.1	1.3	1.3	1.2	...	0.0	0.0	97 604.9	45.0
Madagascar	10.3	9.2	11.7	7.1	2 142.3	1 873.1	1 658.1	3 453.5	21.4	22.7	1 009.9	4.1
Malawi	7.9	8.3	7.5	6.5	136.0	140.0	141.6	96.1	16.6	15.1	132.0	1.2
Mali	1.4	9.3	5.6	2.5	522.6	479.2	452.8	1 049.4	27.8	4.3	1 065.2	5.0
Mauritania	7.3	7.4	6.4	6.2	268.6	258.6	243.5	250.5	27.7	18.4	227.2	1.3
Mauritius	8.8	9.8	6.5	5.7	31.7	31.3	28.7	424.6	169.2	9.5	2 055.0	4.8
Morocco	2.2	3.9	2.2	2.8	8.8	8.2	7.8	733.0	107.6	16.0	24 156.5	7.4
Mozambique	8.2	10.4	7.3	6.1	24 982.1	25 671.2	23 985.3	79 324.4	33.8	18.2	1 684.4	3.6
Namibia	6.7	10.3	8.6	7.2	6.8	7.0	8.3	31.3	52.6	16.2	1 359.9	4.1
Niger	0.1	10.9	4.1	4.3	522.6	479.2	452.8	410.6	18.1	14.5	831.9	6.9
Nigeria	5.4	11.0	10.2	10.1	128.7	125.8	117.8	7 397.6	28.9	53.7	62 082.7	15.7
Rwanda	9.1	14.4	8.8	7.9	551.7	547.0	546.4	419.3	19.4	11.7	593.5	10.5
São Tomé and Príncipe	18.5	25.9	18.1	12.8	12 448.6	13 536.8	14 699.0	993.7	39.0	21.0	...	...
Senegal	5.9	5.8	4.0	3.4	522.6	479.2	452.8	2 403.4	40.2	21.8	1 458.9	2.9
Seychelles	5.3	37.0	23.4	10.2	5.5	6.7	9.3	5.0	80.5	8.0	94.9	1.0
Sierra Leone	12.1	13.0	11.1	9.0	2 961.9	2 985.2	2 976.7	1 360.1	23.2	20.5	222.4	4.5
Somalia	...	...	...	...	1 546.7	1 423.7	1 435.7	...	...	...	...	...
South Africa*	7.2	11.5	6.7	5.9	6.8	7.1	8.3	1 986.0	85.9	19.0	30 832.0	4.3
Sudan	8.8	14.2	8.3	7.4	2.2	2.1	2.2	23.9	19.2	21.0	2 292.2	2.3
Swaziland	8.1	12.6	8.3	6.3	6.8	7.0	8.3	5.8	25.5	10.6	835.0	4.6
Tanzania	7.0	10.3	9.1	8.4	1 251.9	1 245.0	1 194.3	6 365.9	26.1	22.7	2 689.4	5.6
Togo	1.0	8.9	5.3	2.8	522.6	479.2	452.8	510.9	40.0	10.0	614.6	4.6
Tunisia	3.1	5.0	2.9	3.1	1.3	1.3	1.3	33.0	66.9	10.5	8 471.4	4.7
Uganda	6.1	12.0	9.5	8.6	1 831.5	1 723.5	1 723.3	5 037.0	20.9	31.1	2 663.1	7.2
Zambia	10.7	12.9	9.9	7.1	3 603.1	4 002.5	3 761.1	12 598.9	23.4	17.7	1 170.7	2.8
Zimbabwe	6 723.7	2 311 509	...	...	164.4	9 675.8	2654602 447.2	...	...	...	...	...
Africa	7.5	11.6	8.1	6.5	...	...	...	...	...	...	466 880.3	12.4

Note: StatSA modified the reference for the Consumer Price Index in February 2009.
Sources: Authors' estimates and predictions; IMF *World Economic Outlook* (October 2008) and *International Financial Statistics* (March 2009).

160

Table 6 - Balance of Payments Indicators 2007-2010

	Trade balance (USD million)				Current account balance (USD million)				Current account balance (as % of GDP)			
	2007	2008(e)	2009(p)	2010(p)	2007	2008(e)	2009(p)	2010(p)	2007	2008(e)	2009(p)	2010(p)
Algeria	34 108	45 699	15 088	16 148	30 386	38 883	7 458	10 058	22.4	24.5	5.6	7.0
Angola	29 115	56 631	19 890	24 779	7 066	15 376	-7 221	-7 054	11.5	12.9	-8.1	-7.0
Benin	- 643	- 753	- 677	- 805	- 372	- 450	- 494	- 582	-6.7	-7.1	-7.8	-8.3
Botswana	1 622	1 289	1 048	1 004	1 973	1 557	1 280	1 193	16.6	13.5	11.5	10.1
Burkina Faso	- 597	- 789	- 517	- 574	- 618	- 838	- 683	- 755	-9.1	-10.2	-8.7	-9.0
Burundi	- 205	- 244	- 192	- 205	- 116	- 185	- 98	- 150	-12.4	-16.6	-8.4	-12.4
Cameroon	328	1 083	614	625	86	574	50	58	0.4	2.3	0.2	0.2
Cape Verde	- 664	- 891	- 754	- 810	- 132	- 214	- 173	- 128	-8.7	-11.0	-9.6	-6.6
Central African Rep.	- 71	- 172	- 129	- 146	- 104	- 217	- 162	- 190	-6.1	-9.4	-7.4	-8.1
Chad	2 351	2 666	1 420	1 554	- 476	491	- 163	68	-6.8	8.0	-3.8	1.4
Comoros	- 116	- 156	- 154	- 162	- 31	- 45	- 57	- 57	-6.7	-8.1	-9.5	-9.1
Congo. Republic of	3 190	7 183	4 166	4 901	-1 477	88	-2 850	-2 580	-19.3	0.6	-27.4	-22.6
Congo Dem. Rep.	208	918	461	754	- 191	84	- 331	- 302	-1.8	0.7	-2.9	-2.2
Côte d'Ivoire	2 545	3 303	2 287	2 260	- 135	514	- 69	- 293	-0.7	2.2	-0.3	-1.3
Djibouti	- 451	- 577	- 539	- 586	- 204	- 318	- 239	- 232	-24.2	-31.1	-20.7	-19.2
Egypt*	-16 291	-23 415	-28 505	-28 738	2 269	889	-2 188	-3 588	1.7	0.5	-1.2	-1.8
Equatorial Guinea	7 447	11 640	4 994	5 728	110	3 721	-2	104	1.0	24.0	0.0	1.1
Eritrea	- 358	- 363	- 360	- 335	- 49	- 44	- 34	- 5	-3.7	-3.0	-2.1	-0.3
Ethiopia *	-3 943	-5 348	-4 556	-4 501	- 589	-1 170	-1 160	- 922	-3.0	-4.7	-5.0	-3.7
Gabon	4 922	8 295	4 170	4 649	1 707	3 517	- 426	444	14.9	21.3	-3.5	3.4
Gambia. The	- 172	- 187	- 156	- 163	- 80	- 112	- 61	- 70	-12.5	-18.3	-8.8	-10.0
Ghana	-3 879	-3 974	-2 921	-3 347	-1 885	-1 686	-2 154	-2 930	-12.4	-11.5	-13.1	-17.9
Guinea	- 14	- 86	68	104	- 456	- 658	- 443	- 458	-11.8	-14.3	-9.7	-9.2
Guinea-Bissau	- 44	- 84	- 73	- 75	- 8	1	- 56	- 54	-2.2	0.2	-11.6	-10.6
Kenya	-4 258	-6 800	-5 358	-5 481	-1 102	-1 750	- 165	38	-4.1	-4.2	-0.4	0.1
Lesotho	- 799	- 739	- 739	- 715	211	- 59	106	19	12.6	-4.5	8.9	1.4
Liberia	- 291	- 622	- 481	- 502	- 274	- 349	- 73	101	-48.1	-28.8	-5.7	7.0

Table 6 - Balance of Payments Indicators 2007-2010 *(cont.)*

	Trade balance (USD million)				Current account balance (USD million)				Current account balance (as % of GDP)			
	2007	2008(e)	2009(p)	2010(p)	2007	2008(e)	2009(p)	2010(p)	2007	2008(e)	2009(p)	2010(p)
Libya	27 122	34 408	6 656	6 815	23 785	28 376	2 081	4 517	34.1	32.3	3.3	6.5
Madagascar	-1 003	-1 831	-1 506	-1 568	-1 070	-2 119	-1 920	-2 411	-13.9	-25.8	-21.0	-22.9
Malawi	- 601	- 442	- 451	- 493	- 74	- 160	- 89	- 193	-2.1	-5.3	-2.8	-5.9
Mali	- 247	- 205	142	- 106	- 557	- 396	- 76	- 311	-7.9	-4.7	-0.9	-3.7
Mauritania	23	85	-70	- 151	- 321	- 350	- 472	- 537	-11.3	-9.3	-13.2	-14.5
Mauritius	-1 411	-1 995	-1 577	-1 665	- 399	- 910	- 569	- 620	-5.3	-9.9	-6.1	-6.4
Morocco	-14 500	-16 787	-13 802	-15 050	- 600	-3 313	-1 768	-3 129	-0.8	-3.7	-2.0	-3.1
Mozambique	- 635	-1 739	-2 521	-2 240	- 722	-1 716	-1 952	-1 681	-9.0	-11.9	-14.0	-11.2
Namibia	454	- 928	-1 047	-1 196	1 572	298	206	125	18.0	3.6	2.7	1.4
Niger	- 158	- 417	- 432	- 479	- 320	- 657	- 720	- 848	-7.7	-12.8	-15.4	-16.3
Nigeria	26 973	31 517	8 079	9 789	5 873	6 917	-16 721	-13 611	3.5	3.2	-9.1	-6.4
Rwanda	- 404	- 488	- 444	- 492	- 168	- 303	- 254	- 301	-5.0	-7.9	-5.9	-6.2
São Tomé and Principe	-58	-66	-76	-80	-44	-47	-61	-64	-30.2	-29.6	-34.5	-33.4
Senegal	-2 329	-2 936	-2 057	-2 249	-1 259	-1 788	-1 057	-1 261	-11.3	-14.2	-8.7	-9.8
Seychelles	- 426	- 487	- 268	- 284	- 265	- 344	- 135	- 138	-29.1	-40.9	-21.5	-20.0
Sierra Leone	- 100	- 174	- 141	- 154	- 64	- 141	- 123	- 143	-3.8	-5.9	-4.4	-4.5
Somalia	...	...	...	...	...	...	...	...	...	...	...	...
South Africa	-5 749	-5 588	-4 583	-7 459	-21 142	-20 214	-14 491	-19 881	-7.5	-7.8	-6.4	-7.6
Sudan	1 133	6 082	- 297	237	-7 217	-1 841	-7 243	-9 420	-16.3	-3.4	-13.8	-15.9
Swaziland	- 309	- 326	- 163	- 149	- 104	201	383	215	-3.6	7.8	15.4	7.9
Tanzania	-2 634	-3 530	-2 785	-3 504	-1 839	-2 713	-1 912	-2 297	-10.9	-14.8	-9.7	-10.4
Togo	- 499	- 619	- 444	- 506	- 159	- 197	- 27	- 59	-6.4	-7.8	-1.1	-2.2
Tunisia	-2 870	-3 552	-3 401	-3 160	- 915	-1 764	-1 447	-1 223	-2.6	-4.2	-3.2	-2.5
Uganda	- 861	-1 971	-1 494	-1 864	- 378	-1 633	-1 199	-1 635	-2.8	-9.8	-7.3	-8.9
Zambia	841	41	-1 038	- 992	- 783	-1 303	-1 811	-1 984	-6.7	-9.1	-17.0	-17.3
Zimbabwe	- 21	...	...	...	- 165	...	...	...	-3.5	...	...	...
Africa	74 770	121 557	-15 624	-11 642	28 172	51 481	-61 787	-65 161	2.2	3.3	-4.4	-4.1

Note: * Fiscal year July (n-1)/June (n)
Source: Authors' estimates and projections; Various domestic authorities; IMF *World Economic Outlook* (October 2008).

161

Table 7 - Exports, 2007

Three main exports*, with their share in total exports**

	Product I	Product II	Product III	No. of products accounting for more than 75 per cent of exports
Algeria	Petroleum oils and oils obtained from bituminous minerals, crude (63.1%)	Petroleum oils and oils obtained from bituminous minerals, other than crude (10.5%)	Liquefied :-- Natural gas (9.7%)	3
Angola	Petroleum oils and oils obtained from bituminous minerals, crude (96.7%)			1
Benin	Cotton, not carded or combed. (29.8%)	Petroleum oils and oils obtained from bituminous minerals, other than crude (20.8%)	Copper waste and scrap. (10.9%)	5
Botswana	Diamonds, whether or not worked, but not mounted or set. Unworked or simply sawn, cleaved or bruted (56.0%)	Nickel mattes (21.2%)	Copper mattes (3.7%)	2
Burkina Faso	Cotton, not carded or combed. (71.6%)	Sesamum seeds (4.3%)	Guavas, mangoes and mangosteens (2.6%)	2
Burundi	Coffee, not roasted :-- Not decaffeinated (62.1%)	Black tea (fermented) & partly fermented tea in packages exceedg 3 kg (4.3%)	Other black tea (fermented) and other partly fermented tea (3.4%)	6
Cameroon	Petroleum oils and oils obtained from bituminous minerals, crude (52.7%)	Wood sawn or chipped lengthwise, sliced or peeled, whether or not planed, sanded or end-jointed, of a thickness exceeding 6 mm. (9.1%)	Cocoa beans, whole or broken, raw or roasted. (6.1%)	5
Cape Verde	Fish, frozen, excluding fish fillets and other fish meat of heading 03.04. (25.4%)	Cotton, not carded or combed. (12.9%)	Cocoa paste, not defatted (10.2%)	9
Central African Republic	Wood in the rough, whether or not stripped of bark or sapwood, or roughly squared. (30.3%)	Diamonds, whether or not worked, but not mounted or set. Unsorted (21.4%)	Cotton, not carded or combed. (16.8%)	4
Chad	Petroleum oils and oils obtained from bituminous minerals, crude (95.3%)	Cotton, not carded or combed. (2.3%)		1
Comoros	Vessels and other floating structures for breaking up (31.0%)	Cloves (whole fruit, cloves and stems) (19.8%)	Essential oils (terpeneless or not), including concretes and absolutes resinoids extracted oleoresins (19.0%)	4
Congo	Petroleum oils and oils obtained from bituminous minerals, crude (83.2%)			1
Congo Democratic Republic	Diamonds, whether or not worked, but not mounted or set. Unworked or simply sawn, cleaved or bruted (24.6%)	Petroleum oils and oils obtained from bituminous minerals, crude (14.9%)	Cobalt ores and concentrates (14.7%)	6
Cote d'Ivoire	Cocoa beans, whole or broken, raw or roasted (29.4%)	Petroleum oils and oils obtained from bituminous minerals, crude (17.0%)	Cocoa paste, not defatted (6.3%)	9

Table 7 - Exports, 2007 (cont.)

Three main exports*, with their share in total exports**

	Product I	Product II	Product III	No. of products accounting for more than 75 per cent of exports
Djibouti	Sheep (26.9%)	Goats (24.0%)	Petroleum oils and oils obtained from bituminous minerals, other than crude (14.0%)	4
Egypt	Liquefied :-- Natural gas (18.2%)	Petroleum oils and oils obtained from bituminous minerals, crude (11.6%)	Petroleum oils and oils obtained from bituminous minerals, other than crude (8.7%)	68
Equatorial Guinea	Petroleum oils and oils obtained from bituminous minerals, crude (87.9%)	Methanol (methyl alcohol) (3.9%)	Liquefied :-- Natural gas (3.2%)	1
Eritrea	Natural uranium and its compounds (69.1%)	Nuclear reactors, boilers, mchy & mech appliance (6.4%)	Sesamum seeds (3.3%)	2
Ethiopia	Coffee, not roasted, not decaffeinated (42.1%)	Sesamum seeds (16.3%)	Cut flowers and flower buds of a kind suitable for bouquets or for ornamental purposes, fresh (6.5%)	7
Gabon	Petroleum oils and oils obtained from bituminous minerals, crude (71.8%)	Manganese ores and concentrates, in (9.6%)	Wood in the rough, whether or not stripped of bark or sapwood, or roughly squared. (0.0%)	2
Gambia	Cashew nuts :-- In shell (36.0%)	Titanium ores and concentrates. (8.5%)	Ground-nut oil and its fractions, crude. (8.5%)	11
Ghana	Cocoa beans, whole or broken, raw or roasted (45.6%)	Manganese ores and concentrates, in (8.4%)	Petroleum oils and oils obtained from bituminous minerals, other than crude (4.1%)	10
Guinea	Aluminium ores and concentrates. (52.4%)	Aluminium oxide other than artificial (15.3%)	Copper ores and concentrates. (7.9%)	3
Guinea Bissau	Cashew nuts :-- In shell (91.3%)			1
Kenya	Cut flowers and flower buds of a kind suitable for bouquets or for ornamental purposes, fresh (13.7%)	Other black tea (fermented) and other partly fermented tea (11.8%)	Petroleum oils and oils obtained from bituminous minerals, other than crude (5.9%)	51
Lesotho	Diamonds, whether or not worked, but not mounted or set. Unworked or simply sawn, cleaved or bruted (28.9%)	Jerseys, pullovers, cardigans, waist-coats and similar articles, knitted or crocheted, of cotton (18.5%)	Men's or boys' suits, ensembles, jackets, blazers, trousers, bib and brace overalls, breeches and shorts (other than swimwear), of cotton (14.5%)	6
Liberia	Tankers (46.1%)	Other vessels for the transport of goods and/or persons (21.9%)	Natural rubber latex, whether or not prevulcanised (11.6%)	3
Libya	Petroleum oils and oils obtained from bituminous minerals, crude (86.2%)	Petroleum oils and oils obtained from bituminous minerals, other than crude(8.9%)		1

164

Table 7 - Exports, 2007 (cont.)

Three main exports*, with their share in total exports**

	Product I	Product II	Product III	No. of products accounting for more than 75 per cent of exports
Madagascar	Jerseys, pullovers, cardigans, waist-coats and similar articles, knitted or crocheted, of wool or fine animal hair (12.4%)	Shrimps and prawns (10.1%)	Women's or girls' suits, ensembles, jackets, blazers, dresses, skirts, divided skirts, trousers, bib and brace overalls, breeches and shorts (other than swimwear). (8.0%)	26
Malawi	Tobacco, partly or wholly stemmed/s (49.5%)	Raw sugar not containing added flav (8.8%)	Other black tea (fermented) and other partly fermented tea (5.7%)	6
Mali	Cotton, not carded or combed. (70.8%)	Guavas, mangoes and mangosteens (4.4%)	Sesamum seeds (2.0%)	2
Mauritania	Iron ores and concentrates, including roasted iron pyrites. Non agglomerated (45.3%)	Petroleum oils and oils obtained from bituminous minerals, other than crude (19.0%)	Molluscs or aquatic invertebrates other than crustaceans, other than live, fresh or chilled (9.7%)	4
Mauritius	T-shirts, singlets and other vests, knitted or crocheted of cotton (17.5%)	Cane sugar and chemically pure sucrose, in solid form. (15.9%)	Prepared of Preserved Fish - Tunas, skipjack and bonito (Sarda spp.) (9.5%)	24
Morocco	Phosphoric acid and polyphosphoric acids (5.2%)	Electronic integrated circuits and microassemblies : other monolithic integrated circuits. (3.8%)	Natural calcium phosphates, natural aluminium calcium phosphates and phosphatic chalk unground. (3.2%)	72
Mozambique	Aluminium, not alloyed (51.3%)	Petroleum oils and oils obtained from bituminous minerals, other than crude (9.9%)	Electrical energy. (optional heading) (5.1%)	5
Namibia	Diamonds, whether or not worked, but not mounted or set : Unworked or simply sawn, cleaved or bruted (20.2%)	Unwrought zinc, containing by weight 99.99 % or more of zinc. (18.7%)	Natural uranium and its compounds alloys, dispersions (including cermets), ceramic products and mixtures containing natural uranium (12.1%)	7
Niger	Natural uranium and its compounds (83.7%)	Paintings, drawings and pastels (2.2%)		1
Nigeria	Petroleum oils and oils obtained from bituminous minerals, crude (87.5%)	Liquefied :-- Natural gas (6.6%)	Petroleum oils and oils obtained from bituminous minerals, other than crude (2.0%)	1
Rwanda	Coffee, not roasted, not decaffeinated (43.2%)	Tin ores and concentrates. (15.6%)	Other black tea (fermented) and other partly fermented tea (13.7%)	4
São Tomé and Principe	Cocoa beans, whole or broken, raw o (49.5%)	Prefabricated buildings. (4.6%)	Parts and accessories (other than covers, carrying cases and the like) suitable for use solely or principally with machines of headings 84.69 to 84.72. (4.6%)	12
Senegal	Petroleum oils and oils obtained from bituminous minerals, other than crude (14.3%)	Phosphoric acid and polyphosphoric acids (9.5%)	Ground-nut oil and its fractions, crude. (7.1%)	34
Seychelles	Tunas, skipjack and bonito (Sarda spp.) (47.8%)	Yellowfin tunas (Thunnus albacares) (11.0%)	Other Fish, frozen, excluding fish fillets and other fish meat of heading No. 03.04. Skipjack or stripe bellied bonito (7.9%)	5

Table 7 - Exports, 2007 (cont.)

Three main exports*, with their share in total exports**

	Product I	Product II	Product III	No. of products accounting for more than 75 per cent of exports
Sierra Leone	Diamonds, whether or not worked, but not mounted or set : Unworked or simply sawn, cleaved or bruted (31.1%)	Aluminium ores and concentrates. (11.7%)	Titanium ores and concentrates. (11.2%)	8
Somalia	Goats (33.7%)	Live bovine animals : Other than Purebred breeding animals (10.5%)	Pure-bred breeding animals (10.4%)	7
South Africa	Platinum :- Unwrought or in powder form (7.6%)	Diamonds, whether or not worked, but not mounted or set :- Unworked or simply sawn, cleaved or bruted (6.1%)	Gold (including gold plated with platinum) unwrought form. (5.1%)	102
Sudan	Petroleum oils and oils obtained from bituminous minerals, crude (92.3%)			3
Swaziland	Raw sugar not containing added flav (12.7%)	Food preparations not elsewhere specified or included. (10.2%)	Mixtures of odoriferous substances of a kind used in the food or drink (9.9%)	25
Tanzania	Tobacco, partly or wholly stemmed/s (8.5%)	Coffee, not roasted :-- Not decaffe (7.5%)	Fish fillets and other fish meat (whether or not minced), fresh or chilled. (7.4%)	36
Togo	Cocoa beans, whole or broken, raw or roasted (25.3%)	Petroleum oils and oils obtained from bituminous minerals, other than crude (13.0%)	Portland cement, aluminous cement, slag cement, supersulphate cement and similar hydraulic cements, in the form of clinkers. (8.3%)	9
Tunisia	Petroleum oils and oils obtained from bituminous minerals, crude (3.8%)	Trousers, bib and brace overalls, breeches and shorts: -- Of cotton (5.6)	Ignition wiring sets and other wiring sets of a kind used in vehicles, aircraft or ships (4.6)	82
Uganda	Coffee, not roasted :-- Not decaffe (25.6%)	Fish fillets and other fish meat (whether or not minced), fresh or chilled (12.8%)	Tobacco, partly or wholly stemmed (7.3%)	16
Zambia	Refined copper :-- Cathodes and sections of cathodes (62.1%)	Copper ores and concentrates. (6.3%)	Cobalt mattes and other intermediate products of cobalt (5.3%)	4
Zimbabwe	Nickel, not alloyed (22.7%)	Tobacco, partly or wholly stemmed (11.1%)	Nickel ores and concentrates. (9.4%)	13
Africa	Petroleum oils and oils obtained from bituminous minerals, crude (48.6%) [19.5%]	Petroleum oils and oils obtained from bituminous minerals, other than crude (4.3%) [4.0%]	Liquefied :-- Natural gas (3.4%) [22.4%]	37

Note: * Products are reported when accounting for more than 2 per cent of total exports.
** Figures in [ ] represent the share of Africa in the World export for each product.

Sources: COMTRADE Database (Harmonized system, Rev.1) - UN Statistics Division, March 2009.

165

Table 8 - Diversification and Competitiveness

	Diversification index					Annual export growth nominal (%)	Competitiveness Indicator 2003-2007 (%)	
	2003	2004	2005	2006	2007	2003-2007	Sectoral effect	Global competitiveness effect
Algeria	3.1	2.3	2.4	2.3	2.4	35.3	-0.4	15.8
Angola	1.1	1.1	1.1	1.1	1.1	81.4	17.0	44.5
Benin	4.2	3.9	4.8	6.3	6.4	0.1	2.2	-22.0
Botswana	1.3	1.4	1.4	1.8	2.8	8.2	-9.9	-6.4
Burkina Faso	2.3	2.5	1.6	1.7	1.9	21.2	-9.7	11.1
Burundi	2.8	3.4	2.0	5.4	2.6	36.3	3.7	12.7
Cameroun	4.7	4.0	4.1	3.0	3.3	19.7	3.9	-4.1
Cape Verde	14.5	13.6	7.9	10.0	9.0	33.1	-8.2	21.4
Central African Republic	5.4	5.5	4.7	4.6	5.5	0.8	-7.4	-11.7
Chad	2.2	1.4	1.7	1.2	1.1	604.8	-4.8	589.7
Comoros	1.7	2.4	4.6	5.6	4.9	3.3	-31.4	14.8
Congo	1.6	1.5	1.4	1.3	1.4	48.9	15.1	14.0
Congo Dem. Rep.	3.4	4.0	4.7	6.2	7.6	22.8	-2.7	5.7
Cote d'Ivoire	4.8	7.2	7.1	7.7	7.7	6.9	-8.0	-4.9
Djibouti	13.1	15.0	44.6	23.9	5.9	50.7	-0.8	31.6
Egypt	22.1	22.0	22.6	14.0	17.2	50.9	4.8	26.2
Equatorial Guinea	1.2	1.1	1.2	1.2	1.3	57.8	14.1	23.8
Eritrea	31.2	27.8	9.5	22.4	2.1	204.4	-5.7	190.3
Ethiopia	4.6	4.1	4.2	4.5	4.7	34.0	1.4	12.7
Gabon	1.7	1.8	1.7	1.9	1.9	18.3	13.2	-14.8
Gambia	8.2	10.7	6.1	5.2	6.6	6.8	-7.3	-5.8
Ghana	5.3	5.3	5.2	4.7	4.5	14.7	-5.1	0.0
Guinea	3.5	3.3	3.1	3.4	3.2	15.9	16.0	-19.9
Guinea Bissau	2.2	2.3	1.2	1.4	1.2	0.8	-13.0	-6.1
Kenya	18.8	18.4	17.9	19.9	21.9	12.0	-3.7	-4.1
Lesotho	7.3	7.1	7.2	7.9	6.6	13.4	-14.6	5.5
Liberia	3.1	3.4	3.3	5.0	3.5	1.6	0.6	-18.9

Table 8 - Diversification and Competitiveness (cont.)

	Diversification index					Annual export growth nominal (%)	Competitiveness Indicator 2003-2007 (%)	
	2003	2004	2005	2006	2007	2003-2007	Sectoral effect	Global competitiveness effect
Libya	1.4	1.3	1.3	1.3	1.3	52.0	17.5	14.6
Madagascar	10.5	15.7	19.6	19.5	21.2	3.2	-14.4	-2.3
Malawi	3.2	3.8	2.9	3.0	3.8	15.4	-9.2	4.8
Mali	1.5	1.3	1.5	2.9	2.0	1.1	-9.9	-8.9
Mauritania	4.5	4.2	4.1	4.4	3.9	47.9	17.8	10.3
Mauritius	13.9	11.8	12.3	12.7	13.4	4.4	-6.9	-8.5
Morocco	72.1	71.6	63.0	69.6	67.3	17.8	-4.2	2.1
Mozambique	2.8	2.6	3.1	2.7	3.5	50.8	-1.1	32.1
Namibia	10.2	7.9	5.9	5.2	9.1	42.4	6.8	24.8
Niger	2.1	3.7	2.5	2.5	1.4	43.4	21.5	2.1
Nigeria	1.3	1.2	1.3	1.2	1.3	44.8	16.4	8.5
Rwanda	2.0	1.7	2.7	2.5	4.1	-1.5	14.9	-36.2
São Tomé and Principe	2.8	5.8	3.8	5.3	3.9	-5.8	-9.8	-15.9
Senegal	19.6	19.7	10.4	25.4	22.3	12.7	-4.2	-2.9
Seychelles	3.2	3.8	4.7	3.2	3.9	-0.2	-1.7	-18.4
Sierra Leone	4.5	3.4	2.8	5.3	7.3	24.0	-6.6	10.8
Somalia	11.4	8.5	8.8	9.0	6.6	12.4	-5.4	-2.1
South Africa	54.1	51.5	50.0	46.7	45.6	24.0	6.0	-1.9
Sudan	1.6	1.5	1.4	1.3	1.2	55.9	12.4	23.7
Swaziland	17.2	17.0	18.8	20.0	20.0	15.2	-5.8	1.1
Tanzania	27.6	25.5	20.4	31.2	30.1	21.4	-1.1	2.6
Togo	11.0	9.8	13.3	11.8	9.3	-9.3	3.1	-32.3
Tunisia	47.1	44.8	43.2	44.3	35.8	20.9	-4.2	5.3
Uganda	7.3	6.7	7.8	8.0	10.4	21.6	-3.8	5.5
Zambia	5.8	4.1	3.5	2.3	2.5	98.9	27.9	51.1
Zimbabwe	11.2	13.6	15.7	15.6	10.8	7.1	9.8	-22.5
Africa	7.3	5.8	4.7	3.9	4.1	34.1	8.2	6.0

167

Sources: COMTRADE Database (Harmonized system, Rev.1) - UN Statistics Division, March 2009.

Table 9 - International Prices of Exports, 2002-2008

	Unit	2002	2003	2004	2005	2006	2007	2008
Aluminum	($/mt)	1 349.91	1 431.29	1 715.54	1 898.31	2 569.90	2 638.18	2 572.79
Banana (US)	($/mt)	528.58	374.79	524.58	602.84	677.24	675.81	844.21
Coal (Australia)	($/mt)	...	...	...	...	49.09	65.73	127.10
Cocoa	(cents/kg)	177.79	175.09	154.98	153.81	159.19	195.23	257.71
Coffee (Arabica)	(cents/kg)	135.66	141.54	177.40	253.22	252.21	272.37	308.16
Coffee (Robusta)	(cents/kg)	66.18	81.45	79.30	111.45	148.93	190.92	232.09
Copper	($/mt)	1 559.48	1 779.14	2 865.88	3 678.88	6 722.13	7 118.23	6 955.88
Cotton	(c/kg)	101.92	139.91	136.57	121.70	126.66	139.52	157.39
Fish Meal	($/mt)	605.92	610.71	648.58	730.96	1 166.33	1 177.25	1 133.08
Gold	($/toz)	309.97	363.51	409.21	444.84	604.34	696.72	871.71
Groundnut oil	($/mt)	687.08	1 243.17	1 161.00	1 060.44	970.23	1 352.08	2 131.12
Iron ore	(c/dmtu)	29.31	31.95	37.90	65.00	77.35	84.70	140.60
Lead	(c/kg)	45.27	51.50	88.65	97.64	128.97	258.00	209.07

Table 9 - International Prices of Exports, 2002-2008 (cont.)

	Unit	2002	2003	2004	2005	2006	2007	2008
Logs Cameroon	($/CM)	..	..	..	..	318.48	381.32	526.89
Maize	($/mt)	99.27	105.37	111.80	98.67	121.85	163.66	223.12
Oil (crude)	($/bbl)	24.97	28.85	38.30	54.43	65.39	72.70	97.64
Palm oil	($/mt)	390.25	443.25	471.33	422.08	478.35	780.25	948.54
Phosphate (rock)	($/mt)	40.38	38.00	40.98	42.00	44.21	70.93	345.59
Rubber (US)	(cents/kg)	..	..	..	..	231.28	248.03	284.08
Sugar (EU)	(cents/kg)	54.92	59.72	66.97	66.54	64.56	68.09	69.69
Sugar (World)	(c/kg)	15.18	15.63	15.80	21.79	32.59	22.22	28.21
Sugar (US)	(cents/kg)	46.14	47.37	45.47	46.93	48.76	45.77	46.86
Tea (Avg. 3 auctions)	(c/kg)	150.60	151.66	168.56	164.71	187.21	203.61	242.05
Tea (Mombasa)	(c/kg)	149.21	154.36	155.42	147.75	195.23	166.49	221.76
Tobacco	($/mt)	2 744.50	2 646.10	2 740.20	2 790.00	2 740.00	2 917.00	3 270.12

Source: World Bank, *Global Commodity Price Prospects*, March 2009.

169

Table 10 – Foreign Direct Investment, 2002-2007 (USD million)

	FDI inflows						FDI outflows						FDI inflows/GFCF (%)			Inward FDI* Potential
	2002	2003	2004	2005	2006	2007	2002	2003	2004	2005	2006	2007	2005	2006	2007	2006
Algeria	1065	634	882	1081	1795	1665	100	14	258	23	35	290	4.70	6.30	5.10	68
Angola	1672	3505	1449	-1304	-38	-1500	29	24	35	219	191	331	-52.70	-0.60	-17.80	76
Benin	14	45	64	53	53	48	1	0	-1	0	-2	-1	6.30	5.80	4.60	138
Botswana	405	420	392	281	489	495	43	207	-39	56	51	51	14.70	26.90	24.40	78
Burkina Faso	15	29	14	34	34	600	2	2	-9	0	1	-3	2.70	2.40	37.00	127
Burundi	0	0	0	1	0	0	0	0					0.50	...	...	...
Cameroon	602	383	319	225	309	284	-33	4	2	-9	-1	-2	6.70	7.80	6.20	112
Cape Verde	39	34	68	82	131	177	...	1	...	...	...	0	21.90	30.30	33.80	...
Central African Republic	4	13	15	17	18	27	1	...	...	...	...	...	21.50	22.40	29.00	...
Chad	924	713	495	613	700	603	0	0	...	...	...	...	48.20	45.40	34.80	...
Comoros	0	1	1	1	1	1							1.60	1.30	1.60	...
Congo	131	321	-13	724	344	352	4	2	5	3	3	4	47.50	18.30	18.90	97
Congo Dem. Rep.	117	158	10	-76	-116	720	-2	0	0	...	...	...	-7.50	-8.40	44.80	139
Cote d'Ivoire	213	165	283	312	319	427	-4	23	-26	52	-27	0	18.30	17.90	21.20	128
Djibouti	4	14	39	59	164	195	...	...	...	...	...	...	42.00	111.40	121.70	...
Egypt	647	237	2157	5376	10043	11578	28	21	159	92	148	665	32.20	49.80	42.70	83
Equatorial Guinea	323	1444	1651	1873	1656	1726	...	...	...	...	...	...	71.20	52.50	44.70	...
Eritrea	20	22	-8	-1	0	-3	...	...	...	...	...	...	-0.60	0.20	-1.20	...
Ethiopia	255	465	545	265	545	254	...	...	...	...	...	...	11.40	20.80	7.60	134
Gabon	37	206	194	60	268	269	-32	-57	-25	65	106	57	3.30	13.10	11.20	99
Gambia	43	15	49	45	71	64	...	...	...	...	...	...	37.30	57.80	40.20	115
Ghana	59	105	139	145	636	855	-2	11	-1	...	...	...	4.60	19.40	22.30	113
Guinea	30	83	98	105	108	111	0	...	-1	-5	...	...	23.40	20.00	13.70	132
Guinea Bissau	4	4	2	9	18	7	1	1	-8	1	0	-4	19.80	35.10	12.40	...
Kenya	28	82	46	21	51	728	7	2	4	10	24	36	0.60	1.20	13.10	126
Lesotho	27	42	53	57	92	106	0	0	0	...	...	...	11.20	15.50	16.70	...
Liberia	3	372	237	-1384	-205	42	403	173	304	437	346	363	-1587.00	-242.30	41.60	...

Table 10 - Foreign Direct Investment, 2002-2007 (USD million) (cont.)

	FDI inflows						FDI outflows						FDI inflows/GFCF (%)			Inward FDI* Potential
	2002	2003	2004	2005	2006	2007	2002	2003	2004	2005	2006	2007	2005	2006	2007	2006
Libya	145	143	357	1038	2013	2541	-136	63	-286	128	-534	-479	14.40	23.00	25.30	35
Madagascar	61	95	95	86	294	997	…	-5	…	1	…	…	7.60	24.60	62.30	131
Malawi	17	66	108	27	30	55	0	1	2	1	1	1	14.30	15.90	26.20	137
Mali	244	132	101	224	83	360	2	1	1	-1	1	1	26.40	7.60	30.10	123
Mauritania	67	102	392	814	155	153	…	-1	4	2	5	4	97.80	19.50	19.00	…
Mauritius	32	62	11	42	105	339	9	-5	32	48	10	58	3.10	6.70	17.90	…
Morocco	481	2314	895	1653	2450	2577	28	12	31	74	445	652	9.80	13.00	12.20	91
Mozambique	347	337	245	108	154	427	0	0	0	0	0	0	8.50	9.10	22.60	104
Namibia	181	149	226	348	387	697	-5	-10	-22	-13	-12	-3	22.20	23.60	39.90	95
Niger	2	11	20	30	51	27	-2	0	7	-4	-1	1	5.60	7.70	3.50	133
Nigeria	2040	2171	2127	4978	13956	12454	172	167	261	200	228	261	36.70	88.50	69.60	88
Rwanda	2	3	11	14	16	67	…	…	…	…	14	13	3.20	3.30	12.20	135
São Tomé and Principe	4	3	4	16	38	35	…	…	…	15	3	3	64.10	74.50	59.90	…
Senegal	78	52	77	45	220	78	34	3	13	-8	10	9	2.00	9.10	2.70	122
Seychelles	48	58	38	86	146	248	9	8	8	7	8	9	81.20	132.40	246.00	…
Sierra Leone	10	9	61	83	59	81	…	1	…	-8	0	-4	104.80	69.20	81.70	114
Somalia	0	-1	-5	24	96	141	…	…	…	…	…	…	5.10	19.80	26.00	…
South Africa	1573	734	799	6644	-527	5692	-399	565	1352	930	6725	3727	16.10	-1.20	11.50	74
Sudan	713	1349	1511	2305	3541	2436	…	…	…	…	7	11	41.30	42.20	22.90	121
Swaziland	92	-61	71	-50	36	37	-1	16	-1	-24	2	3	-9.80	7.70	7.50	…
Tanzania	388	308	331	568	522	600	0	2	…	-6	20	5	20.00	17.70	17.90	120
Togo	53	34	59	77	77	69	2	-6	-13	-15	-14	-25	18.80	16.70	13.30	130
Tunisia	821	584	639	782	3312	1618	7	5	4	13	33	20	12.10	45.50	19.60	66
Uganda	185	202	295	380	400	368	…	…	…	…	…	…	17.60	15.80	12.30	117
Zambia	303	347	364	357	616	984	…	…	…	…	…	…	19.90	22.80	35.60	129
Zimbabwe	26	4	9	103	40	69	3	0	0	1	0	3	202.00	39.80	153.80	141
Africa	14592	18719	18020	29459	45754	52982	270	1245	2050	2282	7829	6055	16.30	21.40	21.30	…

Note: * The potential Index is based on 12 economic and policy variables. See note on methodology for further details.
Source: UNCTAD, FDI Online Database (March 2009) and *World investment Report* 2008.

172

Table 11 - Aid Flows*, 2002-2007 (USD million)

	ODA net total, All donors						ODA net total, DAC countries						ODA net total, Multilateral					
	2002	2003	2004	2005	2006	2007	2002	2003	2004	2005	2006	2007	2002	2003	2004	2005	2006	2007
Algeria	328	234	315	348	208	390	123	169	235	266	205	289	63	68	80	70	-4	93
Angola	414	493	1 144	423	171	241	286	372	1 016	248	-55	86	129	122	131	176	124	137
Benin	221	301	391	348	375	470	140	196	210	208	228	238	78	106	181	141	147	229
Botswana	37	28	46	48	66	104	37	27	32	30	36	64	2	2	16	20	31	42
Burkina Faso	477	522	643	696	870	930	230	266	331	338	386	412	202	253	306	349	474	503
Burundi	172	227	359	364	415	466	85	121	186	180	222	200	87	106	173	183	193	266
Cameroon	657	895	780	414	1 689	1 933	436	752	572	331	1 505	1 697	220	143	207	81	179	227
Cape Verde	92	143	143	162	138	163	43	90	91	104	99	114	50	53	52	55	38	49
Central African Republic	60	51	110	90	133	176	40	32	55	60	65	118	20	19	55	30	68	58
Chad	231	251	330	380	284	352	67	96	163	162	153	223	162	155	164	214	128	128
Comoros	32	24	25	23	30	44	11	11	14	15	20	20	17	13	12	8	10	25
Congo	1 175	5 417	1 826	1 782	2 049	1 217	351	5 009	1 165	990	1 500	788	824	407	661	794	549	427
Congo Dem. Rep.	57	69	115	1 429	259	127	41	34	48	1 344	169	48	15	35	68	85	89	78
Côte d'Ivoire	1 068	254	161	97	251	165	831	281	197	129	199	112	236	-28	-36	-32	51	53
Djibouti	78	79	64	76	117	112	37	37	39	54	89	75	39	39	27	23	26	37
Egypt	1 237	987	1 456	995	873	1 083	1 124	775	1 176	663	537	787	83	84	260	242	287	214
Equatorial Guinea	20	21	29	38	26	31	14	18	23	30	19	26	7	3	6	9	7	6
Eritrea	230	316	263	354	129	155	121	185	177	226	63	45	96	131	90	132	67	107
Ethiopia	1 303	1 600	1 809	1 916	1 948	2 422	489	1 033	1 025	1 184	1 024	1 242	780	534	747	702	899	1 147
Gabon	72	-11	40	52	31	48	49	-41	24	29	32	34	22	30	16	23	-1	13
Gambia	60	63	55	61	74	72	18	20	12	15	25	33	40	40	43	46	43	36
Ghana	658	968	1 403	1 146	1 176	1 151	405	471	913	602	595	708	247	483	470	526	580	440
Guinea	250	242	273	199	161	224	126	135	178	126	103	122	118	107	95	61	55	92
Guinea-Bissau	59	145	76	66	82	123	26	98	29	27	39	44	34	48	48	39	43	79
Kenya	391	521	654	767	943	1 275	288	320	471	510	760	824	93	199	185	244	167	448
Lesotho	76	79	96	69	72	130	30	33	35	40	38	62	48	47	61	30	34	68
Liberia	52	107	213	232	268	696	27	70	163	144	187	226	25	36	50	87	80	469

Table 11 - Aid Flows*, 2002-2007 (USD million) (cont.)

	ODA net total, All donors						ODA net total, DAC countries						ODA net total, Multilateral					
	2002	2003	2004	2005	2006	2007	2002	2003	2004	2005	2006	2007	2002	2003	2004	2005	2006	2007
Libya**	0	0	0	24	37	19	0	0	0	17	33	15	0	0	0	3	3	2
Madagascar	371	543	1 250	914	750	892	126	225	685	498	261	387	246	319	566	417	485	499
Malawi	376	515	504	581	684	735	225	309	308	325	398	401	142	204	194	254	274	323
Mali	475	554	582	704	825	1 017	257	272	328	371	398	558	164	284	255	327	418	455
Mauritania	355	249	189	183	190	364	147	136	83	105	94	133	210	116	105	77	96	229
Mauritius	24	-15	32	34	19	75	4	-18	15	22	9	44	20	3	20	11	12	33
Morocco	486	539	707	693	1 044	1 090	217	336	394	287	567	628	135	157	244	315	361	344
Mozambique	2 218	1 049	1 243	1 290	1 605	1 777	1 661	697	731	760	938	1 073	555	349	508	528	663	681
Namibia	134	146	173	114	145	205	85	110	124	88	106	144	47	33	34	22	38	60
Niger	299	461	547	520	514	542	114	245	306	254	235	233	181	216	242	266	279	307
Nigeria	294	308	577	6 401	11 432	2 042	215	200	315	5 932	10 820	1 385	81	109	263	470	611	656
Rwanda	358	335	490	574	586	713	199	213	217	281	321	374	159	121	273	292	264	337
São Tomé and Principe	26	38	33	32	22	36	19	25	22	18	18	31	7	12	12	14	3	5
Senegal	449	454	1 053	686	826	843	243	314	755	444	509	451	196	143	299	243	305	360
Seychelles	8	9	10	15	14	3	4	5	6	8	7	1	4	3	3	7	8	2
Sierra Leone	383	337	376	348	344	535	225	208	163	129	180	381	155	125	212	220	164	154
Somalia	191	174	199	238	392	384	102	114	140	145	263	257	44	60	58	93	126	124
South Africa	505	641	628	680	720	794	375	477	459	466	561	597	128	163	168	214	159	196
Sudan	343	613	992	1 824	2 052	2 104	232	332	848	1 455	1 518	1 666	60	278	119	320	447	324
Swaziland	22	34	22	47	35	63	7	13	7	21	12	12	12	20	14	26	23	51
Tanzania	1 257	1 721	1 765	1 489	1 825	2 811	909	966	1 029	858	992	1 831	351	755	734	619	832	973
Togo	51	50	65	82	79	121	39	46	52	59	55	65	9	2	12	23	24	57
Tunisia	265	298	327	364	432	310	145	208	231	269	287	194	77	95	95	103	154	126
Uganda	732	999	1 217	1 195	1 549	1 728	466	587	684	691	938	1 002	260	411	532	502	608	721
Zambia	794	755	1 128	1 165	1 426	1 045	360	592	746	823	1 115	713	432	157	379	340	309	331
Zimbabwe	199	186	187	374	279	465	178	161	166	187	200	371	21	25	20	187	79	93
Africa Unspecified	1 554	2 107	2 404	2 379	2 828	3 706	1 341	1 758	1 944	2 024	2 411	2 946	174	345	459	354	375	683
Africa	21 675	27 127	29 520	35 525	43 492	38 720	13 367	19 142	19 334	24 589	31 490	24 529	7 608	7 743	9 987	10 586	11 484	13 600

Note: ODA: Official Development Assistance.
DAC: Development Assistance Committee of OECD.
* Net disbursements.
** Libya has belonged to the recipient countries of Official Aid (OA) group from 2000 to 2004 and has been re-included in the new list of ODA recipients in 2005.

Source: OECD Development Assistance Committee 2009.

Table 12 - External Debt Indicators

Country	Debt outstanding, at year end of 2007				Total debt outstanding (as % of GDP)				Debt Service (as % of exports of goods and services)				
	Total (USD million)	Multilateral	Of which: Bilateral (as % of total)	Private	2007	2008 (e)	2009 (p)	2010 (p)	2007	2008 (e)	2009 (p)	2010 (p)	
Algeria	5 123	2.5	72.1	25.4	3.8	2.8	3.1	2.7	2.4	1.7	1.5	1.2	
Angola	8 556	3.3	44.6	52.1	13.9	7.4	11.9	10.9	8.0	2.8	2.8	2.7	
Benin	665	60.2	39.8	0.0	12.1	13.2	15.7	16.3	4.4	5.9	7.2	8.0	
Botswana	1 294	64.3	0.0	35.7	10.9	11.9	13.8	14.5	16.1	16.1	16.8	17.3	
Burkina Faso	1 338	67.5	32.5	0.0	19.8	21.4	26.7	29.9	6.5	5.9	4.7	4.7	
Burundi	1 499	80.9	18.9	0.2	160.1	131.3	36.4	37.7	77.6	49.9	1057.7	2.8	
Cameroon	1 132	19.0	71.0	10.0	5.5	5.7	7.8	8.5	10.7	7.5	7.7	7.5	
Cape Verde	921	75.3	0.0	24.7	60.7	50.2	57.3	53.8	8.0	7.2	7.0	6.6	
Central African Rep.	971	61.3	38.7	0.0	56.7	42.6	44.5	38.6	0.0	0.0	0.0	0.0	
Chad	2 057	85.2	14.8	0.0	29.3	34.7	50.9	48.2	2.1	1.8	1.8	2.1	
Comoros	281	78.1	21.9	0.0	60.3	49.8	44.7	41.3	63.1	12.1	10.1	10.6	
Congo	5 936	9.3	81.3	9.4	77.6	44.8	56.9	50.4	6.3	3.9	2.7	2.2	
Congo Dem. Rep.	5 219	30.6	69.4	0.0	50.1	40.8	44.8	38.3	7.7	4.3	4.1	1.8	
Côte d'Ivoire	20 245	24.9	33.1	42.0	103.4	83.2	84.7	81.2	9.6	9.3	9.2	9.0	
Djibouti	504	74.7	25.3	0.0	59.8	52.6	53.1	56.4	6.7	6.7	6.6	6.6	
Egypt	30 906	17.3	69.1	13.6	23.4	17.5	15.9	13.7	6.6	5.6	5.2	5.0	
Equatorial Guinea	136	70.1	28.8	1.1	1.3	0.8	1.4	1.2	0.4	0.1	0.0	0.0	
Eritrea	850	...	...	0.0	64.6	59.2	56.9	55.3	28.9	26.4	24.4	15.1	
Ethiopia	2 292	52.6	43.5	3.9	11.8	11.0	18.6	23.5	5.7	3.9	3.4	6.7	
Gabon	4 252	8.0	68.7	23.3	37.2	13.4	17.7	15.9	10.1	23.8	4.1	3.5	
Gambia. The	314	78.1	0.0	21.9	48.7	56.4	56.5	62.4	193.9	23.7	24.0	23.9	
Ghana	5 749	35.1	27.3	37.6	37.9	46.2	47.7	54.8	2.9	3.1	2.5	2.6	
Guinea	3 242	57.5	42.0	0.5	83.8	66.7	30.7	27.7	8.6	20.4	223.7	4.8	
Guinea-Bissau	1 013	67.4	32.5	0.1	284.5	235.5	223.6	160.3	7.7	11.4	426.9	9.7	
Kenya	5 333	48.9	46.6	4.5	19.8	13.1	14.0	13.7	5.8	4.7	4.0	4.2	
Lesotho	687	86.4	5.1	8.5	41.1	53.8	63.0	58.1	4.7	4.1	4.1	3.5	
Liberia	4 725	7.8	92.2	0.0	829.8	388.8	365.7	7.1	...	...	...	...	

Table 12 - External Debt Indicators (cont.)

Country	Debt outstanding, at year end of 2007				Total debt outstanding (as % of GDP)				Debt Service (as % of exports of goods and services)				
	Total (USD million)	Of which: Multilateral (as % of total)	Bilateral	Private	2007	2008 (e)	2009 (p)	2010 (p)	2007	2008 (e)	2009 (p)	2010 (p)	
Libya	5 574	...	...	42.6	8.0	6.3	8.9	8.0	...	...	...	3.8	
Madagascar	1 996	66.0	28.3	5.7	25.9	28.7	29.0	28.1	1.3	1.5	3.1	3.1	
Malawi	518	55.3	44.7	0.0	14.7	22.9	26.5	31.5	4.6	4.0	3.5	3.1	
Mali	1 577	46.5	53.5	0.0	22.4	22.2	26.5	28.4	6.4	2.9	3.6	4.0	
Mauritania	2 709	47.4	46.2	6.4	95.5	56.6	61.6	69.4	0.8	1.0	2.3	2.7	
Mauritius	741	5.8	87.7	6.5	9.9	8.9	10.1	11.7	3.9	3.3	3.6	3.2	
Morocco	17 852	38.7	38.6	22.7	23.8	20.5	20.9	19.7	9.9	8.1	5.6	5.2	
Mozambique	4 557	44.4	0.0	55.6	56.5	34.5	38.3	38.5	44.4	17.1	17.9	20.2	
Namibia	2 220	...	...	80.3	25.5	29.9	31.5	27.6	3.6	2.0	2.2	3.0	
Niger	682	68.6	31.4	0.0	16.3	15.4	21.2	22.9	12.1	20.1	19.9	21.1	
Nigeria	3 654	34.8	65.2	0.0	2.2	1.7	2.5	2.6	3.4	2.5	2.9	3.1	
Rwanda	579	81.5	18.5	0.0	17.4	17.3	21.0	24.2	3.0	1.9	1.8	2.0	
São Tomé and Príncipe	154	22.4	77.6	0.0	105.7	70.0	65.5	62.3	1626.2	302.8	6.4	6.0	
Senegal	4 786	54.3	0.5	55.2	42.8	44.0	50.6	51.7	6.5	5.8	6.7	7.0	
Seychelles	668	3.9	33.7	62.4	73.2	88.5	124.7	118.6	10.0	9.1	10.7	6.5	
Sierra Leone	335	72.6	0.0	27.4	20.2	14.0	11.8	10.5	4.4	1.2	1.6	1.9	
Somalia	2 944	27.5	72.5	0.0	...	...	...	...	...	...	...	...	
South Africa	75 275	0.7	6.0	93.3	26.5	34.0	44.4	44.3	8.8	8.1	8.8	8.7	
Sudan	31 873	15.6	69.2	15.2	71.8	63.3	69.8	65.4	1.9	3.8	4.4	4.0	
Swaziland	507	60.9	11.8	27.3	17.5	20.1	20.9	19.6	0.0	0.0	0.0	0.0	
Tanzania	6 673	45.1	46.5	8.4	39.7	37.3	35.5	32.6	132.1	1.1	1.3	1.2	
Togo	2 143	51.4	48.6	0.0	85.9	75.5	75.5	45.6	0.5	1.6	2.7	2.5	
Tunisia	20 162	30.9	25.4	43.7	56.8	49.6	49.2	47.9	13.0	10.0	9.6	9.5	
Uganda	1 468	83.1	16.5	0.4	10.8	11.3	14.7	15.5	4.0	3.5	2.7	3.8	
Zambia	674	29.1	70.9	0.0	5.8	5.5	8.6	9.4	1.3	1.1	0.9	0.6	
Zimbabwe	5 643	30.5	12.2	57.3	119.5	...	...	...	8.8	...	...	...	
Africa	311 203	21.8	36.6	41.6	23.6	20.4	24.2	23.0	7.0	4.7	5.0	4.2	

175

Sources: IMF, *World Economic Outlook* (October, 2008); World Bank, *GDF Online Database* (March 2009).

Table 13 - Demographic Indicators

	Total population (thousands) 2008	Urban population (% of total) 2008	Sex ratio (males per 100 females) 2008	Population growth rate (%) 2000-2005	Population growth rate (%) 2005-2010	Infant mortality rate (per 1000) 2008	Total fertility rate (per woman) 2008	Mortality under age 5 (per 1000) 2008	Distribution by age (%) 0-14 2008	Distribution by age (%) 15-64 2008	Distribution by age (%) 65+ 2008
Algeria	34 373	65.3	101.9	1.5	1.5	30.4	2.4	32	27.7	67.6	4.6
Angola	18 021	56.7	97.2	3.0	2.7	116.3	5.8	203	45.3	52.3	2.5
Benin	8 662	41.2	101.7	3.3	3.2	84.1	5.4	119	43.2	53.6	3.2
Botswana	1 921	59.7	99.6	1.3	1.5	36.5	2.9	54	33.7	62.6	3.7
Burkina Faso	15 234	19.5	99.7	3.3	3.4	79.6	5.9	156	46.2	51.8	2.0
Burundi	8 074	10.4	96.0	2.6	2.9	97.5	4.6	164	39.0	58.2	2.8
Cameroon	19 088	56.8	99.9	2.3	2.3	86.2	4.6	143	41.1	55.4	3.6
Cape Verde	499	59.7	91.5	1.7	1.4	25.2	2.7	30	36.9	58.7	4.3
Central African Republic	4 339	38.5	96.5	1.8	1.9	104.9	4.8	178	40.9	55.2	3.9
Chad	10 914	26.6	98.8	3.5	2.8	129.4	6.2	210	45.8	51.3	2.9
Comoros	661	28.0	100.7	2.2	2.3	47.5	4.0	61	38.2	58.7	3.1
Congo	3 615	61.3	99.6	2.4	1.9	79.4	4.4	129	40.7	55.5	3.8
Congo Dem. Rep.	20 591	48.8	104.0	2.2	2.3	86.1	4.6	122	40.9	55.3	3.8
Cote d'Ivoire	64 257	33.9	98.2	3.0	2.8	115.3	6.0	196	47.0	50.4	2.6
Djibouti	849	87.4	99.9	2.0	1.8	84.1	3.9	124	36.6	60.2	3.2
Egypt	81 527	42.7	101.2	1.9	1.8	34.2	2.9	40	32.5	63.0	4.5
Equatorial Guinea	659	39.3	98.3	2.8	2.6	98.7	5.3	167	41.2	55.8	3.0
Eritrea	4 927	20.6	96.6	4.0	3.1	53.5	4.6	74	41.5	56.0	2.4
Ethiopia	80 713	16.9	99.0	2.6	2.6	78.1	5.3	129	43.9	53.0	3.1
Gabon	1 448	85.2	99.7	2.1	1.8	50.5	3.3	79	36.7	58.9	4.3
Gambia	1 660	56.5	98.4	3.2	2.7	76.1	5.1	115	42.5	54.7	2.8
Ghana	23 351	50.0	102.7	2.3	2.1	72.7	4.3	116	38.7	57.7	3.6
Guinea	9 833	34.4	102.0	1.9	2.3	97.2	5.4	145	42.9	53.8	3.2
Guinea Bissau	1 575	29.8	98.1	2.4	2.2	113.0	5.7	194	42.7	53.9	3.4
Kenya	38 765	21.6	99.9	2.6	2.6	63.4	4.9	102	42.8	54.6	2.7
Lesotho	2 049	25.4	89.2	1.1	0.9	69.1	3.3	103	39.2	56.1	4.7
Liberia	3 793	60.2	98.7	3.3	4.1	94.1	5.1	138	42.9	54.0	3.1

Table 13 - Demographic Indicators (cont.)

	Total population (thousands) 2008	Urban population (% of total) 2008	Sex ratio (males per 100 females) 2008	Population growth rate (%) 2000-2005	Population growth rate (%) 2005-2010	Infant mortality rate (per 1000) 2008	Total fertility rate (per woman) 2008	Mortality under age 5 (per 1000) 2008	Distribution by age (%) 0-14 2008	Distribution by age (%) 15-64 2008	Distribution by age (%) 65+ 2008
Libya	6 294	77.5	107.2	2.0	2.0	17.8	2.7	19	30.2	65.7	4.1
Madagascar	19 111	29.5	99.2	2.8	2.7	64.3	4.7	99	43.3	53.7	3.1
Malawi	14 846	18.8	98.7	2.9	2.8	82.5	5.5	119	46.4	50.5	3.1
Mali	12 706	32.2	97.5	2.3	2.4	105.7	5.5	189	44.2	53.4	2.3
Mauritania	3 215	40.9	102.8	2.7	2.4	72.3	4.5	119	39.8	57.6	2.6
Mauritius	1 280	42.4	98.3	0.9	0.7	14.4	1.8	17	23.2	69.8	7.0
Morocco	31 606	56.0	96.6	1.1	1.2	29.9	2.4	35	28.8	65.9	5.3
Mozambique	22 383	36.9	94.4	2.6	2.3	88.7	5.1	150	44.1	52.7	3.2
Namibia	2 130	36.8	97.1	1.9	1.9	34.4	3.4	50	37.4	59.0	3.6
Niger	14 704	16.5	100.3	3.4	3.9	87.5	7.1	170	49.7	48.3	2.0
Nigeria	151 212	48.4	100.4	2.4	2.3	108.7	5.3	186	42.7	54.2	3.1
Rwanda	9 721	18.3	93.8	2.4	2.7	98.9	5.4	153	42.2	55.3	2.5
São Tomé and Principe	160	60.6	98.1	1.7	1.6	71.9	3.8	94	40.9	55.0	4.1
Senegal	12 211	42.3	98.4	2.6	2.6	58.1	5.0	119	43.8	53.8	2.4
Seychelles	84	54.3	101.3	0.4	0.5	19.3	2.1	23	24.5	68.4	7.1
Sierra Leone	5 560	37.7	94.8	3.8	2.7	102.6	5.2	146	43.3	54.9	1.9
Somalia	8 926	36.5	98.3	2.4	2.3	108.4	6.4	178	44.9	52.4	2.7
South Africa	49 668	60.7	97.2	1.4	1.0	47.9	2.5	70	30.8	64.9	4.4
Sudan	41 348	43.5	101.4	2.1	2.2	68.2	4.2	110	39.5	56.9	3.6
Swaziland	1 168	24.9	95.4	0.8	1.3	65.0	3.5	100	40.0	56.7	3.3
Tanzania	42 484	25.5	99.3	2.7	2.9	63.5	5.6	104	44.7	52.3	3.1
Togo	6 459	42.0	98.0	2.7	2.5	70.9	4.3	97	40.2	56.3	3.5
Tunisia	10 169	66.5	101.2	0.9	1.0	19.5	1.8	22	23.7	69.6	6.7
Uganda	31 657	13.0	100.3	3.2	3.3	73.3	6.3	121	49.0	48.4	2.6
Zambia	12 620	35.4	99.5	2.3	2.4	92.8	5.8	157	46.2	50.7	3.0
Zimbabwe	12 463	37.3	93.6	0.0	0.3	56.7	3.4	92	40.2	55.7	4.0
Africa	987 092	39.1	99.4	2.3	2.3	81.8	4.6	134	40.6	56.0	3.4

Sources: United Nations, Department of Economic and Social Affairs, Population Division, World Population Prospects, The 2008 Revision. Special extract.

177

178

Table 14 - Poverty and Income Distribution Indicators

	National poverty line				International poverty line			Gini Coefficient*		Share of consumption (%)	
	Population below the poverty line (%)				Population below the poverty line (%)						
	Survey year	Rural	Urban	National	Survey year	Below USD1	Below USD2	Survey year	Index	Lowest 10%	Highest 10%
Algeria	2000	...	...	15.0	1995	0.9	...	1995	35.3	2.8	26.9
Angola	2001	94.3	57.0	68.0	2000	54.3	...	2000	58.6	0.6	44.7
Benin	2003	52.3	19.9	46.4	2003	47.3	73.7	2003	38.6	2.9	31.0
Botswana	1994	...	...	30.3	1994	31.2	...	1994	61.0	1.3	51.2
Burkina Faso	2003	52.3	19.9	46.4	2003	56.5	81.0	2003	39.6	3.0	32.4
Burundi	2006	37.0	...	36.2	2006	81.3	87.6	2006	33.3	4.1	28.0
Cameroon	2001	49.9	22.1	40.2	2001	32.8	50.6	2001	44.6	2.4	35.5
Cape Verde	2002	55.1	25.0	36.7	2001	20.6	...	2001	50.5	1.8	40.3
Central African Republic	2003	...	...	50.2	2003	62.4	...	2003	43.6	2.1	33.0
Chad	2003	67.0	63.0	64.0	2003	61.9	...	2003	39.8	2.6	30.8
Comoros					2004	46.1	...	2004	64.3	0.9	55.2
Congo	2005	65.1	40.4	50.7	2005	54.1	...	2005	47.3	2.1	37.1
Congo Dem. Rep.	2005	...	...	71.3	2006	59.2	...	2006	44.4	2.3	34.7
Cote d'Ivoire	2008	62.5	29.5	48.9	2002	23.3	48.8	2002	48.4	2.0	39.6
Djibouti	2002	...	...	42.1	2002	18.8	...	2002	40.0	2.3	30.7
Egypt	2005	...	...	19.6	2005	2.0	43.9	2005	32.1	3.9	27.6
Equatorial Guinea	2006	...	...	76.8	...	...	...	...	...	...	...
Eritrea	...										
Ethiopia	...										
Gabon	2005	45.0	30.0	33.0	2005	4.8	...	2005	41.5	2.5	32.7
Gambia	2003	63.0	...	61.3	2003	34.3	82.9	2003	47.3	2.0	36.9
Ghana	2006	39.2	10.8	28.5	2006	30.0	78.5	2006	42.8	1.9	32.5
Guinea	2007	...	...	53.0	2003	70.1	50.2	2003	43.3	2.4	34.4
Guinea Bissau	2002	...	...	65.7	2002	48.8	96.7	2002	35.5	2.9	28.0
Kenya	2005-06	49.1	33.7	45.9	2005	19.7	58.3	2005	47.7	1.8	37.8
Lesotho	2007	...	...	64.0	2003	43.4	56.1	2003	52.5	1.0	39.4
Liberia	2007	...	...	64.0	2007	83.7	...	2007	52.6	2.4	30.1

Table 14 - Poverty and Income Distribution Indicators *(cont.)*

| | National poverty line | | | | International poverty line | | | | Gini Coefficient* | | Share of consumption (%) | |
| | Population below the poverty line (%) | | | | Population below the poverty line (%) | | | | | | | |
	Survey year	Rural	Urban	National	Survey year	Below USD1	Below USD2	Survey year	Index	Lowest 10%	Highest 10%
Libya	2000-05	...	...	14.0	...	...	...	...	...	...	...
Madagascar	2006	...	...	67.5	2005	67.8	85.1	2005	47.2	2.6	41.5
Malawi	2006	47.0	25.0	45.0	2004	73.9	76.1	2004	39.0	2.9	31.7
Mali	2005	...	...	47.5	2006	51.4	90.6	2006	39.0	2.7	30.5
Mauritania	2000	61.2	25.4	46.3	2000	21.2	63.1	2000	39.0	2.5	29.6
Mauritius	...	...	...	...	...	...	...	2006	38.9	...	...
Morocco	2004	22.0	7.9	14.2	2007	2.5	14.3	2007	40.9	2.7	33.2
Mozambique	2002/03	55.3	51.5	54.1	2003	74.7	78.4	2003	47.1	2.1	39.2
Namibia	2004	...	...	28.0	2004	32.8	55.8	2004	60.0	0.6	65.0
Niger	1993	66.0	52.0	63.0	2005	65.9	85.3	2005	43.9	2.3	35.7
Nigeria	2004	...	...	54.4	2004	64.4	90.8	2004	42.9	2.0	32.4
Rwanda	2000	62.5	41.5	56.9	2000	57.0	83.7	2000	46.7	2.3	38.2
São Tomé and Principe	2001	...	...	53.8	...	...	...	...	...	...	...
Senegal	2001	...	...	53.9	2005	33.5	63.0	2005	39.2	2.5	30.1
Seychelles	...	...	...	...	...	...	...	...	...	...	...
Sierra Leone	2004	79.0	56.4	70.2	2003	53.4	74.5	2003	42.5	2.6	33.6
Somalia	...	...	...	...	...	...	...	...	...	...	...
South Africa	2006	...	...	43.2	2000	26.2	34.1	2000	57.8	1.3	44.9
Sudan	...	...	...	...	...	...	...	...	...	...	...
Swaziland	2001	75.0	...	69.2	2001	62.9	22.5	2001	50.7	1.8	40.8
Tanzania	2007	33.3	...	...	2000	88.5	89.9	2000	34.6	3.1	27.0
Togo	2006	...	...	61.7	2006	38.7	...	2006	34.4	3.3	27.1
Tunisia	2005	...	...	3.8	2000	2.6	6.6	2000	40.8	2.4	31.6
Uganda	2006	31.3	...	...	2005	51.5	...	2005	42.6	2.6	34.1
Zambia	2006	...	...	64.0	2004	64.3	94.1	2004	50.7	1.3	38.9
Zimbabwe	1995-96	48.0	7.9	34.9	2004	61.9	...	2004	50.1	1.8	40.3

Note: * The Gini coefficient is defined on income distribution.
Sources: Domestic authorities and World Bank (Povcal 2009), *World Development Indicators*, online Database, *Country DHS*, March 2009.

179

Table 15 - Access to Services

| | Telecommunications | | | | | | Access to electricity | | Water supply coverage (%) | | | Sanitation coverage (%) | | |
| | Main telephone line per 100 inhabitants | Mobile lines per 100 inhabitants | | Internet users per 100 habitants | | Final consumption (GWh) | | | 2006 | | | 2006 | | |
	2000	2007	2000	2007	2000	2007	2000	2006	Total	Urban	Rural	Total	Urban	Rural
Algeria	5.77	9.06	0.28	81.4	0.49	10.3	18 592	26 456	85	87	81	94	98	87
Angola	0.47	0.63	0.19	29.1	0.11	2.9	1 157	2 372	51	62	39	50	79	16
Benin	0.71	1.23	0.77	21.1	0.21	1.7	399	602	65	78	57	30	59	11
Botswana	7.86	7.28	12.85	61.2	2.89	5.3	1 959	2 544	96	100	90	47	60	30
Burkina Faso	0.45	0.64	0.21	10.9	0.08	0.5	...	...	72	97	66	13	41	6
Burundi	0.30	0.41	0.24	2.9	0.07	0.7	...	...	71	84	70	41	44	41
Cameroun	0.60	1.02	0.65	24.5	0.25	2.0	2 719	3 374	70	88	47	51	58	42
Cape Verde	12.12	13.50	4.37	27.9	1.78	7.0	...	...	80	86	73	41	61	19
Central African Republic	0.25	0.28	0.13	3.0	0.05	0.3	...	...	66	90	51	31	40	25
Chad	0.12	0.12	0.06	8.5	0.04	0.6	...	...	48	71	40	9	23	4
Comoros	0.97	2.28	0.00	4.8	0.21	2.5	...	...	85	91	81	35	49	26
Congo	0.69	0.42	2.19	34.2	0.02	1.9	260	381	71	95	35	20	19	21
Congo Dem. Rep.	0.02	0.01	0.03	10.5	0.01	0.4	2 442	3 030	46	82	29	31	42	25
Cote d'Ivoire	1.55	1.35	2.77	36.6	0.23	1.6	2 757	3 307	81	98	66	24	38	12
Djibouti	1.33	1.30	0.03	5.3	0.19	1.3	...	...	92	98	54	67	76	11
Egypt	8.24	14.87	2.04	39.8	0.68	14.0	64 330	98 443	98	99	98	66	85	52
Equatorial Guinea	1.42	1.97	1.16	43.4	0.16	1.6	...	...	43	45	42	51	60	46
Eritrea	0.83	0.77	0.00	1.7	0.14	2.5	173	220	60	74	57	5	14	3
Ethiopia	0.33	1.06	0.03	1.5	0.01	0.4	1 419	2 567	42	96	31	11	27	8
Gabon	3.30	1.99	10.15	87.9	1.27	6.2	989	1 294	87	95	47	36	37	30
Gambia	2.41	4.47	0.40	46.8	0.87	5.9	...	...	86	91	81	52	50	55
Ghana	1.05	1.60	0.65	32.4	0.15	3.7	6 055	6 519	80	90	71	10	15	6
Guinea	0.30	0.53	0.51	21.3	0.10	0.5	...	...	70	91	59	19	33	12
Guinea Bissau	0.81	0.27	0.00	17.5	0.22	2.2	...	...	57	82	47	33	48	26
Kenya	0.93	0.71	0.41	30.2	0.32	8.0	3 408	5 296	57	85	49	42	19	48
Lesotho	1.18	2.64	1.15	22.7	0.21	3.5	...	...	78	93	74	36	43	34
Liberia	0.22	0.05	0.05	15.0	0.02	0.5	...	...	64	72	52	32	49	7

Table 15 - Access to Services (cont.)

	Telecommunications						Access to electricity		Water supply coverage (%)			Sanitation coverage (%)		
	Main telephone line per 100 inhabitants		Mobile lines per 100 inhabitants		Internet users per 100 habitants		Final consumption (GWh)		2006			2006		
	2000	2007	2000	2007	2000	2007	2000	2006	Total	Urban	Rural	Total	Urban	Rural
Libya	11.32	13.83	0.75	73.0	0.19	4.2	10 132	21 573	71	72	68	97	97	96
Madagascar	0.34	0.68	0.39	11.3	0.19	0.6	…	…	47	76	36	12	18	10
Malawi	0.40	1.26	0.42	7.5	0.13	1.0	…	…	76	96	72	60	51	62
Mali	0.39	0.65	0.10	20.5	0.15	0.8	…	…	60	86	48	45	59	39
Mauritania	0.74	1.29	0.60	41.6	0.19	1.0	…	…	60	70	54	24	44	10
Mauritius	23.69	28.63	15.18	73.6	7.34	26.9	…	…	100	100	100	94	95	94
Morocco	4.94	7.67	8.12	64.1	0.69	21.1	12 838	19 260	83	100	58	72	85	54
Mozambique	0.47	0.31	0.28	15.4	0.11	0.9	1 013	9 418	42	71	26	31	53	19
Namibia	5.86	6.66	4.36	38.6	1.60	4.9	2 386	3 163	93	99	90	35	66	18
Niger	0.18	0.17	0.02	6.3	0.04	0.3	…	…	42	91	32	7	27	3
Nigeria	0.44	1.07	0.02	27.3	0.06	6.8	8 688	16 250	47	65	30	30	35	25
Rwanda	0.22	0.24	0.48	6.5	0.06	1.0	…	…	65	82	61	23	34	20
São Tomé and Principe	3.28	4.88	0.00	19.1	4.64	14.6	…	…	86	88	83	24	29	18
Senegal	1.99	2.17	2.42	29.3	0.39	6.6	1 337	1 757	77	93	65	28	54	9
Seychelles	25.39	26.21	32.05	89.3	7.40	36.9	…	…	87	100	75	…	…	…
Sierra Leone	0.42	0.00	0.26	13.2	0.11	0.2	…	…	53	83	32	11	20	5
Somalia	0.35	1.15	1.13	6.9	0.21	1.1	…	…	29	63	10	23	51	7
South Africa	10.93	9.56	18.37	87.1	5.29	8.2	162 516	198 114	93	100	82	59	66	49
Sudan	1.16	0.90	0.07	21.3	0.03	9.1	2 058	3 553	70	78	64	35	50	24
Swaziland	3.01	3.85	3.12	33.3	0.95	3.7	…	…	60	87	51	50	64	46
Tanzania	0.51	0.40	0.33	20.6	0.12	1.0	1 913	2 213	55	81	46	33	31	34
Togo	0.79	1.51	0.93	18.1	1.85	4.9	521	623	59	86	40	12	24	3
Tunisia	9.99	12.33	1.25	75.9	2.72	16.7	8 979	13 021	94	99	84	85	96	64
Uganda	0.25	0.53	0.51	13.6	0.16	2.4	…	…	64	90	60	33	29	34
Zambia	0.80	0.77	0.95	22.1	0.19	4.2	6 039	8 312	58	90	41	52	55	51
Zimbabwe	1.97	2.58	2.10	9.2	0.40	10.1	10 494	11 559	81	98	72	46	63	37
Africa	3.10	3.77	2.56	29.57	0.55	5.4	345 789	477 329	64	83	51	37	52	28

Sources: Telecommunications: International Telecommunication Union - online database,March 2009.
Electricity: International Energy Agency - online database, 2009
Water supply coverage and sanitation coverage: WHO and UNICEF, 2009.

181

Table 16 - Basic Health Indicators

	Life expectancy at birth (years)			Undernourishment prevalence (%)	Food availability (Kcal/person/day)	Total health expenditure					Health personnel (per 100 000)		
		With AIDS	Without AIDS			as % of GDP	Per capita* (USD)	Distribution			Survey year	Physicians	Nurses
								Public (%)	Private (%)				
	2008	2008	2008	2003-05	2003-05		2006						
Algeria	72.4	...	...	...	3 100	3.6	123.0	77.3	22.7		2005	92.9	238.2
Angola	47.1	47.1	48.5	46	1 880	2.7	71.0	86.6	13.4		2005	16.5	245.4
Benin	61.5	61.5	62.7	14	2 290	5.3	29.0	53.3	46.7		2005	11.4	39.3
Botswana	54.4	54.4	68.8	26	2 200	7.2	378.0	76.7	23.3		2005	36.2	231.0
Burkina Faso	53.1	53.1	54.2	10	2 620	6.4	27.0	56.9	43.1		2006	2.1	25.9
Burundi	50.5	50.5	52.7	63	1 630	3.0	4.0	24.6	75.4		2005	6.5	75.9
Cameroon	51.1	51.1	55.7	23	2 230	5.2	51.0	28.1	71.9		2005	18.4	43.9
Cape Verde	71.4	...	...	...	2 380	5.6	129.0	81.5	18.5		2006	41.8	90.8
Central African Republic	47.0	47.0	51.6	43	1 900	3.9	14.0	35.6	64.4		2005	4.5	28.8
Chad	48.8	48.8	51.4	39	1 980	3.6	22.0	35.6	64.4		2005	3.4	23.8
Comoros	65.4	...	...	...	1 800	3.2	16.0	55.5	44.5		2005	14.8	75.9
Congo	53.6	53.6	57.2	22	2 330	2.1	42.0	40.8	59.2		2005	21.6	118.9
Congo Dem. Rep.	57.3	57.3	62.6	76	1 500	4.3	6.0	37.1	62.9		2004	10.2	50.6
Cote d'Ivoire	47.7	47.7	48.6	14	2 520	3.8	35.0	23.0	77.0		2004	11.4	55.7
Djibouti	55.4	55.4	57.7	...	2 170	6.7	62.0	75.4	24.6		2004	16.3	32.5
Egypt	70.1	...	...	...	3 320	6.3	93.0	40.7	59.3		2007	227.3	283.3
Equatorial Guinea	50.3	50.3	52.5	68	...	1.5	274.0	78.3	21.7		2004	32.4	48.2
Eritrea	59.6	59.6	61.0	68	1 530	4.5	10.0	37.3	62.7		2004	4.9	57.5
Ethiopia	55.2	55.2	57.3	46	1 810	4.9	7.0	60.4	39.6		2004	1.5	13.7
Gabon	60.5	60.5	65.1	...	2 760	3.7	267.0	78.7	21.3		2004	31.1	549.1
Gambia	55.9	...	...	30	2 140	4.3	13.0	58.3	41.7		2003	10.2	112.8
Ghana	56.6	56.6	58.5	9	2 690	6.2	35.0	36.5	63.5		2004	14.7	89.3
Guinea	57.8	57.8	59.3	17	2 540	5.7	20.0	12.3	87.7		2005	5.5	53.9
Guinea Bissau	47.8	47.8	49.1	...	2 050	6.2	13.0	24.7	75.3		2004	12.1	66.9
Kenya	54.3	54.3	61.4	32	2 040	4.6	29.0	48.2	51.8		2007	27.6	121.9
Lesotho	45.2	45.2	62.8	15	2 430	6.7	49.0	61.6	38.4		2003	4.6	...
Liberia	58.3	58.3	60.1	40	2 010	5.6	10.0	63.9	36.1		2004	3.1	18.3

Table 16 - Basic Health Indicators (cont.)

	Life expectancy at birth (years)			Undernourishment prevalence (%)	Food availability (Kcal/person/day)	Total health expenditure						Health personnel (per 100 000)		
		With AIDS	Without AIDS				Per capita* (USD)	Distribution			Survey year			
	2008	2008	2008	2003-05	2003-05	as % of GDP	2006	Public (%)	Private (%)			Physicians	Nurses
Libya	74.1	...	...	...	3 020	2.9	255.0	70.2	29.8		2002	120.0	353.4
Madagascar	60.4	...	...	37	2 010	3.2	9.0	62.8	37.2		2004	28.7	31.2
Malawi	53.1	53.1	64.5	29	2 130	12.3	20.0	72.1	27.9		2004	2.1	56.3
Mali	48.5	48.5	49.5	11	2 570	6.0	30.0	51.7	48.3		2004	9.3	58.0
Mauritania	56.7	...	...	8	2 790	2.2	19.0	68.6	31.4		2004	10.9	65.7
Mauritius	72.1	72.1	72.9	6	2 880	4.3	223.0	50.4	49.6		2006	111.9	245.3
Morocco	71.3	...	...	...	3 190	5.1	95.0	35.9	64.1		2004	55.6	88.9
Mozambique	47.9	47.9	56.0	38	2 070	4.7	17.0	69.4	30.6		2004	2.6	19.7
Namibia	61.2	61.2	70.2	19	2 290	4.9	167.0	64.4	35.6		2004	30.0	308.2
Niger	51.4	...	...	29	2 140	4.0	10.0	52.7	47.3		2004	2.9	21.2
Nigeria	47.9	47.9	50.3	9	2 600	4.1	32.0	30.1	69.9		2003	25.9	156.2
Rwanda	50.2	50.2	52.2	40	1 940	10.4	32.0	63.7	36.3		2007	2.7	31.9
São Tomé and Principe	65.6	...	...	...	2 600	10.5	58.0	85.4	14.6		2004	54.0	170.5
Senegal	55.6	...	...	26	2 150	5.4	40.0	31.5	68.5		2004	5.2	28.7
Seychelles	73.0	...	...	...	2 380	6.8	573.0	74.2	25.8		2007	142.6	478.0
Sierra Leone	47.6	47.6	48.8	47	1 910	3.5	9.0	49.0	51.0		2004	3.1	34.2
Somalia	49.9	...	...	...	...	...	...	...	...		1997	4.8	23.1
South Africa	51.6	51.6	64.8	...	2 900	8.6	456.0	41.9	58.1		2007	75.3	329.3
Sudan	58.2	58.2	59.6	21	2 290	3.8	38.0	37.1	62.9		2005	21.7	48.6
Swaziland	45.8	45.8	63.9	18	2 320	5.9	138.0	62.0	38.0		2004	15.3	612.9
Tanzania	55.7	55.7	61.6	35	2 010	5.5	18.0	59.2	40.8		2007	4.8	102.4
Togo	62.6	62.6	66.5	37	2 020	5.5	19.0	27.8	72.2		2004	3.7	35.3
Tunisia	74.0	...	...	...	3 280	5.3	159.0	43.7	56.3		2006	99.7	301.6
Uganda	52.7	52.7	58.8	15	2 380	7.2	25.0	26.9	73.1		2004	7.9	57.9
Zambia	45.5	45.5	55.1	45	1 890	5.2	49.0	46.8	53.2		2004	11.2	168.7
Zimbabwe	44.5	44.5	65.3	40	2 040	8.4	36.0	52.6	47.4		2004	16.0	71.8
Africa	54.3	...	...	30	2 307	5.7	57.7	52.2	47.8		...	...	...

Note: * At average exchange rate

Source: Life expectancy at birth : United Nations, Department of Economic and Social Affairs, Population Division, World Population Prospects, The 2008 Revision. Special extract.
Undernourishment prevalence and food availability: FAO, FAOSTAT (online database, March 2009), The State of Food Insecurity in the World 2008.
Total health expenditure and public health expenditure: WHO, The World Health Report 2005 and 2007.
Health Personnel: Reports from Ministry of Health, DHS, Pop censuses, MI.

Table 17 - Major Diseases

	Healthy life expectancy at birth (years)			People living with HIV/AIDS (000)	HIV/AIDS Adult prevalence (%) 2007	AIDS deaths in adults & children (000)	Malaria notified cases		Tuberculosis notified cases	Measles incidence (reported cases)	Vaccination (%)	
	Total	Male	Female				Survey year	Notified cases			MCV	DTP3
		2003							2007	2007	2007	
Algeria	61.0	62.0	60.0	21	0.1	1.0	2002	307	21 369	0	92	95
Angola	33.0	35.0	32.0	190	2.1	11.0	2002	1409 328	41 292	1 014	88	83
Benin	44.0	45.0	43.0	64	1.2	3.3	2001	779 041	...	341	93	97
Botswana	36.0	35.0	36.0	300	23.9	11.0	2003	22 418	7 622	1	79	96
Burkina Faso	36.0	36.0	35.0	130	1.6	9.2	2002	1451 125	3 960	12	94	99
Burundi	35.0	37.0	33.0	110	2.0	11.0	2002	1808 588	6 284	43	99	99
Cameroon	41.0	42.0	41.0	540	5.1	39.0	1998	664 413	24 062	100	74	82
Cape Verde	61.0	63.0	59.0	...	...	...	2000	143	274	0	74	81
Central African Republic	37.0	38.0	37.0	160	6.3	11.0	2003	95 644	...	49	99	84
Chad	41.0	42.0	40.0	200	3.5	14.0	2001	386 197	5 879	441	77	70
Comoros	55.0	55.0	54.0	<200	0.1	...	2001	3 718	...	0	65	75
Congo	46.0	47.0	45.0	79	3.5	6.4	1998	17 122	9 002	84	67	80
Congo Dem. Rep.	37.0	39.0	35.0	...	...	...	2003	4386 638	99 810	55 577	79	87
Cote d'Ivoire	39.0	41.0	38.0	480	3.9	38.0	2001	400 402	23 033	5	67	76
Djibouti	43.0	43.0	43.0	16	3.1	1.1	2003	5 036	3 195	24	74	88
Egypt	59.0	60.0	58.0	9	...	0.5	2003	45	9 841	1 684	97	98
Equatorial Guinea	46.0	46.0	45.0	11	3.4	...	1995	12 530	...	5	37	41
Eritrea	50.0	51.0	49.0	38	1.3	2.6	2003	72 023	3 641	55	80	80
Ethiopia	41.0	42.0	41.0	980	2.1	67.0	2003	565 273	128 844	1 446	65	73
Gabon	51.0	53.0	50.0	49	5.9	2.3	1998	80 247	3 766	0	62	81
Gambia	50.0	51.0	48.0	8	0.9	...	1999	127 899	1 916	0	85	90
Ghana	50.0	50.0	49.0	260	1.9	21.0	2003	3 552 869	12 743	6	95	94
Guinea	45.0	46.0	44.0	87	1.6	4.5	2000	889 089	9 411	3	94	93
Guinea Bissau	41.0	41.0	40.0	16	1.8	1.1	2002	194 976	...	1	80	96
Kenya	44.0	45.0	44.0	...	...	...	2002	124 197	106 438	1 516	80	81
Lesotho	31.0	33.0	30.0	270	23.2	18.0	...	...	2 319	2	80	91
Liberia	35.0	37.0	34.0	35	1.7	2.3	1998	777 754	...	1	95	88

Table 17 - Major Diseases (cont.)

	Healthy life expectancy at birth (years)			People living with HIV/AIDS (000)	HIV/AIDS Adult prevalence (%) 2007	AIDS deaths in adults & children (000)	Malaria notified cases		Tuberculosis notified cases 2007	Measles incidence (reported cases) 2007	Vaccination (%) 2007	
	2003						Survey year	Notified cases			MCV	DTP3
	Total	Male	Female									
Libya	64.0	65.0	62.0	...	...	...	...	...	2 119	59	98	98
Madagascar	49.0	50.0	47.0	14	0.1	1.0	2003	2114 400	21 857	0	97	95
Malawi	35.0	35.0	35.0	930	11.9	68.0	2002	2853 317	24 461	143	82	87
Mali	38.0	38.0	37.0	100	1.5	5.8	2003	809 428	5 166	2	87	88
Mauritania	45.0	46.0	43.0	14	0.8	1.0	2002	167 423	2 969	11	67	75
Mauritius*	62.0	65.0	60.0	13	1.7	...	2002	22	106	13	98	97
Morocco	60.0	61.0	59.0	21	0.1	1.0	2003	73	25 562	2 248	95	95
Mozambique	37.0	38.0	36.0	1 500	12.5	81.0	2003	5087 865	37 651	267	75	75
Namibia	43.0	44.0	43.0	200	15.3	5.1	2003	444 081	15 205	21	69	86
Niger	36.0	35.0	36.0	60	0.8	4.0	2002	681 707	9 276	282	67	78
Nigeria	42.0	42.0	41.0	2 600	3.1	170.0	2003	2608 479	82 417	2 613	86	69
Rwanda	38.0	40.0	36.0	150	2.8	7.8	2003	856 233	7 638	26	99	97
São Tomé and Principe	54.0	55.0	54.0	...	...	...	2003	63 199	93	0	86	97
Senegal	48.0	49.0	47.0	67	1.0	1.8	2000	1120 094	10 297	9	84	94
Seychelles	61.0	65.0	57.0	...	...	...	...	...	...	1	99	99
Sierra Leone	29.0	30.0	27.0	55	1.7	3.3	1999	409 670	9 418	0	82	79
Somalia	37.0	38.0	36.0	24	0.5	1.6	2003	23 349	11 130	1 149	34	39
South Africa	44.0	45.0	43.0	5 700	18.1	350.0	2003	13 446	315 315	31	83	97
Sudan	49.0	50.0	47.0	320	1.4	25.0	2003	3 084 320	29 270	327	80	91
Swaziland	34.0	35.0	33.0	190	26.1	10.0	2003	36 664	8 888	0	58	68
Tanzania	40.0	41.0	40.0	1 400	6.2	96.0	2003	10 712 526	59 371	7 726	90	83
Togo	45.0	46.0	44.0	130	3.3	9.1	2001	431 826	2 436	8	80	88
Tunisia	62.0	64.0	61.0	4	0.1	0.2	...	...	2 282	4	98	98
Uganda	43.0	44.0	42.0	940	5.4	77.0	2003	12343 411	40 909	3 776	86	85
Zambia	35.0	35.0	35.0	1 100	15.2	56.0	2001	2 010 185	46 320	535	97	92
Zimbabwe	34.0	33.0	34.0	1 300	15.3	140.0	2002	1252 668	40 277	242	80	85
Africa	44.6	43.8	45.3	21 085	4.5	1 390.0	...	...	1 335 134	81 903	83	83

Notes: DTP: Diphtheria, tetanus toxoids and pertussis antigen. MCV: Measles Contaning Vaccine.
Sources: UNAIDS and WHO, Country epidemic updates December 2008; Malaria notified cases: WHO, Roll Back Malaria (RBM) December 2008 online Database; Tuberculosis notified cases: WHO, 2009, Global Tuberculosis Database; Vaccination coverage and Measles incidence: WHOSIS, December 2008.

185

186

Table 18 - Basic Education Indicators

	Estimated adult illiteracy rate, 2005-08 (%) (people over 15)			Estimated youth illiteracy rate, 2005-08 (%) (people between 15 and 24)			Public expenditure on education 2002-08 (% of GDP)
	Total	Male	Female	Total	Male	Female	
Algeria	25	16	34	8	5	11	...
Angola	...	...	...	...	...	...	2.6
Benin	59	47	72	41	24	58	4.4
Botswana	17	17	17	10	13	6	8.1
Burkina Faso	71	63	78	60	49	71	4.5
Burundi	...	...	...	31	31	30	5.1
Cameroon	...	...	...	7	6	8	3.9
Cape Verde	16	11	21	9	7	12	5.7
Central African Republic	...	...	...	26	20	32	1.4
Chad	...	...	...	26	21	30	1.9
Comoros	25	20	30	40	34	47	3.8
Congo	13	8	18	2	1	2	1.8
Congo Dem. Rep.	...	...	...	14	9	18	...
Cote d'Ivoire	...	...	...	34	26	41	4.6
Djibouti	...	...	...	12	9	15	8.3
Egypt	28	16	39	26	21	32	3.8
Equatorial Guinea	...	...	...	2	1	3	0.6
Eritrea	...	...	...	26	17	34	2.4
Ethiopia	...	...	...	39	34	44	5.5
Gabon	14	10	18	...	...	...	3.8
Gambia	...	...	...	36	28	43	2.7
Ghana	35	28	42	6	5	8	5.4
Guinea	...	...	...	...	...	...	1.7
Guinea Bissau	35	25	46	35	23	47	...
Kenya	...	...	...	3	3	4	7.1
Lesotho	45	...	59	8	15	1	13.3
Liberia	44	40	49	26	12	40	...

Table 18 - Basic Education Indicators (cont.)

	Estimated adult illiteracy rate, 2005-08 (%) (people over 15)			Estimated youth illiteracy rate, 2005-08 (%) (people between 15 and 24)			Public expenditure on education 2002-08 (% of GDP)
	Total	Male	Female	Total	Male	Female	
Libya	13	6	22	2	0	4	...
Madagascar	...	...	...	17	14	19	3.4
Malawi	28	21	35	25	17	34	4.2
Mali	77	69	84	59	48	70	4.6
Mauritania	44	37	52	49	42	57	2.9
Mauritius	13	10	15	5	6	4	3.9
Morocco	44	31	57	27	21	34	5.5
Mozambique	56	43	67	34	21	46	4.7
Namibia	12	11	13	7	8	5	6.9
Niger	70	56	84	73	64	83	3.4
Nigeria	28	20	36	9	8	10	...
Rwanda	...	...	...	13	12	13	4.9
São Tomé and Principe	12	7	17	...	...	...	...
Senegal	57	47	68	44	36	52	4.8
Seychelles	...	...	...	...	...	...	6.3
Sierra Leone	62	50	73	...	...	...	3.8
Somalia	...	...	...	...	...	...	...
South Africa	12	11	13	8	8	8	5.4
Sudan	...	...	...	18	14	22	...
Swaziland	...	...	...	8	8	7	7.6
Tanzania	28	21	34	7	5	8	...
Togo	...	...	...	20	10	29	2.5
Tunisia	22	14	31	4	1	7	7.2
Uganda	26	18	34	18	12	23	5.2
Zambia	...	...	...	9	8	11	2.0
Zimbabwe	9	6	12	2	1	3	4.6
Africa	...	...	...	20.2	16.1	24.2	4.5

StatLink http://dx.doi.org/10.1787/324125036081

187

Source: UNESCO Institute for Statistics (UIS) Database, (March 2009), Domestic authorities.

188

Table 19 - School Enrolment

	Primary School, 2006-07								Secondary School, 2006-07				Enrolment ratio in technical and vocational programmes 2006 (000)		
	Gross enrolment ratio			Net enrolment ratio			Pupil/ teacher ratio		Gross enrolment ratio			Pupil/ teacher ratio	Total secondary	Lower secondary	Upper secondary
	Total	Male	Female	Total	Male	Female		Total	Male	Female					
Algeria	109.7	113.2	106.0	95.0	96.0	95.0	53.0	83.2	80.3	86.3	20.8	...	...	...
Angola	193.8	200.9	186.8	36.9	60.0	25.4	...	...	...	...	...	...	...	141.6
Benin	100.1	104.4	95.6	82.7	87.3	77.8	17.0	32.5	41.3	23.4	23.9	...	...	...
Botswana	112.2	113.0	112.0	84.0	83.0	85.0	78.0	74.9	73.2	76.7	13.7	...	...	...
Burkina Faso	66.5	71.7	61.2	47.0	52.0	42.0	31.0	13.8	16.2	11.4	31.3	23.0	1.7	3.3
Burundi	103.2	108.1	98.4	75.0	75.9	73.0	55.0	13.3	15.2	11.3	18.9	11.9	2.0	4.4
Cameroon	109.6	117.9	101.3	76.2	81.6	70.8	43.0	41.4	46.0	36.8	24.7	118.0	58.3	15.7
Cape Verde	101.5	104.6	98.3	85.0	85.0	84.0	67.0	67.7	65.3	70.1	23.1	2.1	2.0
Central African Republic	81.7	93.7	69.5	55.8	62.8	48.6	...	15.2	22.7	7.5	34.2	...	...	...
Chad	75.6	90.1	61.0	60.0	70.9	49.5	12.0	35.1	40.0	30.2	13.8	...	...	...
Comoros	85.4	90.7	79.9	56.0	59.5	50.0	33.0	42.9	46.7	39.1	34.3	...	...	...
Congo	105.9	110.0	101.8	55.0	57.7	52.0	44.0	22.0	27.8	16.1	14.5	...	...	...
Congo Dem. Rep.	101.1	106.2	95.5	61.0	62.5	59.4	...	...	...	...	29.4	...	...	...
Côte d'Ivoire	72.1	80.6	63.7	55.1	58.6	51.3	24.0	22.8	27.3	18.1	27.9	1.73	0.10	1.45
Djibouti	44.1	48.7	39.5	38.0	42.0	34.0	27.0	86.2	89.5	82.6	16.6	...	...	...
Egypt	104.7	107.5	101.7	96.0	98.0	94.0	56.0	...	...	...	...	...	...	...
Equatorial Guinea	122.0	125.0	119.0	87.0	91.4	83.0	...	30.3	38.2	22.5	51.3	2.1	...	1.5
Eritrea	62.2	68.8	55.6	47.0	50.0	43.0	43.0	34.4	40.7	28.0	54.2	123.6	...	...
Ethiopia	90.8	96.7	84.8	71.0	74.0	68.0	...	45.0	49.0	40.9	41.7	...	...	...
Gabon	139.8	139.1	140.6	92.4	91.9	93.0	34.0	45.9	49.5	42.1	19.7	31.5	...	18.4
Gambia	77.0	75.0	80.0	64.0	62.0	66.0	37.0	31.2	40.8	21.2	35.6	...	...	...
Ghana	97.7	98.3	97.0	72.0	73.0	71.0	26.0	48.2	49.4	47.1	31.6	23.0	...	15.6
Guinea	90.8	97.8	83.6	74.0	79.0	69.0	...	37.4	33.0	41.7	26.6	1.5	...	...
Guinea Bissau	69.7	83.5	55.9	45.0	53.0	37.0	45.0	...	...	...	...	...	...	...
Kenya	107.4	107.3	104.4	75.0	75.0	76.0	78.0							
Lesotho	114.4	114.5	114.2	72.0	71.0	74.0	12.0							
Liberia	83.4	88.2	78.5	37.0	...	...								

Table 19 - School Enrolment (cont.)

	Primary School, 2006-07							Secondary School, 2006-07				Enrolment ratio in technical and vocational programmes 2006 (000)		
	Gross enrolment ratio			Net enrolment ratio			Pupil/ teacher ratio	Gross enrolment ratio			Pupil/ teacher ratio	Total secondary	Lower secondary	Upper secondary
	Total	Male	Female	Total	Male	Female		Total	Male	Female				
Libya	110.4	113.0	103.1	...	...	...	...	109.7	99.7	120.0	4.8	...	...	...
Madagascar	141.4	143.7	139.1	98.0	98.0	99.0	61.0	...	...	...	...	32.0	5.1	15.9
Malawi	116.5	114.4	118.6	87.0	84.0	90.0	27.0	27.6	30.4	24.8	...	...	...	...
Mali	83.1	92.3	74.0	63.0	70.0	56.0	35.0	27.1	33.9	20.3	...	51.2	...	10.3
Mauritania	103.2	100.4	106.3	80.0	78.0	83.0	65.0	20.8	21.9	19.6	31.0	3.2	0.9	2.3
Mauritius	101.4	101.4	101.4	95.0	95.0	96.0	47.0	88.4	88.9	88.0	17.2	...	...	...
Morocco	107.2	113.0	101.3	89.0	91.0	86.0	26.0	49.2	53.4	44.8	18.7	118.5	18.0	72.4
Mozambique	104.8	112.6	96.9	76.0	79.0	73.0	65.0	13.2	15.7	10.8	32.2	26.3	22.7	3.0
Namibia	109.2	109.7	108.8	87.0	84.0	89.0	40.0	56.3	52.7	59.9	25.1	...	...	...
Niger	50.6	58.0	42.7	43.0	50.0	37.0	51.0	9.7	11.9	7.6	30.9	6.3	1.2	5.1
Nigeria	92.5	96.1	88.5	63.0	68.0	58.0	53.0	32.4	35.6	29.2	40.2	...	...	...
Rwanda	147.4	146.3	148.4	94.0	92.0	95.0	55.0	13.4	14.2	12.7	26.3	...	...	...
São Tomé and Principe	130.4	131.6	129.1	97.0	98.0	96.0	28.0	45.3	43.7	46.9	21.7	...	...	...
Senegal	83.5	83.6	83.5	72.0	72.0	72.0	85.0	22.1	25.3	18.8	26.4	...	...	...
Seychelles	125.3	126.1	124.6	98.4	98.9	100.0	26.0	105.4	105.7	105.0	12.8	...	...	...
Sierra Leone	147.1	154.9	139.3	65.2	54.9	62.7		...	...	...	...	...	...	...
Somalia	8.4	11.1	5.8	9.8	12.7	6.9	76.0	...	...	...	...	...	...	...
South Africa	98.0	103.4	92.9	86.0	86.0	86.0	64.0	94.7	91.5	97.9	30.8	...	...	...
Sudan	66.4	71.3	61.2	41.2	44.9	37.0	73.0	32.7	33.8	31.6	21.5	44.1	...	44.1
Swaziland	119.5	123.3	115.7	84.2	82.9	85.6	48.0	44.6	45.4	43.8	18.1	...	...	...
Tanzania	111.9	112.8	110.9	98.0	98.0	97.0	12.0	...	...	...	...	...	...	...
Togo	97.1	104.2	94.6	77.0	82.0	72.0	52.0	40.4	53.7	27.1	29.6	...	...	...
Tunisia	97.3	97.3	97.4	96.0	96.0	97.0	39.0	83.2	79.3	87.4	17.2	112.9	65.3	47.6
Uganda	116.7	116.3	117.2	81.8	82.3	81.2	48.0	18.3	20.3	16.4	20.9	...	...	...
Zambia	119.0	120.7	117.2	94.0	94.0	94.0		30.4	33.4	27.3	34.0	...	...	...
Zimbabwe	101.2	101.7	100.6	88.0	87.0	88.0		...	...	...	...	...	...	...
Africa	**99.6**	**99.9**	**92.0**	**75.0**	**75.9**	**71.5**	**45.0**	**44.5**	**47.4**	**41.8**	**26.2**	**732.8**	**175.2**	**404.8**

Sources: UNESCO Institute for Statistics (UIS) Database, March 2009; Domestic authorities.

190

Table 20 - Employment and Remittances*

		Unemployment rate			Participation rate (>15) 2007	Inactivity rate (>15) 2007			Worker remittances (USD million)					
	Year	Total	Men	Female	Total	Total	Men	Female	2003	2004	2005	2006	2007
Algeria	2007	13.8	12.9	18.4	57.3	42.7	22.5	63.1	1 750	2 460	1 950	2 527	2 906
Angola	2006	25.2	...	...	81.7	18.3	10.8	25.5	...	...	...	...	...
Benin	...	...	...	...	72.1	27.9	14.3	41.5	55	63	173	173	173
Botswana	2008	17.6	15.3	19.9	55.7	44.3	36.6	51.8	39	93	125	117	117
Burkina Faso	1998	2.4	2.3	2.6	83.3	16.7	10.2	22.9	50	50	50	50	50
Burundi	1990	0.5	0.7	0.3	89.9	10.1	9.6	10.5	...	...	0	0	0
Cameroon	2001	7.5	8.2	6.7	63.8	36.2	24.6	47.6	76	103	103	103	103
Cape Verde	2008	17.8	15.0	28.0	60.1	39.9	24.6	53.5	109	113	137	137	143
Central African Republic	...	...	...	...	76.8	23.2	12.9	32.7	...	...	...	...	...
Chad	1993	0.69	1.1	0.3	74.1	25.9	22.7	29.0	12	12	12	12	12
Comoros	1991	20.0	21.3	16.9	73.1	26.9	17.0	36.8	13	15	11	11	11
Congo	...	...	...	...	69.1	30.9	17.2	44.2	...	...	...	...	...
Congo Dem. Rep.	...	...	...	...	71.6	28.4	10.3	45.7	...	159	163	167	179
Cote d'Ivoire	1998	4.1	...	...	62.5	37.5	15.3	60.8	142	...	...	...	...
Djibouti	1991	43.5	41.9	46.7	67.3	32.7	23.0	42.2	...	...	...	...	...
Egypt	2008	8.4	...	...	47.3	52.7	28.8	76.2	2 961	3 341	5 017	5 330	5 865
Equatorial Guinea	1983	24.2	27.4	18.5	66.6	33.4	8.5	57.4	...	...	...	...	...
Eritrea	1984				70.0	30.0	14.2	44.6					
Ethiopia	2006	16.7	11.5	22.1	85.3	14.7	9.0	20.3	47	134	174	172	172
Gabon	1993	18.0	19.3	16.4	70.9	29.1	20.2	37.9	6	7	7	7	7
Gambia	...	...	...	...	76.9	23.1	16.2	29.9	65	62	57	64	64
Ghana	1999	10.1	9.4	10.1	72.5	27.5	26.7	28.4	65	82	99	105	105
Guinea	1994	3.09	4.6	1.7	84.1	15.9	11.1	20.6	111	42	42	42	42
Guinea Bissau	...	...	...	...	71.4	28.6	10.1	46.4	23	28	28	28	29
Kenya	1999	9.8	...	...	80.8	19.2	12.7	25.6	538	620	805	1 128	1 300
Lesotho	1999	27.3	21.5	33.1	70.9	29.1	25.0	32.4	287	355	327	361	371
Liberia	2007	5.6	6.8	4.2	69.9	30.1	15.5	44.6	...	484	620	685	685

Table 20 - Employment and Remittances* (cont.)

	Year	Unemployment rate			Participation rate (>15) 2007	Inactivity rate (>15) 2007			Worker remittances (USD million)				
		Total	Men	Female	Total	Total	Men	Female	2003	2004	2005	2006	2007
Libya	2007	13.5	...	...	52.7	47.3	22.5	74.1	8	10	15	16	16
Madagascar	2005	2.8	2.0	3.6	85.2	14.8	11.6	17.9	16	12	11	11	11
Malawi	2004	7.8	5.4	10.0	77.8	22.2	20.5	23.7	1	1	1	1	1
Mali	2004	8.8	7.2	10.9	50.1	49.9	34.9	63.5	154	156	177	212	212
Mauritania	2004	33.0	25.2	...	70.1	29.9	20.1	39.8	2	2	2	2	2
Mauritius	2007	8.5	5.3	14.4	59.5	40.5	22.8	57.6	215	215	215	215	215
Morocco	2007	9.5	9.6	9.4	51.4	48.6	20.2	75.3	3 614	4 221	4 590	5 454	5 700
Mozambique	1997	2.2	3.4	1.3	82.9	17.1	22.8	11.9	70	58	57	80	80
Namibia	2004	21.9	19.3	25.0	53.8	46.2	41.0	51.2	12	15	18	17	17
Niger	2001	1.5	1.7	0.9	63.5	36.5	12.5	60.7	26	60	66	66	66
Nigeria	1986	3.9	3.7	4.4	54.5	45.5	29.4	61.3	1 063	2 273	3 329	3 329	3 329
Rwanda	1996	0.6	0.9	0.4	80.0	20.0	20.8	19.2	9	10	21	21	51
São Tomé and Principe	2006	16.7	11.0	24.5	56.5	43.5	29.2	57.3	1	1	2	2	2
Senegal	2006	11.1	7.9	13.6	73.7	26.3	13.8	38.5	511	633	633	633	874
Seychelles	2005	5.5	6.1	4.9	...	...	...	...	2 661	4 129	4 650	4 703	4 910
Sierra Leone	2004	2.8	3.1	2.5	66.1	33.9	32.6	35.1	26	25	2	33	38
Somalia	...	...	...	...	71.1	28.9	11.5	45.7	...	...	...	...	...
South Africa	2007	23.0	20.0	26.7	53.4	46.6	39.8	53.0	424	424	424	424	424
Sudan	...	...	...	...	51.5	48.5	28.4	68.7	1 223	1 403	1 016	1 156	1 156
Swaziland	1997	22.5	20.0	26.0	65.1	34.9	31.5	38.0	65	83	95	99	99
Tanzania	2006	4.3	2.8	5.8	88.6	11.4	9.7	13.0	9	11	18	15	15
Togo	...	...	...	...	68.9	31.1	13.3	48.2	149	179	193	193	193
Tunisia	2005	14.2	13.1	17.3	48.3	51.7	29.1	74.3	1 250	1 432	1 393	1 510	1 669
Uganda	2003	3.2	2.5	3.9	85.9	14.1	9.7	18.4	306	311	323	665	849
Zambia	2000	12.9	14.1	11.3	70.1	29.9	19.5	40.2	36	48	53	58	59
Zimbabwe	2004	4.2	4.2	4.1	69.7	30.3	20.3	40.1	...	...	...	...	...
Africa	...	...	...	...	...	...	...	...	18 198	23 932	27 204	30 133	32 322

191

Note: * See note on methodology for definitions.
Source: Employment: ILO, KILM database, March 2009.
Workers remittances: World Bank. Global Development Finance, March 2009.

Table 21 - Corruption Perception Index

	2002		2003		2004		2005		2006		2007		2008	
	Index	Country Rank / 102	Index	Country Rank / 133	Index	Country Rank / 145	Index	Country Rank / 158	Index	Country Rank / 163	Index	Country Rank / 179	Index	Country Rank / 180
Algeria	...	...	2.6	88	2.7	97	2.8	97	3.1	84	3	99	3.2	92
Angola	1.7	98	1.8	124	2	133	2	151	2.2	142	2.2	147	1.9	158
Benin	...	...	...	...	3.2	77	2.9	88	2.5	121	2.7	118	3.1	96
Botswana	6.4	24	5.7	30	6	31	5.9	32	5.6	37	5.4	38	5.8	36
Burkina Faso	...	...	...	...	...	...	3.4	70	3.2	79	2.9	105	3.5	80
Burundi	...	...	...	...	...	...	2.3	130	2.4	130	2.5	131	1.9	158
Cameroon	2.2	89	1.8	124	2.1	129	2.2	137	2.3	138	2.4	138	2.3	141
Cape Verde	...	...	...	...	...	...	...	...	...	...	4.9	49	5.1	47
Central African Republic	...	...	...	...	...	...	...	...	2.4	130	2	162	2	151
Chad	...	...	...	...	1.7	142	1.7	158	2	156	1.8	172	1.6	173
Comoros	...	...	...	...	...	...	...	...	...	...	2.6	123	2.5	134
Congo	...	...	2.2	113	2.3	114	2.3	130	2.2	142	2.1	150	1.9	158
Congo. Dem. Rep.	...	...	...	...	2	133	2.1	144	2	156	1.9	168	1.7	171
Côte d'Ivoire	2.7	71	2.1	118	2	133	1.9	152	2.1	151	2.1	150	2	151
Djibouti	...	...	...	...	...	...	...	...	...	...	2.9	105	3	102
Egypt	3.4	62	3.3	70	3.2	77	3.4	70	3.3	70	2.9	105	2.8	115
Equatorial Guinea	...	...	...	...	...	...	1.9	152	2.1	151	1.9	168	1.7	171
Eritrea	...	...	...	...	2.6	102	2.6	107	2.9	93	2.8	111	2.6	126
Ethiopia	3.5	59	2.5	92	2.3	114	2.2	137	2.4	130	2.4	138	2.6	126
Gabon	...	...	...	...	3.3	74	2.9	88	3	90	3.3	84	3.1	96
Gambia	...	...	2.5	92	2.8	90	2.7	103	2.5	121	2.3	143	1.9	158
Ghana	3.9	50	3.3	70	3.6	64	3.5	65	3.3	70	3.7	69	3.9	67
Guinea	...	...	...	...	...	...	...	...	1.9	160	1.9	168	1.6	173
Guinea Bissau	...	...	...	...	...	...	...	...	...	...	2.2	147	1.9	158
Kenya	1.9	96	1.9	122	2.1	129	2.1	144	2.2	142	2.1	150	2.1	147
Lesotho	...	...	...	...	...	...	3.4	70	3.2	79	3.3	84	3.2	92
Liberia	...	...	...	...	...	...	2.2	137	...	...	2.1	150	2.4	138

Table 21 - Corruption Perception Index (cont.)

	2002		2003		2004		2005		2006		2007		2008	
	Index	Country Rank / 102	Index	Country Rank / 133	Index	Country Rank / 145	Index	Country Rank / 158	Index	Country Rank / 163	Index	Country Rank / 179	Index	Country Rank / 180
Libya	...	...	2.1	118	2.5	108	2.5	117	2.7	105	2.5	131	2.6	126
Madagascar	1.7	98	2.6	88	3.1	82	2.8	97	3.1	84	3.2	94	3.4	85
Malawi	2.9	68	2.8	83	2.8	90	2.8	97	2.7	105	2.7	118	2.8	115
Mali	...	...	3	78	3.2	77	2.9	88	2.8	99	2.7	118	3.1	96
Mauritania	...	...	...	...	...	...	...	...	3.1	84	2.6	123	2.8	115
Mauritius	4.5	40	4.4	48	4.1	54	4.2	51	5.1	42	4.7	53	5.5	41
Morocco	3.7	52	3.3	70	3.2	77	3.2	78	3.2	79	3.5	72	3.5	80
Mozambique	...	...	2.7	86	2.8	90	2.8	97	2.8	99	2.8	111	2.6	126
Namibia	5.7	28	4.7	41	4.1	54	4.3	47	4.1	55	4.5	57	4.5	61
Niger	...	...	...	...	2.2	122	2.4	126	2.3	138	2.6	123	2.8	115
Nigeria	1.6	101	1.4	132	1.6	144	1.9	152	2.2	142	2.2	147	2.7	121
Rwanda	...	...	...	...	...	...	3.1	83	2.5	121	2.8	111	3	102
São Tomé and Príncipe	...	...	...	...	...	...	...	...	...	...	2.7	118	2.7	121
Senegal	3.1	66	3.2	76	3	85	3.2	78	3.3	70	3.6	71	3.4	85
Seychelles	...	...	...	...	4.4	48	4	55	3.6	63	4.5	57	4.8	55
Sierra Leone	...	...	2.2	113	2.3	114	2.4	126	2.2	142	2.1	150	1.9	158
Somalia	...	...	...	...	...	...	2.1	144	...	...	1.4	179	1	180
South Africa	4.8	36	4.4	48	4.6	44	4.5	46	4.6	51	5.1	43	4.9	54
Sudan	...	...	2.3	106	2.2	122	2.1	144	2	156	1.8	172	1.6	173
Swaziland	...	...	...	...	...	...	2.7	103	2.5	121	3.3	84	3.6	72
Tanzania	2.7	71	2.5	92	2.8	90	2.9	88	2.9	93	3.2	94	3	102
Togo	...	...	...	...	...	...	...	...	2.4	130	2.3	143	2.7	121
Tunisia	4.8	36	4.9	39	5	39	4.9	43	4.6	51	4.2	61	4.4	62
Uganda	2.1	93	2.2	113	2.6	102	2.5	117	2.7	105	2.8	111	2.6	126
Zambia	2.6	77	2.5	92	2.6	102	2.6	107	2.6	111	2.6	123	2.8	115
Zimbabwe	2.7	71	2.3	106	2.3	114	2.6	107	2.4	130	2.1	150	1.8	166

Note: The Corruption Perception Index (CPI) Score relates to perceptions of the degree of corruption as seen by business people and country analysts, and ranges between 10 (highly clean) and 0 (highly corrupt).
Source: Transparency International 2009.

193

Table 22 - **Civil Tensions***

	1996	1997	1998	1999	2000	2001	2002	2003	2004	2005	2006	2007	2008
Algeria	29.6	30.2	30.3	33.4	29.9	35.6	16.0	2.5	15.4	5.8	0.3	7.4	11.0
Angola	...	...	...	...	...	...	...	...	10.1	0.7	0.5	0.0	0.2
Benin	...	...	...	...	...	...	...	...	0.7	0.0	0.2	0.0	0.0
Botswana	0.0	0.0	0.0	0.0	0.0	0.0	0.0	0.0	0.0	0.0	0.0	0.0	0.0
Burkina Faso	0.0	0.8	0.3	0.6	2.4	0.6	0.6	0.0	0.5	0.2	0.5	0.1	1.3
Burundi	...	...	...	...	...	...	...	...	...	...	...	...	2.1
Cameroon	5.8	11.3	0.3	0.4	0.6	0.2	0.1	0.2	0.5	0.8	0.9	0.0	1.6
Cape Verde	...	...	...	...	...	...	...	...	...	...	...	0.0	0.0
Central African Republic	...	...	...	...	...	...	...	...	...	...	...	...	2.9
Chad	1.1	1.4	0.6	5.0	6.7	4.1	2.6	4.0	1.0	2.8	9.4	4.0	3.5
Congo	...	...	...	...	...	...	...	...	0.5	0.5	0.2	0.1	0.0
Congo Dem. Rep.	...	...	...	...	...	...	...	...	5.4	4.7	7.8	7.0	8.6
Côte d'Ivoire	4.0	0.9	0.8	5.3	6.9	0.7	3.4	4.7	6.3	4.7	4.6	2.0	1.7
Djibouti	...	...	...	...	...	...	...	...	...	...	...	...	0.7
Egypt	5.7	10.1	0.0	0.2	1.9	1.8	0.5	1.4	1.7	3.3	1.7	0.1	6.3
Equatorial Guinea	0.5	0.0	0.5	0.0	0.0	0.0	0.0	0.2	0.3	0.0	0.0	0.0	0.0
Ethiopia	11.8	3.0	0.4	6.2	1.4	2.1	10.6	3.8	6.5	3.3	1.7	2.7	3.2
Gabon	2.3	0.2	0.6	0.2	0.0	0.0	0.4	0.0	0.1	1.1	0.6	0.8	0.5
Gambia	...	...	...	...	...	...	...	...	...	...	...	...	0.0
Ghana	1.2	0.0	0.1	1.1	0.5	1.0	1.0	0.3	0.5	0.0	0.0	0.0	0.7
Guinea	...	...	...	...	...	...	...	...	...	...	...	...	1.6
Kenya	2.5	6.4	8.5	0.0	0.0	1.9	0.5	1.7	1.1	2.8	1.4	16.0	9.8
Lesotho	...	...	...	...	...	...	...	...	...	...	...	...	0.0
Liberia	...	...	...	...	...	...	...	...	...	...	...	2.2	0.7
Libya	...	...	...	...	...	...	...	...	...	...	...	0.0	0.2
Madagascar	...	...	...	...	...	...	...	...	1.7	2.2	1.2	1.8	0.0
Malawi	...	...	...	...	...	...	...	...	...	1.4	1.4	0.7	0.0
Mali	0.8	3.4	0.3	2.2	0.0	0.0	0.0	0.1	0.1	0.6	0.5	1.7	3.1
Mauritania	...	...	...	...	...	...	...	...	...	...	...	...	3.6
Mauritius	0.0	0.0	0.0	1.3	0.0	0.0	0.0	0.0	0.5	0.2	0.0	0.0	0.0
Morocco	2.9	0.4	0.5	0.1	0.1	0.0	0.0	0.0	0.9	0.5	0.0	1.3	1.8
Mozambique	8.4	0.0	0.0	0.7	1.7	0.0	0.0	1.1	1.0	0.2	0.0	0.5	1.0
Namibia	0.9	0.0	0.0	1.9	1.0	0.0	0.0	0.0	0.0	0.0	0.0	0.0	0.0
Niger	...	...	...	...	...	...	...	...	1.4	0.9	0.3	4.2	5.7
Nigeria	7.3	12.8	2.5	11.8	6.6	9.9	4.8	2.6	7.6	1.0	5.4	6.8	9.9
Rwanda	...	...	...	...	...	...	...	...	0.0	0.0	0.1	0.0	0.9
Senegal	0.1	4.9	0.7	1.4	1.4	1.2	1.9	1.7	2.3	1.2	1.1	1.6	0.8
Seychelles	...	...	...	...	...	...	...	...	...	...	...	...	0.0
Sierra Leone	...	...	...	...	...	...	...	...	...	...	...	...	0.1
South Africa	21.2	10.1	4.9	9.3	4.7	0.6	0.8	0.3	2.7	0.8	2.2	4.7	5.0
Sudan	...	...	...	...	...	...	...	...	...	...	...	...	8.8
Swaziland	...	...	...	...	...	...	...	...	...	...	...	...	0.0
Tanzania	1.2	0.5	0.2	0.0	0.0	1.5	0.0	0.1	0.1	1.3	0.0	0.5	0.1
Togo	...	...	...	...	...	...	...	...	...	...	...	...	0.0
Tunisia	0.0	0.0	0.1	0.6	0.1	0.0	0.7	0.6	0.0	0.7	0.0	0.0	0.7
Uganda	19.5	3.8	2.6	2.4	0.0	6.0	3.6	4.3	9.8	2.2	1.9	5.3	1.7
Zambia	1.2	1.1	1.2	0.9	0.1	4.4	0.3	1.4	0.5	0.5	0.7	2.0	0.5
Zimbabwe	2.1	2.2	2.8	1.3	4.2	3.2	4.1	1.2	0.9	1.1	1.0	6.4	8.3

Note: The AEO Indicator for Civil Tensions was called Political Troubles indicator in past editions of the report. Computation methodology has been improved in 2008 and for all the data series. For more details, see the methodological note of the Statistical Annex.

Source: Authors' calculations based on Marchés Tropicaux et Méditerranéens, between 1996 and 2007, and Agence France Presse for 2008. The change in the source might affect the comparability of 2008 indicator to its historical values.

StatLink http://dx.doi.org/10.1787/324268640831

194

Table 23 - Softening of the Regime*

	1996	1997	1998	1999	2000	2001	2002	2003	2004	2005	2006	2007	2008
Algeria	1.3	3.6	0.2	0.5	0.2	0.0	0.7	0.5	0.9	0.5	0.3	0.1	0.1
Angola	...	...	...	...	...	...	...	...	0.3	0.2	0.5	0.0	0.6
Benin	...	...	...	...	...	...	...	...	0.1	0.0	0.2	0.1	0.0
Botswana	0.0	0.0	0.0	0.1	0.0	0.0	0.0	0.0	0.0	0.0	0.0	0.0	0.1
Burkina Faso	0.4	0.4	0.0	0.0	0.3	0.0	0.2	0.0	0.3	0.0	0.0	0.0	0.1
Burundi	...	...	...	...	...	...	...	...	...	...	...	...	0.1
Cameroon	0.7	2.0	0.2	0.0	0.0	0.2	0.0	0.2	0.6	0.2	0.0	0.1	0.1
Cape Verde	...	...	...	...	...	...	...	...	...	...	...	0.0	0.2
Central African Republic	...	...	...	...	...	...	...	...	...	...	...	...	0.1
Chad	4.5	4.0	0.0	0.5	0.1	0.3	0.7	0.4	0.0	0.1	0.1	0.0	0.3
Congo	...	...	...	...	...	...	...	...	-0.1	0.3	0.0	0.4	0.0
Congo Dem. Rep.	...	...	...	...	...	...	...	...	0.1	0.3	0.3	0.2	0.2
Côte d'Ivoire	1.5	2.1	0.2	0.0	0.6	-0.4	0.4	1.7	-0.1	0.9	0.3	1.2	0.7
Djibouti	...	...	...	...	...	...	...	...	...	...	...	...	0.0
Egypt	0.1	0.0	0.0	0.4	0.5	0.0	-0.3	0.3	0.6	0.1	0.5	0.0	0.4
Equatorial Guinea	0.0	2.6	0.0	0.2	0.2	0.1	0.4	0.4	0.1	0.0	0.4	0.0	0.2
Ethiopia	0.1	0.1	0.2	0.0	0.0	0.4	0.0	0.0	0.1	0.5	0.5	0.6	0.3
Gabon	0.0	0.5	0.1	0.0	0.0	0.0	0.3	0.1	0.2	0.2	0.2	0.3	0.0
Gambia	...	...	...	...	...	...	...	...	...	...	...	...	0.1
Ghana	0.9	0.1	0.0	0.0	0.3	0.0	0.0	0.0	0.1	0.0	0.0	0.0	0.1
Guinea	...	...	...	...	...	...	...	...	...	...	...	...	0.1
Kenya	0.9	0.7	0.2	0.0	0.0	0.3	0.0	0.6	0.2	0.0	0.0	0.3	2.0
Lesotho	...	...	...	...	...	...	...	...	...	...	...	...	0.0
Liberia	...	...	...	...	...	...	...	...	...	...	...	0.1	0.1
Libya	...	...	...	...	...	...	...	...	...	...	...	0.4	0.4
Madagascar	...	...	...	...	...	...	...	...	0.7	0.0	0.1	0.1	0.0
Malawi	...	...	...	...	...	...	...	...	...	0.0	0.4	0.1	0.1
Mali	1.4	1.8	0.2	0.4	0.3	0.0	0.3	0.0	0.0	0.0	0.0	0.2	0.5
Mauritania	...	...	...	...	...	...	...	...	...	...	...	...	-0.9
Mauritius	0.0	0.1	0.0	0.0	0.0	0.0	0.0	0.3	0.0	0.0	0.0	0.0	0.0
Morocco	0.9	0.6	0.1	0.0	0.4	0.0	0.2	0.3	0.8	0.3	0.4	0.2	0.3
Mozambique	0.1	0.0	0.0	0.0	0.2	0.4	0.2	0.0	0.0	0.0	0.0	0.0	0.0
Namibia	0.0	0.4	0.0	0.0	0.0	0.3	0.0	0.1	0.0	0.0	0.0	0.0	0.1
Niger	...	...	...	...	...	...	...	...	0.0	0.3	0.4	0.0	0.2
Nigeria	1.1	1.8	1.6	0.9	0.1	0.0	0.2	0.1	0.3	0.1	-0.2	0.1	0.4
Rwanda	...	...	...	...	...	...	...	...	0.1	0.4	0.0	0.3	0.2
Senegal	0.5	0.7	0.0	0.6	0.3	0.4	0.0	0.0	0.2	0.3	0.2	0.2	0.2
Seychelles	...	...	...	...	...	...	...	...	...	...	...	...	0.0
Sierra Leone	...	...	...	...	...	...	...	...	...	...	...	...	0.2
South Africa	2.6	2.3	0.2	0.5	0.2	0.5	0.2	0.1	0.2	0.2	0.0	0.1	0.5
Sudan	...	...	...	...	...	...	...	...	...	...	...	...	0.5
Swaziland	...	...	...	...	...	...	...	...	...	...	...	...	0.0
Tanzania	0.2	0.1	0.0	0.4	0.0	0.4	0.2	0.0	0.1	0.0	0.0	0.0	0.1
Togo	...	...	...	...	...	...	...	...	...	...	...	...	0.3
Tunisia	1.4	0.7	0.0	0.0	0.2	0.4	0.8	0.2	0.0	0.3	0.1	0.0	0.2
Uganda	0.0	0.4	0.1	0.1	0.2	0.0	0.1	0.2	0.1	0.1	0.6	0.4	0.5
Zambia	1.4	0.0	0.4	0.2	0.0	0.3	0.3	0.4	0.1	0.0	0.1	0.2	0.1
Zimbabwe	0.1	0.1	0.0	0.0	0.3	0.1	0.4	0.6	0.1	0.0	0.2	0.1	1.0

Note: * Aggregation methodology changed for all the series with respect to AEO 2007/08. For more details, see note on methodology.

Source: Authors' calculations based on Marchés Tropicaux et Méditerranéens, between 1996 and 2007, and Agence France Presse for 2008. The change in the source might affect the comparability of 2008 indicator to its historical values.

StatLink http://dx.doi.org/10.1787/324268640831

Table 24 - State Pressure over Civil Liberties*

	1996	1997	1998	1999	2000	2001	2002	2003	2004	2005	2006	2007	2008
Algeria	2.9	1.5	0.6	0.6	0.1	1.9	3.7	1.1	2.2	0.0	0.5	0.3	4.9
Angola	...	...	...	...	...	...	...	...	1.3	0.1	0.3	0.5	0.8
Benin	...	...	...	...	...	...	...	...	0.1	0.1	0.4	0.0	0.5
Botswana	0.1	0.1	0.0	0.2	0.0	0.0	0.0	0.0	0.3	0.1	0.0	0.4	0.0
Burkina Faso	0.0	0.5	0.1	1.1	0.4	0.3	0.7	0.6	0.7	0.1	0.1	0.1	0.8
Burundi	...	...	...	...	...	...	...	...	...	...	...	...	1.2
Cameroon	1.9	1.5	0.5	0.4	0.2	0.6	0.2	0.5	0.6	0.0	0.4	0.5	1.6
Cape Verde	...	...	...	...	...	...	...	...	...	...	...	0.0	0.2
Central African Republic	...	...	...	...	...	...	...	...	...	...	...	...	0.5
Chad	0.7	0.3	0.3	0.0	0.3	0.6	0.4	1.6	0.2	1.7	4.1	1.6	4.9
Congo	...	...	...	...	...	...	...	...	0.3	0.3	0.1	0.6	0.2
Congo Dem. Rep.	...	...	...	...	...	...	...	...	1.2	2.3	5.0	3.9	3.5
Côte d'Ivoire	0.5	0.6	0.2	2.3	1.6	0.4	0.8	1.6	2.3	1.7	3.1	0.2	1.5
Djibouti	...	...	...	...	...	...	...	...	...	...	...	...	0.6
Egypt	2.3	1.6	1.4	0.5	1.9	0.9	2.9	1.2	1.0	2.8	1.4	5.3	6.0
Equatorial Guinea	0.0	0.3	1.0	0.0	0.0	0.2	1.4	0.1	1.9	0.0	0.3	0.2	0.5
Ethiopia	1.6	1.0	0.6	0.0	0.2	0.9	2.1	0.3	0.3	3.1	1.0	0.5	1.6
Gabon	0.2	1.2	0.2	0.5	0.1	0.0	0.1	0.3	0.6	2.0	0.7	0.1	0.2
Gambia	...	...	...	...	...	...	...	...	...	...	...	...	0.9
Ghana	0.6	0.2	0.6	0.6	0.0	0.2	0.3	0.0	0.1	0.0	0.0	0.0	0.1
Guinea	...	...	...	...	...	...	...	...	...	...	...	...	2.5
Kenya	-0.3	2.1	0.9	0.0	0.0	0.2	0.3	0.5	0.6	0.4	0.8	9.6	7.1
Lesotho	...	...	...	...	...	...	...	...	...	...	...	...	0.0
Liberia	...	...	...	...	...	...	...	...	...	...	...	0.1	0.5
Libya	...	...	...	...	...	...	...	...	...	...	...	0.1	0.5
Madagascar	...	...	...	...	...	...	...	...	0.7	0.3	0.4	1.5	0.0
Malawi	...	...	...	...	...	...	...	...	...	0.8	2.1	0.8	0.3
Mali	0.1	1.3	0.0	0.1	0.3	0.3	0.1	0.3	0.1	0.0	0.2	1.2	1.8
Mauritania	...	...	...	...	...	...	...	...	...	...	...	...	8.3
Mauritius	0.1	0.0	0.0	0.1	0.0	0.0	0.0	0.6	0.1	0.2	0.0	0.0	0.0
Morocco	1.3	0.9	0.4	0.3	0.8	0.7	0.6	0.8	1.4	0.1	0.2	1.1	3.2
Mozambique	0.1	0.2	0.6	0.3	0.9	0.3	0.0	0.1	0.4	0.0	0.0	0.0	0.4
Namibia	0.0	0.1	0.0	0.3	0.4	0.1	0.1	0.2	0.1	0.0	0.1	0.0	0.0
Niger	...	...	...	...	...	...	...	...	0.4	0.4	0.4	2.2	1.7
Nigeria	31.3	0.6	1.2	1.0	1.1	0.7	0.6	0.6	2.3	0.7	0.8	2.4	3.4
Rwanda	...	...	...	...	...	...	...	...	1.0	0.0	0.0	0.0	0.2
Senegal	0.4	0.8	0.7	0.1	0.0	0.4	0.3	0.4	0.2	0.7	0.7	0.7	0.9
Seychelles	...	...	...	...	...	...	...	...	...	...	...	...	0.0
Sierra Leone	...	...	...	...	...	...	...	...	...	...	...	...	0.2
South Africa	4.6	3.0	1.4	1.1	0.5	0.3	0.5	-0.2	0.9	1.1	0.3	1.0	1.5
Sudan	...	...	...	...	...	...	...	...	...	...	...	...	5.0
Swaziland	...	...	...	...	...	...	...	...	...	...	...	...	0.9
Tanzania	0.3	0.1	0.1	0.0	0.1	0.1	0.0	0.1	0.0	0.4	0.0	0.0	0.0
Togo	...	...	...	...	...	...	...	...	...	...	...	...	0.0
Tunisia	0.7	0.4	0.4	0.6	0.3	0.5	0.7	0.4	1.6	0.7	0.1	0.2	3.0
Uganda	0.8	0.0	0.2	0.2	0.0	1.5	0.3	0.6	2.8	0.7	1.6	2.4	0.9
Zambia	0.9	2.1	1.0	0.7	0.3	0.9	1.2	0.4	0.2	0.3	0.3	0.0	0.2
Zimbabwe	1.0	0.9	1.9	1.3	1.2	2.6	3.5	2.3	3.7	3.0	2.5	5.7	9.8

Note: The AEO Indicator for State Pressure over Civil Liberties was called Political Hardening indicator in past editions of the report. Computation methodology has been improved in 2008 and for all the data series. For more details, see the methodological note of the Statistical Annex.

Source: Authors' calculations based on Marchés Tropicaux et Méditerranéens, between 1996 and 2007, and Agence France Presse for 2008. The change in the source might affect the comparability of 2008 indicator to its historical values.

StatLink http://dx.doi.org/10.1787/324268640831

OECD PUBLISHING, 2, rue André-Pascal, 75775 PARIS CEDEX 16
PRINTED IN FRANCE
(41 2009 02 1 P) ISBN 978-92-64-06170-5 – 2009